FIVE STAR WHITE TRASH

MW01285308

EVICTION NOTICE
NOTICE NONPAYMENT OF RENT

FIVE STAR WHITE TRASH

A Memoir of Fraud and Family

GEORGIANN DAVIS

NEW YORK UNIVERSITY PRESS New York

NEW YORK UNIVERSITY PRESS
New York
www.nyupress.org

Please contact the Library of Congress for
Cataloging-in-Publication data.
ISBN: 9781479840397 (hardback)
ISBN: 9781479840434 (library ebook)
ISBN: 9781479840427 (consumer ebook)

This book is printed on acid-free paper, and
its binding materials are chosen for strength
and durability. We strive to use environmentally
responsible suppliers and materials to the
greatest extent possible in publishing our books.

The manufacturer's authorized representative
in the EU for product safety is Mare Nostrum
Group B.V., Mauritskade 21D, 1091 GC
Amsterdam, The Netherlands.
Email: gpsr@mare-nostrum.co.uk.

Manufactured in the United States of America

10 9 8 7 6 5 4 3 2 1

Also available as an ebook

CONTENTS

AUTHOR'S NOTE

All quotes and dates I share in this book are my approximations. Details are as I remember them, but I've changed some names and other information that could identify a person, to protect privacy. All incidents are real to the best of my recollection, which is one reason why I want to forewarn you that many of the stories I share contain disturbing details about bodies, mental health, the criminal legal system, familial trauma, and physical violence. People represented in my stories may have different interpretations of the events that unfolded. But here, in this book, I analyze my lived experiences as humanely as possible from my perspective. By drawing on research to analyze my lived experiences, I hope this book reveals as much about U.S. society as it does about me.

The summer before fifth grade, my Aunt Maria took me to the Gap for school clothes. Married to a judge, she just knew preppy clothes would help me fit in at my new school. I trusted her. She was Sandra Bullock classy with natural beauty and a modest style. Her social circles were filled with college-educated white people unlike anyone my immediate family socialized with. My parents had moved us from our three-bedroom apartment in a racially mixed area near Chicago's Midway Airport, to an elaborate four-bedroom home in a suburb of Chicago that we couldn't afford. Inside its three-car garage, you'd find a red convertible Mercedes and a navy-blue Cadillac that was outlined in fake gold trim with a matching grill. My parents didn't want my brother and I to go to school with all of the Black and Brown kids who were moving into the neighborhood, so we fled, like many of our white neighbors, to a suburb that had some of the best public schools.[1] We used credit cards to go on elaborate Caribbean vacations and buy real fur coats—I had a white one with Disney characters on it. All of us always got what we wanted and more. I made it halfway through the seventh grade before dropping out.[2] My brother, Theo, was expelled his sophomore year of high school after stabbing someone in the hall. We never fit in. We were white, but not the right kind of white.[3] We were five star white trash.[4] We had borrowed money and tried to use it to buy class.[5]

Theo was better looking than me by societal standards and definitely more athletic.[6] He was a football player who, at the time, resembled a young David Silver from the 1990s series *Beverly Hills, 90210*, with his pronounced jawline, muscular body, and dirty brown hair that matched his eyes. Today, when I'm scrolling social media and see a photo of Justin Bieber looking way too thin for his body, I have to do a double take because he looks like my brother. Theo was a terrible student. I mean, he really struggled. I, on the other hand, was a nearly 300-pound obnoxious asshole little sister who made fun of her brother for not being able to tell time or do long division. I was an above-average student with a mullet who learned the clarinet in fourth grade and was appointed first chair the next year in my new school. I always towered over the girls my age and was even taller than most of the boys. When mom would give me $10 to get my mullet trimmed at the hair place next to the local grocery store, I would sign in as George. Leaning in to people's assumptions about my body was easier than correcting them. I know that gender is just a performance that acts as a signpost for what's between our legs. All of us are expected to "do gender" in stereotypical ways.[7] If you have a penis, you present like a guy. If you have a vagina, you present like a girl. I always ignored those expectations. I'd like to think I was a savvy gender-rebellious kid. And in some ways, I was. But, to strangers, I was whoever their beliefs wanted me to be—often becoming George because I feared what would happen if I forced them to face their flawed assumptions about gender.

I'm nothing like my mother, Ann, who has always been gorgeous and very feminine. Her hair was layered and dyed blonde to help her look like Farrah Fawcett, whom she always said she resembled. And, in her thirties, she got permanent makeup—black eyeliner and a mole on her upper left cheek tattooed in black ink—to complement her style and admiration of Marilyn Monroe. She was a casual dresser most days, in gym shoes, slacks, and boring tops, but when she dressed up, she went all out in true five star white trash style with long flashy earrings, one-of-a-kind dresses from Chicago boutiques, and heels that matched. She was always more into chasing money than pursuing school, but she did manage to earn a high school diploma.

Mom and dad eloped in their early twenties, soon after they started dating. They were both from Greek families, and mom was even born in Greece. My dad, George, worked at a gas station learning on the job how to be a mechanic. Like my mom, he didn't care about formal education. He didn't finish high school. To me, he always looked like Bill Murray—tired, with his face too small for its skin. His short hair was always overgrown and messy. His mechanic hands were rough and stained with oil owing to his refusal to wear gloves when working on cars, and the navy Dickies he always wore looked like they hadn't been washed in weeks but somehow still looked cleaner than the beat-up t-shirts that he wore. In teenage photos I've seen of him, he had shoulder length dark black hair, a black leather jacket, and a crooked nose from someone breaking it during a fight. He looked like a stoner, even though he never seriously did any drugs. Although his name was George, many people called him by his nickname, Marks, which was short for his last name, Markozis. Everyone spelled his nickname M-A-R-K-S, but when I started studying sociology in college, I changed it to M-A-R-X for Karl Marx. Dad was my working-class hero who lived his own manifesto. I was the only one in the family to take to or understand why I chose the new spelling, but that didn't stop me.

In Greek families, children are to be named after their grandparents. Theo, my brother, was named after our maternal grandfather, Papou Theo, a man who always neatly parted his silver hair and who I rarely saw without a suit and tie. When I was born, it was my paternal side's turn in the naming tradition. I should have been named after my paternal grandmother,

Katerina. But in a big "fuck you" to Katerina, mom decided to name me after herself and her mother, my Yiayia Gia, a petite woman who was always found in the kitchen with her salt-and-pepper hair and wrinkly skin. Mom combined her name with Yiayia's name and came up with Georgiann. Marx was wrapped around mom's little finger, so he didn't put up a fight, despite looking like he always just got out of one.

Even so, everyone in my birth family, along with those who knew me since I was kid, call me Missy. I guess with all of the similar Greek names around it got too confusing. I got "Missy" tattooed when I was 14, quotes and all, on my left ankle under the face of a brown bear. I despise that tattoo even more than my first—a frog on the other side of the same ankle—but not enough to pursue tattoo removal. I'm just thankful that the ink is slowly fading away.

Papou and Yiayia raised my brother and me during much of our single-digit years—either when they spent time in the U.S. visiting for months on end, or when Theo and I spent a summer with them at their condo in Greece. When I tell people I spent some childhood time in Greece, I imagine them thinking my family was as rich as we pretended to be. But the reality was that Greece with my grandparents was free childcare for my parents, and it was a way for Theo and me to be taken care of while my parents worked.

My Papou had immigrated to the U.S. when his eldest daughter, my mother, was a child. Papou chose Chicago because he had friends from Greece in the Windy City, which is where many Greek immigrants had settled to start their new lives.[8] He came to the U.S. on his own, and he roomed with his friends until he managed to get a warehouse job and save up enough money to bring my Yiayia and mother over to join him in his new country. They later had my Aunt Maria and Aunt Athena. Unlike my mother, Maria and Athena were born in the U.S. They were each born five years apart. After my grandparents' kids each finished high school, they decided to move back to Greece with frequent long trips to the U.S. that resulted in them dividing their time between the two countries.

My grandparents were more like parents to me than my parents ever were. Yiayia cooked us dinner whenever she was staying with us. Her recipes ranged from Greek chicken, which was a bit too dry for my liking, to pastitsio, a Greek lasagna that I loved. Yiayia also did all of our laundry and even ironed our socks.

Both Yiayia and Papou would regularly argue with my mother for not mothering us. And they would yell at my father, calling him lazy and unmanly for not making enough money to support his family. My parents always fought back. One year they even kicked them out of our house, forcing them to move into Aunt Athena's for the remainder of their U.S. visit. My parents didn't care when I begged and pleaded with them to not make Papou and Yiayia leave. They wanted them gone for "controlling our lives." I was so sad when they left our home, but not as sad as I would get every time they would go back to Greece. When they would leave the U.S. to return to Greece, I would cry for days and be unable to sleep. I made Yiayia sleep next to me in my bed whenever we were under the same U.S. roof, and just like that, she was gone, thousands of miles away. I was all alone again. It felt like my caregivers were abandoning me and leaving me out in the wild to survive. I would write down my feelings in a notebook after they'd leave, often telling myself that I dreaded eating McDonald's again and digging for clothes to wear out of a pile in our laundry room.

I didn't have a relationship with my paternal grandparents, who were also Greeks living in Chicago. I believe my paternal grandfather died before I was born. I only met my paternal grandmother a handful of times before she died in the 1990s. We didn't talk to Marx's parents because they didn't get along with mom. That's all I knew when I was a kid.

I've always parented mom, and to a lesser extent my dad. I didn't ask for it to be that way. Nor did they. It just happened. For me, this role reversal, which I found out later actually has a name—"parentification"—was how I showed my parents love.[9] I tended to their emotional needs, and sometimes even their financial needs, more than they tended to mine. And, as the years went by and I got more experience under my belt, I got really good at it. I didn't really have a choice.

Mom and I have always been very close. I believe her when she tells me that "I could kill you. But I will kill for you, too." When Theo and I were growing up, she spoiled us with anything we wanted, from fast food to expensive toys—which is an approach some working-class parents take to bring joy to their kids, unlike some middle-class parents who aim to shape their kids' desires in a different way.[10] I felt her love with every meal she purchased and every Cabbage Patch Kids doll I owned. Her gifts made me feel like the kid I was. But it was me, not Theo, who listened to all of her problems and offered whatever emotional support I could. And presents, as opposed to parenting, only get you so far. I grew up with a lot of anxiety.

* * * * *

"Is this a dagger which I see before me,
The handle toward my hand? Come, let me clutch thee."
I still remember many of my lines from when I was Macbeth in my middle school's adaptation of the William Shakespeare classic. My brother Theo was in eighth grade and I was in sixth.

It was 1992, and the play's director and sixth grade science teacher, Mr. Sinds, asked me at the open casting call what role I was interested in. Not knowing anything about the story or characters, I said, "Umm, Macbeth." I wasn't intentionally trying to be a girl who defied gender norms. I thought "Beth" in "Macbeth" meant the character was a girl, and I couldn't for the life of me understand why anyone would audition for a role that wasn't the star of the show.

We put on two performances, and both times, I, along with Shannon, who was Lady Macbeth, received standing ovations. Mom and Yiayia had front-row seats both nights. And after each performance they presented me with the biggest bouquet of flowers. Marx, Aunt Maria, and Theo joined them the second night and brought flowers of their own, which made me feel like the star I wanted to be. I finished the sixth grade as one of the most popular, and fattest, people in the middle school. I was an

A/B student who swore, wore 2- or 3XL men's clothes, and had friends everywhere.

On the school bus, I was known as the "nut cracker" who would stand up for anyone being picked on by threatening to kick the bully in his balls as soon as we got to our stop. In my experience, the bullies were always the insecure boys trying to prove their worth to others.[11] Since I was more than double their size, they were afraid of me and mistakenly assumed I was tough. They often backed down with tears and apologies that went something like, "I'm sorry! I was just joking. Please, Missy, don't hurt me!" I never had to physically fight anyone, but was never afraid of the possibility because I knew Theo would always have my back. When I was emasculating the bullies, Theo would go along with my threats and warn them, "You should listen to her. She'll fuck you up." Before we even got off the bus, I would let the bullies know I wasn't going to hurt anyone but didn't want anyone to be picked on ever again. Each time, the bullies would be relieved and usually ended up apologizing to the kid they were picking on. I didn't expect anything in return from the bullies or those being bullied, but I kept stepping in. I just hated it when folks treated others like shit for no apparent reason other than an attempt to gain masculinity points by going after easy targets.[12] Because there were a lot of boys on the bus all trying to prove themselves to one another, I was a busy "nut cracker."

I went through a lot during the summer after I finished the sixth grade. And, much to the confusion of my family, friends, and school personnel, when the start of seventh grade rolled around, I started refusing to go to school. I would beg and plead with my mother to let me stay by her side. I was more deeply attached to mom than Marx, probably because she shared all of her emotions with me while dad shielded me from many of his. I worried that she would not be okay without me. I started panicking whenever I wasn't with her. Every day she would send me to school with a handwritten note in which she lied and said I had a doctor's appointment and that she would be picking me up early. While it was true that I was seeing a lot of doctors, I didn't have daily appointments. I never stayed at school that year for more than two or three hours a day. That was our compromise. But even with that agreement, I would still hysterically cry as we drove up to the school. Before I would get out of our car, I made her promise over and over again that she would pick me up at our agreed-upon time. I didn't trust her, even though she was always there waiting for me as promised.

It's not that I didn't like school. I just felt mom needed me more than I needed school. In the two or three morning classes I did make it to, I was still earning As or Bs. And, for all of the others, I would meet with each teacher and find out what we would be doing and what assignments we had, and then I would do all of that work on my own and turn it in the next day. I would also complete any extra credit assignments the teachers would give me—mostly book reports or essays on what the class was studying. At first, school officials were understanding and would work with me as I tried to stay in school, but then, after a few months went by, teachers started getting hostile with me.[13] I remember when Mr. Booth, who taught social studies, and Ms. Kasper, who taught English, cornered me in the hall and scolded me with their fingers, calling me a lazy loser who wouldn't amount to anything. They warned me that if I didn't start attending their classes, they would have no problem failing me. Not long after that interaction, I stopped attending altogether—that is, I dropped out of the seventh grade.

The principal came to my house a few weeks after I dropped out of the seventh grade and talked privately with mom before inviting me to join them at our kitchen table. Marx wasn't home.

"Missy, what is going on?" he asked me before reminding me why he was there: "You have to go to school."

"I don't want to go to school anymore. I want to be with my mom," I told him.

He wasn't listening: "What about going to a different school?" he asked before suggesting a private Greek school not far from home. "How about St. Demetra's? You can go there instead of our school."

"I know," I answered, as mom sat there quietly. "I don't wanna go there either."

He threatened us: "Missy, you're breaking the law. You have to go to school. If you don't go, I will have to report you and your mom to the police."

I feared what was going to happen to mom and me, but I was more scared of not being by mom's side. I replied, "I can't go. I'm sorry. I just can't go."

Under the attendance laws at that time, my parents and I were required to meet with a truant officer, a nerdy-looking white man dressed in a suit and tie, whose office was in one of the county's courthouses. Mom met with the truant officer first, while I sat alone in the lobby. Marx was at work, so Mom was representing both of them at that meeting.

I knew this meeting was coming, as I had already had a school-mandated psychiatric evaluation in preparation for it, in which an older large Indian doctor asked me to draw all sorts of images ranging from a self-portrait, to someone I had a crush on, to my brother and more. I remember asking him, "Do you want me to make the people happy or sad? Do you want them to be big like me and you or skinny?" To which he answered, "Whatever you want," before proceeding to just sit there watching me draw request after request. I drew all sorts of people, some that were meant to be me, others that were meant to be my friends. In my drawings, I was playing basketball, swimming, or riding a bike with friends. In one setting, I was with mom, Marx, and Theo. We were all sitting together on a couch sharing popcorn while watching TV. In real life, we never did that, though. I somehow knew to lie.

After the evaluation, mom, who brought me to meet with the psychiatrist, took me to TGI Friday's for lunch. It was then that she told me she was going to admit me to a mental care facility, which she called a "group home," because she was told I needed psychotherapy.[14] I cried and didn't finish eating. I didn't know what a group home was, or what it involved, but I knew it wasn't what I wanted because it would involve me being permanently away from mom. But mom ignored my tears as she drove up to the group home, where we spoke to a couple of people. I blocked out most of what transpired in the few hours that we were there, except for being relieved that mom couldn't leave me there after all. We didn't have insurance to cover their services. She was afraid of what was going to happen to her because of my truancy, but I reassured her everything would be okay.

Being uninsured in that moment saved my life.

A few days later, after meeting with my mom, the truant officer called me into his office. He had a comforting tone and a slight smile on his face. When I started crying, he told me what I've longed to hear, "Don't cry. You don't ever have to go back to school." I knew that mom had just told him what I went through that summer and all about my meeting with the psychiatrist, but I didn't know what he just learned about my body—because I didn't have the truth myself. He had answers still hidden from me.

* ★ ✮ ★ *

My parents got into the Italian ice business in their early twenties. It was my family's primary source of income for about 20 years. They managed to purchase two Italian ice stores; mom had worked at one of the stores as an employee before arranging a rent-to-own agreement with its owner. Both stores were walk-up Italian ice shops that were only open from March to October. When the Italian ice season was over and the stores were closed, we would struggle without any income. So, my parents had the idea to open up a year-round sandwich business to supplement the Italian ice off season, but the sandwiches weren't a success, and the shop closed after only a few years. This forced my mom into waitressing when the Italian ice stores were closed for the season and Marx to return to mechanic jobs at independent auto repair shops, something he did before my family got into the Italian ice business. Because the Italian ice stores sat on large lots with plenty of parking, in the month of December, my family would sometimes sell Christmas trees on one of the lots.

Unlike my brother, I grew up working in our family business, learning everything from how to prepare Italian ice to how to do payroll by hand with only a calculator and an IRS publication guide, all before I was 13 years old. And when I refused to go to school, I did so because I wanted to help my parents as they financially struggled. I was worried for my family, and I wanted to do everything that I could to help out. When I was at school, I was overcome with severe anxiety that my parents wouldn't be okay without me—this was my cost of parentification.[15] I needed to be there for them, whether that meant listening to money problems or working at one of the stores. I even sold Christmas trees in the winter. I was the most successful sales person, always selling them at the top of the price range, making the most profit for our family. One time a Christmas tree customer asked me to take him and his family to the most economical trees we had on the lot. I had no idea, at 11 years old, what "economical" meant but, instead of admitting that to the customer, I assumed it had something to do with being good for the environment (confusing two "e" words that to this day still sound similar to me: economical and environmental). Always wanting to maximize my family's earnings, I always took the customers I was helping to see the Douglas firs first, the most expensive trees we sold, and did everything I could to avoid showing them the rows of the cheap Scotch pines. This particular customer who wanted an economical tree ended up buying a Douglas fir like most of my customers, and after I gave the tree a fresh cut with a chainsaw and tied up the tree to the roof of his car, I brought the cash from the sale to mom, asking her what "economical" meant. We laughed as she placed the customer's cash, and my tip, in our money drawer.

* ★ ☆ ★ *

It was a hot summer day in 1992. I had just finished the sixth grade as the popular "nut cracker" who did well in school and was Macbeth in the middle school play. I was with mom at one of our Italian ice stores, running around outside with friends. I was holding my left side, which mom noticed.

"Missy," she yelled from the walkup window, "come inside!"

"What do you want?" I asked before confirming her concern that my left side was indeed hurting.

Given that I was almost 12 years old, she assumed my abdominal pain was a sign that I was about to get my first period. She brought me to the washroom and used toilet paper to wipe herself. She showed me her discharge, asking me if I had something similar. I didn't, and I remember being quite disgusted with her nonchalant presentation of bodily fluid.

Later that evening, when the pain still didn't go away, she took me to an urgent care center. When she was younger, she had a painful ovarian cyst, and she was worried I might have the same. I knew her concern was real, because like so many others without health insurance, we only saw a doctor when absolutely necessary.[16] We didn't do checkups. We only went to an ER or similar facility because we knew they wouldn't turn us away before offering a medical assessment, unlike a primary care physician who insisted on getting paid at the time of treatment. Over 30 years later, this pattern hasn't changed for many families without adequate, if any, health insurance. Though the Affordable Care Act expanded insurance coverage, many people still can't afford health insurance and are forced to go to the ER.[17]

They drew blood, took a urine sample, and ordered a chest x-ray. Since I was complaining about abdominal pain and weighed about 330 pounds, they were concerned. When everything came back normal, the urgent care doctor ordered a pelvic and abdominal ultrasound. I remember the ultrasound technologist pushing the wand-like transducer deep into my abdomen sliding it around with gel that made me cold. She kept pushing, twisting, and turning it deeper and deeper into my fat abdomen before eventually giving up and telling my mom that she needed to ask for assistance. I remember mom getting worried and asking if everything was okay, to which the tech responded, "Yes, I just need some assistance with the pelvic portion of the scan because of her size." The doctor came in and explained that the tech wasn't able to locate my ovaries or uterus because of the size of my abdomen. He was going to try himself.

"Ow!" I yelled as I felt like the doctor was punching me with the transducer, as he and the ultrasound tech stared at the monitor it was attached to. "I'm sorry," he said, "but we are having a hard time completing the scan because of your excess visceral adipose tissue." I was thankful when he eventually gave up.

"What's going on? Is everything okay?" Mom asked, getting visibly distraught by picking at her lips. The doctor answered her with a simple, "Don't worry." He then asked me to wait in the lobby so that he could speak to my mother alone. Mom started wiping her tears away with a tissue that she got from a box on the counter. "Mommy, don't cry. I'm fine. It doesn't hurt anymore." I tried to comfort her but my effort seemed to have the opposite effect and she ended up crying even more.

I remember walking to the lobby by myself, wishing there was more I could do for mom. My left side pain that brought us there was gone—or maybe, I thought, it was just masked by the discomfort I felt from the poking and prodding during the ultrasound. But that didn't matter to me. I was now focused on mom and what I could do to make her feel better.

After mom met with the doctor, she came and got me. Her eyes were swollen. And her face was red. She had been accumulating tissues, with several used ones all crumbled up in her hand.

"What's wrong?" I was getting scared. "Am I going to be okay? What happened?"

She didn't answer any of my questions. Instead, she whispered, "The doctor wants to talk to both of us," before leading me to an office behind the receptionist's counter.

The doctor looked at me and said, "I've talked to your mother. You need to go for further testing and you need to meet with a specialist."

"I don't hurt anymore though," I told him, hoping this would make a difference.

Mom started crying again. "Mommy, I'm fine." My words weren't helping her, which made me feel like I wasn't being heard.

Frustrated, I told both of them, "I'm fine now. It doesn't hurt anymore. It's gone."

The doctor looked at me and offered some answers, "You need to go on a diet. You weigh more than adult men. You need to eat fruits and vegetables. And exercise every day. No chips. No ice cream. No soda. You have to go on a strict diet. That pain you felt is likely related to your size and isn't our immediate concern. I am concerned, however, that you won't ever be able to have children."

Children? Was that what mom was worried about? I was relieved. I could fix all of this. I just needed to clarify my wishes and mom would feel better:

"I don't want any kids! I want another dog!" I smiled.

Mom's crying went up a couple of notches. I didn't get why she was so sad.

The rest of that summer, and several years that followed, were filled with countless visits to an array of medical specialists all over Chicagoland. For the first time in my life, I had access to more medical providers than ever, despite my family being uninsured. But no one told me what was going on, or rather, when they did give me answers, they were lies. I was a medical anomaly, which made it possible to get medical care pro bono, but it would be years before I understood why.

* ★ ✮ ★ *

As I was going through secretive medical shit and pleading with mom to not make me attend my seventh-grade classes, Theo was barely passing his first year of high school. I wished I was carefree like him and did not worry about our parents every time our water or electricity was shut off because we couldn't pay our utility bills. I often felt like I was the only one in my family who was anxious every time a sheriff, dressed in plain clothes, showed up at our door to serve us with foreclosure paperwork. Because I was a minor, I couldn't legally be served with whatever foreclosure or collection lawsuits we were facing. Mom knew this, so she would have me answer the door, saying I was home alone. If we couldn't be served, then we could prolong the legal process. The sheriff would sometimes give me his card, but I would throw it away, pleased that I was doing something useful for our family. Still, I worried what would happen if I wasn't around to answer the door. To this day, about 30 years later, the sound of a doorbell sends chills down my spine.

The year after the truant officer cleared me from ever going back to school, Theo would have his first run-in with the law. He was a sophomore in high school and was getting bullied by seniors. Rick, a white guy with long hair, was the leader. The bullies would leave their senior halls and find Theo in the sophomore halls and push him around and call him names. Apparently, Rick was pissed off that Theo was pursuing his girlfriend who was, like Theo, a sophomore. Theo got into a number of fistfights with Rick and his friends, which mom and I heard all about. Because I was almost always with mom, I knew that she reached out to Theo's Dean of Students several times to report what he was going through. The Dean seemed to be empathetic, but he always shifted the conversation to Theo's poor academic performance as if it were entirely a separate issue.[18]

Theo's last day in school ended with him in handcuffs and Rick in the hospital with multiple stab wounds and a punctured lung. Theo had a pocket Snap-on multi-tool that Marx had bought him as a Christmas present. It was a small pliers, screwdriver, bottle opener, and knife all in one. The perfect gift for a mechanic to give his son. When Rick and his friends approached him, Theo pulled out his Christmas gift and stabbed Rick several times in his chest. I was with mom at one of our stores when she got multiple phone calls from the police department and high school administrators. She said over and over again while distraught, "I told you so many times he was being bullied. You should have done something." We both freaked out that Theo had been arrested and was in jail. And we were worried that Rick might die. We only knew that he was rushed to the hospital with multiple stab wounds. If Rick died, Theo would be charged with murder. No one in our family had ever been arrested before.

Mom dropped me off at home before going to the police station to meet with the police sergeant and several other law enforcement personnel. She asked the sergeant if he knew of a good attorney, and without any hesitation, he answered, "If it were my kid, I'd hire Thomas Shores."

At home, I was getting bits and pieces of information about the stabbing from Theo's friends who kept calling. Billy, one of Theo's high school best friends, told me that he heard Theo stabbed Rick with a protractor. He said everyone in the school was worried that Rick was going to die. He also said that he thought Theo was never going to get out of jail. I was worried Billy might be right, wishing mom would have let me go with her to the police station. The hours of waiting and not knowing anything were excruciating.

When mom finally came home with Theo, I remember being surprised that he seemed unphased. By then they knew that Rick was going to survive. Theo was released under our mother's supervision because he was a minor without a prior criminal record. Billy even came over that evening singing, "Murder was the case that they gave youuuuuuuu"—modified lyrics off of a new soundtrack album featuring Snoop Dogg—while Theo rehashed the stabbing. He laughed about it.

"Dumbass!" I shouted at Theo, "Aren't you scared? You are going to go to jail forever and you think it's funny." I was angry and confused while my parents sat in silence, worried for their son.

Theo explained, "Nah, it was self-defense. He shouldn't have come at me like that."

Theo got expelled from school. White flight into white schools didn't pay off for my parents the way they had hoped. Three and half years after we had left a racially mixed school district for a more affluent white one in the south suburbs, both of their kids were no longer in school. I was a seventh-grade dropout, and Theo was kicked out of school and facing a serious criminal case.

Mom retained Thomas Shores, the criminal defense attorney that the sergeant highly recommended. I was with mom when she delivered Thomas Shores his $10,000—in cash, as requested—retainer fee to represent my brother. Shores assured us both that Theo wouldn't do any prison time.[19] The $10,000 was everything our family had saved over the summer from our Italian ice business, as we did every summer, to last us until the spring when we would reopen our seasonal stores.

We also needed that money to defend ourselves in a years-long eminent domain case. Eminent domain is the process by which the government can, with fair compensation, take one's private property if there is a public need for it.[20] In our case, a public library wanted to acquire the site of our first Italian ice store. Eminent domain doesn't have to be controversial. However, in our case, we questioned the fairness of their offered compensation because it was mostly based on the physical structure of the building and the land that it had been on for decades, while underestimating the value of its location and proximity to our customer base. But now we didn't have the money to cover those legal fees. Our eminent domain battle, coupled with Theo's criminal case, was the beginning of our end.

Theo's case was working its way through the criminal legal system, with many continuances.[1] After many months, the prosecutor surprisingly dropped the case and accepted that the stabbing was an act of self-defense. This outcome reinforced Shores's reputation as one of Chicagoland's best criminal defense attorneys, and left my mom feeling the 10 grand we spent on retaining Shores was well spent. Meanwhile I was still seeing doctors all around Chicagoland. Medical curiosity and voyeurism continued to trump the fact that we were uninsured. Mom was just as worried about me as she was about Theo, which I didn't understand because I never felt the abdominal pain again and I was free to learn on my own without school.

I took it upon myself to sign up for a homeschooling program through the Red Apple Academy. They ran TV commercials. I called up the number on the screen, pretending to be my mother, and enrolled myself in the eighth grade. They sent a huge box of textbooks and instructor's manuals, which I sorted into neat piles on our kitchen table as soon as they arrived. I did my best to teach myself basic algebra, a whitewashed version of U.S. history, and whatever I could about the periodic table of elements.[2] I even took the exams they included, using the answer keys to assess my performance. I ignored the tuition bill that was included with the materials, so Red Apple Academy never sent another box. I continued learning by reading the *Chicago Sun-Times* every day when I wasn't serving customers at our Italian ice stores. Their journalists' style of writing was accessible and thought-provoking. And I liked the size of the newspaper, the way it was folded like an oversized book, unlike the *Chicago Tribune*, which I found physically bulky with stuffy writing. I also really loved reading *Highlights*, a magazine geared to children, but I only ever saw them in medical waiting rooms. Knowing this, mom always brought a big purse to my doctor's appointments so she could steal as many issues as she could find for me while we waited to be seen.

By the time I saw a reproductive endocrinologist at the Learning Medical Center in the Illinois Medical District when I was around 13 years old, weighing in on the scale at about 367 pounds, I had accumulated a huge pile of stolen *Highlights* magazines. Mom sat in a corner of the cold, sterile room. When a nurse told me to get undressed and put on a gown, I was wearing a men's Michael Jordan black sweatshirt, black mesh shorts despite it being winter, the latest Air Jordans without socks, and a backwards black FILA flat cap that covered my mullet. She said I needed to take everything off including my bra and underwear.

"I don't wear a bra," I told her, while she scribbled something down in my chart.

"Should I keep my hat on?" I asked.

"That's up to you," she answered in a hurried tone as if I was a bother.

The doctor, an old white man, knocked before entering with a crowd of at least six younger looking medical residents, also all white and male.

"Hello, mom. Hello, Georgiann," he said with a smile on his face as he shook both of our hands.

Pointing to my hat he continued, "That's a nice hat you've got on. I need one to cover my bald head!" I laughed while the residents stood around him in silence. "These guys," he said gesturing to the residents, "are here to learn from me and you. Would you mind if they stay with us while we talk?"

I looked at mom for guidance before saying, "It don't matter to me." To which she added, "No problem, doctor."

"Great," he responded, "Now Georgiann, I'm. . . ."

I interrupted. "My name is Missy."

"Oh, I'm sorry." He looked at the chart he had in his hand. "I have here Georgiann."

"Yeah, my nickname is Missy. Everyone calls me that."

"Well nice to meet you, Missy. I'm going to ask that you put your legs here in these metal stirrups so I can take a look at your private parts."

"Why?" I was pissed. I was 13. I didn't want to show anyone my genitals, let alone a group of doctors I just met. And to do this in front of my mom? I was horrified.

"It's part of the exam, Missy. I won't hurt you and I will be quick. I just have to take a peek."

I reluctantly followed his orders while filled with embarrassment.

The doctor sat on a stool with wheels and rolled over to the exam table. I had my feet in the stirrups but still managed to protect my privacy by keeping my fat thighs together until he placed a gloved hand on each knee and forced my legs open while asking me to "relax."

"Missy, you don't shave your pubic area, do you?"

"Huh?"

"That's fine. I was just checking," he answered me and then told the residents behind him, in medical lingo, to take notice of my lack of pubic hair.

"Now, mom, would it be alright if we measure her vaginal canal?"

"No problem," she softly answered shaking her head up and down.

"Missy, I'm going to measure your vaginal canal now. Let me know if I'm hurting you at all."

"Okay."

I felt pressure as he placed something in my vagina. "Are you alright, Missy?" he asked.

"Yeah," I said before he muttered something to the residents before breaking it down for my mom and telling her that he thought my vaginal canal was considerably small but should still be able to handle penile penetration.

And the doctor was right. Not long after he examined my vaginal canal, I had unprotected sex with a 16-year-old white lanky boy named Chuck, an employee I hired to work at the Italian ice store I ran, who eventually became my friend.[3] He had spent the night at my house one summer evening when I was 15 years old, and we just made out. I didn't tell Chuck anything about how a doctor had examined my vagina to make sure it could handle a penis. I didn't tell Chuck that I sat in the doctor's office mortified with my legs spread wide open. And I didn't tell him the doctor left me traumatized, as his exam was happening not only in front of a group of male medical residents I had just met, but also in front of my mother.

I kept all of that to myself, as well as what happened next.

As the doctor rolled away from me and towards the sink to wash his now ungloved hands, he told us he was almost done and just needed to check my breasts. I couldn't believe what was transpiring as he stood over me caressing my breasts while pointing out something about my nipples to the residents who stood over his shoulders.

I felt like a lab rat.

"Missy," he asked me. "Do you exercise? I'm really worried about your weight."

"No." My fatness didn't bother me but it clearly bothered doctors. I imagine if I hadn't dropped out of middle school, I would have felt differently about my weight given that I would have been bombarded with the anti-fat messages that are rampant throughout middle schools.[4] But I was lucky. My abnormal childhood protected me from my societally perceived abnormal body.

He looked as serious as the residents who were scribbling in notepads when he turned away from me and said, "Mom, we have a lot going on here. I'm just as concerned about

Georgiann's reproductive matters as I am about her morbid obesity. Has she always been this obese?"

I had no idea that "morbid" meant death and disease and that "obesity" was a pathologizing medical term for fat.[5] But my ignorance didn't prevent me from feeling judged.

Mom answered, "She was a normal baby, but starting around second or third grade, she kept getting heavier and heavier."

I imagine mom was feeling just as judged when the doctor repeated what the urgent care doctor told us: "She is heavier than most male adults," before also adding that I would likely be "bedridden" before I was 20 years old.

He continued ignoring me but not my legs, which he described to mom as "enormous" before saying that they would only get bigger if my weight was not under "control." Mom sat there picking her lips while nodding in agreement as he insisted "something must be done."

"I'm going to refer you to a bariatric surgical practice at Star Medical Center. They are my colleagues and they perform surgeries that restrict how much you can eat, leaving excess weight to fall right off."

Mom asked, "Is it a major surgery? Is it painful?"

"It is a major surgery, but" he continued, asserting an oversimplified and even unsubstantiated claim, "it is incredibly successful."[6] He went on to say, "I'm not sure what they can do given her age, but I will leave that up to their practice. I'm surprised she doesn't have diabetes yet, but she will soon if she doesn't lose weight."

The doctor seemed to have forgotten that our appointment was about my reproductive issues until mom reminded him: "Doctor, will she ever be able to have children?"

"I'm afraid not," he answered. "We will need to do surgery in the near future because there is an increased risk of malignancy, but we should wait a few years so that she continues developing. We have until she's 18 years old. For now, we need to get her morbid obesity under control."

"Malignancy?" Mom's eyes got big as tears started rolling down her cheeks. "Does she have cancer, doctor?"

"I have cancer?" This was the first I was hearing I might die.

The endocrinologist reassured me that I wasn't going to die, but he did so by saying that I'd be fine if my premalignant "ovaries"—that's what he called them—were removed soon after I finished going through puberty.

I was still sitting on the exam table naked and humiliated with only my hat and a medical gown on, when mom asked, "Can you do both surgeries at the same time?"

"I'm afraid not," he answered again, before explaining "that would necessitate too big of an incision."

* * * * *

The footlong meatball Subway sandwich with cheese, bag of chips, and large coke never tasted as good as it did the night before I had my stomach stapled. I was supposed to be on a bland liquid diet for 24 hours before my surgery, but I only made it to the early evening before giving in to my hunger. It was February 1995. At the time, bariatric surgery for children was quite rare.[7] Yet, here I was about to undergo a major surgery that is at best preventative and at worst cosmetic. I didn't have any health issues like diabetes or high blood pressure. I was just really fat. But doctors insisted that health problems were in my future if I didn't lose weight. There was no mention of the lifelong health implications of drastically reducing the size of my stomach—especially at such a young age.[8] Instead, the bariatric surgeon, and his staff, drew on beliefs that fatness is synonymous with poor health to scare us into thinking stomach stapling was the answer to my obesity "problem." No one mentioned society's expectations about feminine beauty and whiteness, which the medical community relies on, and which insist that weight loss would make my 14-year-old body more sexually desirable to boys.[9]

"I can't take it anymore," I had cried to mom before the surgery. "I'm so hungry. Please, mommy, please get me something to eat."

"You can't! You heard the nurse, Missy, you can't eat anything big. You don't want to get sick, do you? Want another chicken soup?"

"No! I'm hungry!" I yelled. "I need real food."

Mom finally gave in to my cries and had Marx take me to Subway, thinking it was a lighter option than my usual fast-food choices of Taco Bell and McDonald's. We rarely had food in the house other than some stale sugary cereals, barbeque potato chips, an open gallon of milk chasing its expiration date, and a shitload of flavored canned drinks from cream soda to orange crush. Fast food was our grocery store. While I ran into the Subway, Marx went next door to pick up milk of magnesia. It was mom's idea to flush out the Subway that I was going to eat with a liquid laxative. Her plan seemed to work. I was up most of the night shitting my brains out. I also remember calling my maternal grandparents, who were staying at my Aunt Athena's house.

"Yiayia, I'm so scared I'm going to die," I muttered through the tears. "I don't want to die, Yiayia! Please, Yiayia, please. I'm scared."

She tried to calm me, continuously repeating, "No cry. Missy-mou. No cry."

Papou cried with me when he grabbed the phone, reassuring me that God would watch over me. As Papou rambled on, alternating between Greek and English, I held on to the gold cross I was wearing around my neck, silently asking God to let me live. Earlier that day, Papou had taken me to Holy Sky Greek Orthodox Church where the priest, Father Leo, offered me holy water and prayed over me for a successful surgery. I finally fell asleep thinking about what it was going to be like to finally be thin.

* ★ ☆ ★ *

"Just chicken broth and water." I answered the pre-operative nurse's question about what I had eaten the day before with a lie as mom had instructed me to do. The nurse continued, "And you fasted after midnight?" "Huh?" I confusedly looked at mom, who jumped in, "Yes, she hasn't had anything since yesterday night." I started sloppy crying again, with tears running down my face and boogers falling out of my nose, telling mom and the nurse that I didn't want the surgery and was afraid of dying. The nurse assured me I was going to be fine before looking at my mother and telling her that she can give me something to help me calm down. Mom thanked her, and before long the nurse was back with two pills that I was instructed to swallow with only my saliva.

"I can't swallow the pills," I told the nurse.

"Missy, you have to try," mom insisted. "They will help you."

"You know I can't swallow pills. I just can't," I said in tears.

The nurse instructed me to chew them, which I did.

"EWWW!! These are nasty! And taste like shit!" I blurted out with white pill dust all over my tongue and teeth. "Can I have some water?"

"I'm sorry," the nurse explained, "You can't right now because the doctor needs you to have an empty stomach."

Whatever they gave me worked. I smiled and waved goodbye to mom as they rolled me into the operating room. I remember thinking about Marx and wondering if our sandwich shop was going to be busy that day, before being instructed to move myself from the gurney to the operating room table, as the nurses in the room told me I was too big for them to move me themselves.

* ★ ☆ ★ *

"I'm alive. I'm alive," I kept saying as I drifted in and out of a deep sleep. The surgery was over and I was on my own in the recovery room, with only the nurses repeatedly checking on me. I didn't want them to think I had died, resulting in me being buried alive, as I had seen happen in horror movies. So, I kept repeating, "I'm alive."

"Where's my mom?" I asked the nurse.

"You will see her soon. She's in the waiting room. How do you feel? Are you in pain?"

"My throat hurts. And I'm really tired," I answered.

"Your throat hurts from the tube the anesthesiologist placed down your throat."

"Am I okay?" I really wanted to know.

"Yes, everything went well. But you had a big mess on the operating table. You must have had a lot of stool in your colon. We had to give you a sponge bath."

"Okay," I answered, not making the connection that the liquid pre-op diet was meant to avoid such a scenario, or worse, vomiting while under anesthesia, which could cause fluid or food to get into my lungs.

I was hooked up to countless tubes all over my body, one of which led from a morphine pump. I had a vertical six- to eight-inch incision down my chest, from underneath the center of my breastbone to my belly button. The incision was closed with shiny silver staples that looked like the ones you'd see in any old random office stapler, only quite a bit thicker. My mouth was really dry and my throat was scratchy, which I was only offered small ice cubes to (unsuccessfully) soothe. With each ice cube that melted in my mouth, I would feel my stomach, the organ, tightly pulsate, leaving me in incredible pain. Each ice cube felt like a dozen meatball sandwiches. On my legs were uncomfortable plastic knee-high sock-type things, controlled by a compression machine, that intermittently would tightly squeeze each leg at the same time to prevent blood clots from forming. And I was catheterized with a tube in my urethra that ran from my bladder to a see-through plastic circular bag filled with my urine that hung from the side of my hospital bed.

"Missy, does it hurt?" mom asked me as she pressed my morphine control button while standing over my hospital bed.

"Yeah, it hurts a lot, but I'm okay."

"You will feel better soon. Do you want me to put the TV on?"

"No, I just want to sleep," I told her as she pressed my morphine control button again, not knowing that the dosage was preset and that pushing the button before it was time for another dose didn't do anything.

Mom pressed that morphine button all night long as she slept in the mauve leather recliner next to my hospital bed.

Aunt Maria and Yiayia visited me in the hospital the day after my stomach was stapled. Mom left me alone for a few hours but would be back soon. Aunt Maria had with her a huge tray of cookies that she must have picked up on the way to the hospital. How fucking stupid, I thought.

"Mariaaaaa, I can't eat those. I can't eat anything but ice chips right now," I told her, feeling bad that she must have felt so stupid. "They stapled my stomach."

"I know," she said, "I brought these for the nurses so they treat you better."

What I great idea, I thought. It turns out I was the stupid one.

"Missy, have you been up walking yet?"

"Not really. It hurts really bad."

"Missy," she said my name again before raising her voice, "You have to get up and move! I'm going to give these cookies to the nurses and find out why they aren't getting you up."

Yiayia sat down besides my bed and gestured towards my two tattoos—both on my left ankle.

"Shame on you. Why you do this?" she asked in the little English she spoke, before shifting into Greek with her overused phrase that poorly translates to, "Don't you know any better?"

"Yiayia, I like them. Don't be mad at me."

She clicked her tongue, smacked her lips, and moved her right hand in a slow circular motion as a nonverbal Greek expression of disgust. Aunt Maria came back and said that the nurses were, as she predicted, excited to get the cookies. She then insisted that I get out of bed and slowly step over to the recliner with her assistance. And when my lunch arrived, a few ounces of apple juice, a cup of broth, and more ice chips, she sat there demanding that I eat what I was served. I tried the best I could, but could barely consume more than a couple of sips of juice and spoons of broth before feeling like my stomach was going to explode.

* ★ ☆ ★ *

As the nurse went over my discharge instructions, which included sticking to a liquid diet and following up with the surgeon in his office, my mom's friend Thomas—a Black man in his mid-twenties—drove his rented red two-door Honda Civic hatchback up to the hospital's main entrance. We only had one car at the time because our other vehicles had been repossessed by the banks, given that we weren't able to make the payments. Marx had gone to work in our new-to-us two-door navy blue Chevy that he had bought from a buy-here, pay-here car lot. So, Thomas was my only way home. There was no way that I was going to be able to comfortably maneuver my cut-up fat body over his folded front passenger seat to get into the back seat, so I rode shotgun and mom crawled her way into the back. As Thomas drove over cracks and bumps in the road that were brought on by Chicago's cold winter and salted streets, I hugged my abdomen tightly to minimize the painful jiggle. "Thomas," I said, being silly, "slow the fuck down, my staples are going to fall out!"

For the next week or so, I wasn't able to, nor did I want to, swallow more than a couple of spoons of chicken broth and a few sips of chocolate protein shakes. My hunger was gone, and it was rapidly taking my weight with it. When I went to my one-week post-op appointment with the bariatric surgeon, my weigh-in was followed by a nurse applauding that I had already dropped 19 pounds in only seven days. The surgeon was equally pleased as he assessed my incision and removed the remaining external staples (many had already fallen out on their own) with a medical device that looked like an overpriced staple remover. He placed a liquid bandage on the incision and instructed me to slowly ease into a thicker liquid diet.

My next follow-up was a three-week post-op appointment that we didn't go to because the surgeon's billing department called our home inquiring about an outstanding bill that we couldn't pay. We were embarrassed and afraid to face the office staff, so my one-week post-op appointment was my first and last follow-up visit. We shouldn't have taken for granted that the surgeon was going to write off his professional fees like the hospital did.

During our initial consultation, the surgeon had told us not to worry about the cost of his services but instead to focus on the necessity of the medical intervention, given that I was almost 400 pounds at 14 years old. There was no discussion of the cost of the surgery, and the surgeon seemed to focus more on changing my appearance than on addressing health concerns. Instead, he framed it as an educational opportunity where he could teach medical residents and fellows about pediatric bariatric surgery. We should have gotten that in writing. It might have helped when I later learned that his office hired a collection agency which took legal action to recover not only the cost of their medical services but also legal fees through a court judgment. The judgment was on my credit report for years before I eventually learned about it when I was about 20 years old. I called the surgeon's office as soon as I learned of the judgement, asking the billing depart-ment if I could set up a payment plan to clear my debt and have it removed from my credit report. But because years had passed and the judgment had already been issued through a collection agency, it was out of their hands. Fortunately, thanks to my inter-net searches of how to fix bad credit, I learned that I was not le-gally responsible for the outstanding medical debt because I was a minor at the time of the weight loss surgery. I got all three major credit bureaus to wipe away that judgment from my credit report, on my own, in less than a month. They said it was mistakenly tied to my credit report instead of my mom's because we have very similar names and were associated with the same address.

I navigated living with a stapled stomach by trial and error. I ate how and what I used to—just much less. I did start to avoid meat, fibrous vegetables, and acidic fruits because they often caused a burning pressure that started in my chest between my breasts and that would run up through my throat. These foods were the ones that often got stuck where the surgeon had cre-ated a small opening that was supposed to act like a small drain slowing how quickly food would pass from the stapled portion of my stomach and into the rest of my stomach. Once the food got through the narrow opening and made its way to the larger side of the stapled stomach, the normal digestion process would take over. But when food got stuck in the clamp, which hap-pened all the time, I felt like shit.

The only way I could get relief was by throwing up, which became habitual for me and happened almost any time I ate something other than cereal, dairy products like milk and ice cream, bread, crackers, Popeyes Cajun mashed potatoes, or any other food that dissolved in my mouth or that I could easily chew down to a pureed consistency. I would later learn that two months before my stomach was stapled, the *Annals of Surgery*, one the most reputable journal for surgeons, published the results of a longitudinal study of weight loss surgeries that ended with the researchers recommending against stomach stapling.[10] The researchers found that patients who had their stomach stapled were drawn to soft high-caloric foods because of postsurgical complications.

Stomach stapling made me into a medically-induced bulimic who was regularly complimented on my dramatic weight loss. Including the 19 pounds I lost by the time of my post-op appointment, I had lost close to 100 pounds before my one-year "surgiversary"—a term used across the surgical weight loss community to commemorate one's surgical date. I had grown increasingly comfortable throwing up in public in front of anyone, and everywhere from a crowded parking lot to in the car at a red light. The bag my fast food came in often doubled as my vomit bag. I also went through many rolls of duct tape using it as a makeshift belt to hold up my shorts and pants that didn't have belt loops.

Soon after I turned 15, I convinced my mother to enroll me in a private driving school. I was comfortable driving, given that I had been driving illegally since I was 14, but I needed the driver's ed course to get my Illinois State Driver's License as soon as I became eligible on my 16th birthday, which was in October of 1996. It felt good to be back in a classroom, even if temporarily, where I was around people my age. I was also falling in love with my rapidly changing body. I was losing so much weight it was hard to see the surgery as anything but successful.

With one surgery done, I only had one more to go.

The closest I ever got to a "Leave It to Beaver" family life was the time I spent with the Kowalski family. They were a white family who lived next door to us in a Pleasantville-like suburb of Chicago. Our subdivision was lined with trees and filled with four plus-bedroom homes with attached two- to four-car garages and manicured lawns. Beginning in early 1990 when we moved into their neighborhood and for years after that, I spent nearly every fall and winter evening with them. I had the time because our Italian ice stores were closed for the season. Jan, the mother, made dinner every night as Robert, the father, tended to the lawn or worked on the 1957 Chevy he was restoring. They had only one child, Timothy, who was seven years younger than me. I was friends with their entire family, not just Timothy. I would help Jan make dinner, prepare the table, and I would volunteer to do dishes after we ate. We watched evening sitcoms together—*Full House*, *Home Improvement*, *Family Matters*, *Step by Step*, and *Boy Meets World* were my favorites. Like many girls in the early 1990s, I had a huge crush on Jonathan Taylor Thomas, which Jan would playfully tease me about. Their home life was so different than mine. I often wondered what it would be like if I was a Kowalski.

On weekends, I would peer out from our washroom window waiting for the Kowalski's garage door to open. They would open it soon after they got up and they would leave it open all day long. I saw the open garage door as my personal invitation to their world. I went to their home so many times that my footsteps wore out the landscaping rocks to form a direct trail from my front door to their garage driveway. As far as I could tell, they always welcomed me over. I would do chores around their house, watch over Timothy, and tell elaborate made-up stories about my family including lies like my mother was an amazing cook or that my brother and I were close. I was protective of my family and wanted my Kowalski friends to like all of us and not just me.

"Missy," Jan whispered to me. "Come to the washroom with me for a second."

It was a Saturday afternoon. I was 11 years old, and Timothy, she, and I were making sandwiches together in the kitchen. When we entered the washroom, Jan softly closed the door.

"Missy," Jan asked while blushing with a small smile on her face, "Are you wearing a bra?"

"Yeah," I said.

"I don't think you have it on right. It must be uncomfortable."

She was right. It was all twisted up in the back and it was way too small for my fat body. She must have noticed my bra through the worn-out white t-shirt I was wearing.

"Yeah, it hurts," I said before delivering a lie. "My mom gave it to me this morning, but it must have gotten messed up when I was playing."

In our home we had a laundry room near the entrance to our garage. In that room on the floor was a huge pile of clean clothes. When clothes were finished drying, we would just throw them on the laundry room floor. When any of us needed clean clothes, we would go to the laundry room and search the pile for whatever we wanted to wear.

That morning, as I waited for Kowalski's garage door to open, I decided to put on one of my mother's bras that I found in the pile of clothes. Mom had been telling me for months that I needed to wear one. My breasts were getting bigger and my worn-out t-shirts were exposing my body in ways I no longer felt comfortable about, given mom's comments about my appearance. I found bras to be such an awkward and strange piece of clothing. I had no idea how to properly get it on, but I did my best. It was really tight on my back and under my breasts and the cups were way too loose. Having never worn a bra, I didn't know what I was doing but assumed I did something right since it was staying on my body.

"I think you should ask your mom to take you for a fitting at a department store," Jan said.

"Okay."

In a comforting voice Jan continued, "I'm going to step outside the washroom so that you can take it off now and not feel so uncomfortable. I will be right outside the door if you need any help."

"Okay."

After Jan left the washroom, I struggled to unhook the bra but couldn't. The underwire was poking my skin in all sorts of places.

"Jan," I asked, "Can you please help me?"

Jan entered the washroom and helped me remove the bra, which she folded up into her hand, presumably to protect my privacy in front of Timothy and his dad, Robert. She then placed the bra in a plastic grocery bag and left it hanging on the garage entry door that I entered and left from.

"Missy," she whispered to me, "I left a bag for you on the door for you to take home when you leave."

"Okay, thank you," I said. "Thanks for helping me, Jan."

I never told mom about my bra fiasco. I just continued to go braless for years and preferred it that way. Mom still made remarks here and there, telling me that I left "nothing to the imagination" and that I needed to start wearing a bra. But she never took me for a fitting, and I wasn't going to try to put on one of her bras again.

* ★ ☆ ★ *

It was Christmas morning, and I was an impatient 12-year-old waiting for the Kowalskis to open their garage door. So, I picked up the phone and called them.

"Merry Christmas," Jan answered. She didn't know it was me on the line. She just answered the phone that way every Christmas.

"Hi, Jan. It's me, Missy. Can I come over?"

"Merry Christmas, Missy!" Jan said with a smile I could hear. "Come on over! We are having cinnamon rolls and Timothy is opening presents from Santa Claus."

"So cool! I will be right over."

As I hung up the phone, mom looked at me and asked, "Why don't you go live with the Kowalskis? Ass kisser!" She wasn't serious, but I could tell she was hurt.

"Mommy, I just want to see Timothy open up his presents."

"Whatever, traitor!" She yelled as she laid on our love seat watching Court TV in a small room on the first floor of our home that we called our "TV room."

Our TV room was meant to be an office, I think, given that it didn't have a closet. But we crammed a 35-inch TV, two love seats, and an oversized chair into it. The TV room was where mom slept. On top of the TV were all sorts of papers and unpaid bills, some loose change, and lots of dust.

Marx was upstairs sleeping in his room, and Theo was probably doing the same in his room, which was next to mine. It was early in the morning.

"Don't stay there long. We are going to the Old Country Buffet for Christmas," mom reminded me.

I loved the Old Country Buffet. They had all sorts of comfort food, from mashed sweet potatoes with cinnamon and marshmallows to macaroni and cheese to a carving station where a chef let you choose roast beef, turkey, or ham. And on Christmas, they also offered prime rib, which was my favorite.

"That place is so good," I said, reassuring mom I would be back soon.

To this day, mom and her sisters, my Aunts Maria and Athena, have an up and down kind of relationship. Some years they will go months not speaking because of something that one sister said or did to the other. On this particular Christmas, mom wasn't talking to Aunt Maria nor Aunt Athena, so we were on our own, given that neither my mother nor father cooked.

I remember once in my life when mom used the oven—and it was to heat a precooked HoneyBaked Ham. She was never a typical mother, nor did she desire to be one, so she was never bothered when people, from her parents to our neighbors, judged her by where or what we ate, how dirty our home was, or how she was more like an older sibling to us than the matriarch of the household. She knew what society expects a mother to be, but she didn't care. Marx accepted her lifestyle even if he didn't like it. And although he could have assumed the unfulfilled role and mothered us himself, he never did, which is why our kitchen was the cleanest place in our house since we only ate take-out fast food.[1]

After Timothy and I exchanged presents and I ate a cinnamon roll or two, I told the Kowalskis that I needed to go back home because my family was going to the Old Country Buffet. I remember thinking it was such a fancy thing to do on Christmas, but now, more than 30 years later, I find reliving the whole experience depressing. I think about all of the employees, mostly Black and Brown immigrant folks, who were away from their families and forced to check the mostly white people in at the register, cook their food, tend to their buffet, and frantically clean their tables. And I think about how I would see large families sitting together lovingly exchanging wrapped Christmas presents with one another while eating from their plates filled to the rim with working-class comfort food. When they finished, they left a table full of plates, many with half-eaten food, along with an inconsiderate mess of wrapping paper all over the floor for someone else to clean up.

My parents gave Theo and me our Christmas presents after we got back from the Old Country Buffet. Marx always drove, and mom usually sat in back with Theo, while I sat in front next to my dad. It was far more uncomfortable for me to try to fit my fat body in the backseat than it was for mom and Theo to just sit in the back. So that's how we always rolled.

As soon as we pulled up to our home, mom said, "Merry Christmasssssss, Missssssssy and Theoooooooo!" She instructed Marx to pop the trunk.

"Go get your presents Missssssssy and Theoooooooo! They are all in the trunk!"

Mom did all of the Christmas shopping, and our trunk was filled with all sorts of bags filled with unwrapped stuff, from FootLocker to Big and Tall to Kmart. She would get us every-thing we wanted and more.[2] She always hated wrapping gifts. When we were really young and believed in Santa Claus, Marx would do most of Santa's wrapping.

Big and Tall had some of the best clothes. It was a men's store, but their styles not only fit my body but also my preferences for hooded sweatshirts with professional sports logos and t-shirts with sayings from the The Simpsons on them, which I appreci-ated even though I never watched the show. From Footlocker, she got Theo and me the latest Air Jordan gym shoes and a package of eight pair of white Nike socks for each of us. From K-Mart she would get us Super Nintendo games—a lot of them, and anything else she knew we'd love from pajamas to scented soaps to stuffed animals. I always loved stuffed animals and even collected them for a while.

I can count on one hand how many times our family had a Christmas tree in our home, which is funny given that we sold them for a couple of years in the parking lot of one of our Italian ice stores. I wasn't fanatical about Christmas, but I did love how a Christmas tree smelled up a home.

The Kowalskis always put up a tree, which I often helped decorate. They also hung stockings above their fireplace, which displayed countless little Christmas trinkets. They put lights up on the outside of their home and a Christmas wreath on their front door. Our home was the only dark one on the block. When I complained to mom about our home standing out like a Scrooge, causing me embarrassment, she laughed and told me, "Whatever. Tell them we're Jewish and don't celebrate Christmas."

* ★ ✳ ★ *

When I dropped out of school, I was afraid the Kowalskis would disown me. But they didn't. I don't know if it's because they believed me when I told them that my parents wanted to home-school me instead of sending me to the public school, or if they pitied me. Jan always told me that I was the daughter she never had, and that I would always be part of her family.

A year later, when Theo got expelled for the stabbing and it was major news in our neighborhood, I figured my time with the Kowalski family was over. There was no way they'd let me, a stabber's sister, in their home. I avoided the Kowalskis after the stabbing. I no longer saw their open garage door as my personal invitation into their world. Instead, if I saw Timothy or his parents on their driveway, I would slowly close the blinds so they wouldn't know that I was home. This continued for a few weeks until I was getting our mail and saw their garage door slowly open. I tried to run back inside fast enough but Jan saw me.

"Missy!" Jan loudly said, waving from her garage, "How are you? Where have you been?"

"Hi, Jan." I waved back as my heart sunk. "I'm okay," I lied, "just busy with school."

"Do you want to come over later? We are getting pizza."

"Yeah," I hesitated. "I have to ask my mom first."

"Our door is always open for you, Missy!"

"Thanks!"

I was excited and nervous at the same time. I didn't have to ask mom for permission to go to their house, but I did need her advice.

"Ma, I saw Jan outside. She told me to go over there for pizza."

"Then, go," mom said. "That's what you want, right?"

"Yeah, but they are going to hate me because of Theo."

"No, they won't. You didn't do anything wrong. That was Theo. Not you."

I had been telling mom since the stabbing that the Kowalskis must hate us now and be scared of me. She told me to tell them it was self-defense and if they didn't like it that I should say "fuck you to their Griswold family." The Griswolds are a fictional family in a series of 1980s comedy films. They were portrayed as an idealized family navigating over-the-top situations during road trip vacations and holiday gatherings. Mom uses "Griswold" as an insult for anyone that she feels is cheesy or corny.

I was so nervous as I walked over to the Kowalskis. I prepared myself for the questions about the stabbing that they might ask. I was very protective of my family but I also loved the Kowalskis, so I knew this wasn't going to be easy. The pizza was on the table when I got there.

"Hello, stranger!" Jan cheerfully welcomed me in as I knocked and slowly opened their door. "Help yourself. We just sat down."

"Little Caesars is so good!" I said with a smile on my face before stating the chain's tagline, "Pizza! Pizza!"

As we ate pizza on paper plates, we talked about Timothy's school. He went to a private Catholic school instead of our neighborhood public school. The Kowalskis said they wanted him to go to a Catholic school until high school in order for him to be exposed to their faith.

When Timothy was done eating, he ran over to the TV to play Super Nintendo while his parents and I cleaned up the table. It was Robert who brought up the elephant in the kitchen.

"We heard about Theo. It's really unfortunate that. . . ."

I interrupted him. "It was self-defense. I would never do that though. I hope you all aren't mad at me."

Jan jumped in, "Missy, we aren't upset with you. We love you."

"Theo isn't allowed on our property," Robert stated matter-of-factly, "but you are always welcome in our home."

"I don't like him at all," I said.

Timothy called me over to play Donkey Kong Country with him on his Super Nintendo and we never spoke about the stabbing again.

* * * * *

At our home, I did most of the lawn care in the spring and summer, and I shoveled all of the snow in the winter. However, I didn't have a lot of time in the spring and summer to cut the grass and pull weeds, given that I spent every day running one of our family's Italian ice stores. The grass would get really long and the weeds would get out of control. I hated how it looked and knew our neighbors were judging us, so I would try to get up at 8am once a week, after not getting home until midnight the night before, to cut our grass. But I was often too tired and instead would use the energy I did have to yell at Theo for not doing anything around the house. We'd scream back and forth at each other for close to an hour. Usually nothing would come of it. But sometimes I would come home at midnight to find that he heard my cry for help and took time out of his day to cut the grass. Those times, however, were few and far between, which is why one of our neighbors anonymously left a note in our mailbox that read, "Clean up your pigsty! You pigs!!" I was mortified when I read it and broke down in angry tears, yelling at mom, Marx, and Theo.

"I can't do everything around here!" I screamed and cried, "Do something! Please! Please!"

It was midnight and I was aggressively yanking the pull cord on our gas lawnmower trying to get it to start.

"Chill the fuck out, Missy," Theo calmly said as he watched me go hysterical in our garage. "I will do it tomorrow."

Mom and Marx told me to quiet down before someone calls the police.

"Missy," mom yelled, "Stop it! You can't run the lawnmower this late you will wake up the whole neighborhood!"

Shaking, with tears running down my red face, I gave up trying to get our lawnmower to start and ran into the house, hearing mom tell Theo, "This is all your fault."

I woke up early the next morning to cut our grass. Only mom was up at the time. When I was outside going up and down our lawn with the mower, I saw Robert and Jan doing something in their garage. I stopped what I was doing to show them the anonymous note I kept in my pocket. They didn't seem surprised by it, leading me to believe that a lot of the neighbors were gossiping about our family. I was still emotional about the letter to which Robert responded that he would take care of our lawn for us. He said he would be our landscaper for a small amount of money. He worked at a factory during the day, went to school at night as a nontraditional student pursuing a college degree, and on his off days he worked in the stockroom at our local grocery store. He said he could use the extra money and that he loved doing yard work. I tried to convince my parents to hire him, but they wouldn't, saying it was a waste of money that we didn't have in light of the eminent domain situation at one of our Italian ice stores and the legal fees associated with my brother's criminal case.

Later that winter, lots of weeds starting showing up inside our home, only this weed was the kind that mom started selling for people to smoke.

I rarely saw my parents when the Italian ice stores were open. Mom ran one store, while I ran the other. Marx took care of the sandwich shop and would be there until 9 or 10pm, and I didn't know or care what the fuck Theo was doing, as he spent all of his time with his friends. He did not work like the rest of us. I would be at my store until after 11pm. Mom closed her store at 10pm and would then pick me up from my store on the way home. We wouldn't all be back at home until around midnight. And then the next morning, we would do it all again.

I found running an Italian ice store a lot of fun. I got to hire people whom I thought would not only be good employees but who would also make great friends—a problematic process not very different from academic searches, which many of my professor colleagues are reluctant to publicly acknowledge.[1] Most of the employees were teenagers, like me, and the interactions I had with them offered a sense of normalcy to my otherwise unusual life. Since I wasn't in school, the employees I hired were the only people I knew who were my age. We talked about dating, movies, music, and alcohol, and I lived vicariously through their homecomings, proms, high school graduations, and college tours. I thought about trying to enroll in the nearby high school that most of my friends I hired went to, but since years had passed since I dropped out of the seventh grade, I didn't think that would even be a possibility.

I wasn't really conscious of the fact that I no longer felt I needed to always be by mom's side. As time went on, it was clear to me that my attachment to my mother was not separation anxiety and/or some sort of school phobia as some psychiatrists I saw assumed. But I don't fault the psychiatrists for their misdiagnosis, given that I withheld so much information from them in our private sessions in order to protect my family. I told them about the family life I wish I had, not the one I was living. When I refused to go to school, I did so because I felt a deep obligation to help my parents, especially my mother, survive whatever they were navigating. If I was in school, I couldn't help them. By running a store entirely on my own, from when it opened to when it closed, doing everything in between that needs to happen—serving customers, cleaning the Italian ice freezers, handling payroll, and ordering supplies—I was at ease doing my part to keep our family afloat. Much the same is true of the many kids in Chinese immigrant families who help out in their family businesses.[2] When I was 14, I even completed an in-person food service sanitation community education course that was offered at a community college.

I was at my Italian ice store just before 10am to 11pm every day from March to October. Most days I ate lunch and dinner at the Chinese restaurant next door—throwing up whatever my stapled stomach couldn't handle. And I would often treat my employees to whatever they wanted me to bring back for them. Sometimes I would ask one of them to drive me to pick up fast food for all of us, since we only had Italian ice at our store. And, of course, I gorged on Italian ice all of the time. It was the only thing I ate that I always knew I could keep down.

Every summer when the end of August rolled around, I found myself sad that most of the teenagers I hired to work with me at my Italian ice store would need to quit in order to focus on high school. And many of the others also needed to quit before going back to college. Aside from losing similarly aged friends for the school year, I also knew that the Italian ice season was coming to an end and our family would again have to survive another fall and winter on whatever Italian ice money we collectively managed to save during the spring and summer.

* * * * *

In the winter of 1995, Theo was finally working. Only he didn't work at our Italian ice stores like I did. He sold weed. It was a family affair. Danny, one of my mom's friends, hooked mom up with several pounds of marijuana at $700 a pound. She wasn't in the street gang that Danny belonged to, but through him she had access to its resources.[3] I'm not sure how mom approached Danny about selling weed, but I know she saw it as a way to make easy money, which we needed in the winter to pay our bills. Mom wasn't a rare white petite unicorn in the drug world. Spend any time in the street drug trade and you will quickly learn that despite popular tropes, drug dealers aren't all masculine men of color. In fact, research shows that women drug dealers experience empowerment in the business.[4] Mom kept the weed in a gym bag next to her makeshift bed, which was one of the love seats in our TV room. Theo helped her break down the weed into dime bags that went for $10 and quarters that went for $25. They had a little electronic scale that they used to break down the bricks and make up baggies. I sat there watching TV while they happily worked together. They mostly sold the weed to my brother's friends and a few Italian ice store employees. My brother smoked some of it, too. I'm not sure the business was all that successful, as we were still financially struggling every winter.

But when the weather turned and spring was in the air, I joined them at 15 years old, mostly selling bags to Italian ice store employees and their friends. At any given time, I carried about a quarter pound of dime bags with me that mom and Theo had put together. I kept them all in a crunched-up Italian ice store paper bag hidden behind the felt liner of the trunk in my new 1995 Plymouth Neon. To find the weed, you would have to pull down the felt and expose the electrical wires for the left turn signal. I was afraid I'd get caught by the police and be seriously fucked, because not only was I driving without a license, but I was also selling drugs. I decided it would be best to hide the weed in a creative hiding space in my car, unlike mom and Theo who just kept their supply in a gym bag. My car was a bright yellowish color that mom referred to as "Monkey Shit Green." My car stood out like a sore thumb, and I loved it for that reason. I even got personalized license plates for it that read "Go Luce." Luce was short for Lucifer, a nickname mom gave me when we found out I couldn't have biological kids.

Early that spring, when Marx and I had been on our way to my Italian ice store, I saw from what seemed like a mile away a 1995 monkey shit green Plymouth Neon on display in front of a Chrysler dealership. It was gorgeous. Tied to the driver's side mirror were colorful balloons that were swaying in the spring breeze. I pulled into the dealership despite Marx's hesitation to check it out. I explained to him that if I had this car, we wouldn't have to carpool to my Italian ice store every morning, and mom wouldn't have to pick me up on the way home from her store. He was worried that I'd get caught driving illegally without a license. By this time, I had a "blue slip," which allowed me to legally drive as long as there was a licensed driver in the car, but my proposal involved me driving on my own. I made a convincing enough argument that he eventually agreed to take out an auto loan on my behalf. The finance rate sucked because his credit wasn't good, but that wasn't going to stop me from getting my dream car, which I assured him I would make all of the payments for as well as cover the required insurance. A few hours later, I ended up driving my new car to my Italian ice store. I was late opening up my store that day—which was a very rare occurrence—but seeing my monkey shit green car parked outside the back door was worth it.

I did get caught driving illegally three times. Once for making an illegal left turn, once for speeding, and once because someone reported to the police that I had a lot of weed in my car—but all three times I was let go despite not having a driver's license. I simply would cry, show my blue slip, and tell the police officer that I was sorry and would be more careful. And just like that, they'd let me illegally drive away. The time I got pulled over for having suspected weed in my vehicle, the cop told me he was responding to a tip and asked me if he could check my trunk. I said yes as I popped it open. I was worried I was going to be arrested on the spot for having illegal drugs on me with the intent to distribute them. But he just glanced in the trunk and didn't bother to look behind the felt where I kept my supply. Word on the street was that a former girlfriend of an Italian ice store employee reported the tip because she was jealous of my friendship with her ex. These aren't my #CrimingWhileWhite empathetic revelations—a 2014 Twitter trend in which white folks shared their experiences with the criminal legal system that didn't end as horribly as they do for so many Black and Brown folks.[5] As Kara Brown, a former senior writer at *Jezebel*, asks, "[Is] anyone legitimately surprised to learn that white people are able to get away with damn near anything by the police?"[6]

Selling weed helped me make money to pay for my car. But I didn't sell weed for long. We made most of our Italian ice store income on summer Sundays, and one particular hot Sunday we grossed close to $2,000. That night, I counted out the bills, mostly singles, fives, and tens, and then put the huge pile of cash in a large Italian ice store paper bag. I would give it to mom when I got home. The paper bag was meant to conceal the fact that it was a mound of cash. I placed the paper bag in a 1996 Atlanta Olympics purple and blue duffle bag, next to a bra I never wore, a bottle of ck one fragrance, a travel-size baby powder that I used on the heat rashes I got in between my legs, and an illegal cloned yellow cell phone that I used when selling weed. I had sold some weed earlier that day, so the duffle bag also had in it a second paper bag that was filled with weed, as well as close to $1,000 of weed money. I kept the weed money in its own bag with the weed to keep it separate from the Italian ice money. Instead of returning the weed bag back to its hiding space in my trunk after the sale, I got lazy and just threw it in the duffle bag, which sat on a desk at the back of my store.

When I was almost finished closing up for the night, I gathered up the things I needed to bring home—sleeves of cups, spoons, and flavored syrups—for mom to take to her store the next day. We often swapped supplies between the stores, in order to make sure a given store didn't run out of something. As I loaded up the car, I placed my duffle bag in the trunk as well knowing that I was going to be leaving within 10 or 15 minutes as soon as I finished mopping and Tonya, a friend and employee, finished putting away the dishes we had just cleaned.

I was in the front of the store almost done mopping when I saw a young short guy in a light grey hoodie, with the hood pulled up over his head in 90-degree summer weather, walking around the front of my walkup store. It was dark because I had turned off the external lights—something I did at 11pm every night after serving our last customer. The guy had his hands in the hoodie's pouch when he came up to one of the walkup windows. We made eye contact.

"Is Missy here?" he asked, loud enough so I could hear him through the shut window.

"No," I answered, scared out of my fucking mind, but knowing somehow that it would be best to pretend to be someone else. "She left already."

He nodded and walked away. I dropped the mop and immediately ran to the back of the store and told Tonya what just happened. As soon as I told her we both heard a loud BOOM! A gunshot makes an unmistakable crack, and we heard it near the back of the store followed by the sound of glass shattering. I stupidly tried to open the back door, but it wouldn't open.

Tonya and I ran to the front of the store. We were trapped inside. After feeling it was safe to do so, she agreed to slide through the walkup sliding glass window to see why we couldn't open the back door. There was no way in hell that I would have been able to fit through that window. I ran to the back of the store to meet her at the back door, which she was able to open by removing a screwdriver that someone had placed in the padlock clasp that I closed and secured every night when leaving the store. The rear passenger window of my monkey shit green car was shot, leaving glass everywhere. As I looked into the car, I saw the back seat was pulled down. I knew right then that my duffle bag was gone. My heart dropped as I went back into the store to call mom.

"We got robbed!" I cried to mom over the phone.

"What the fuck happened?" she asked, before screaming, "No! No! No! Where's the money? Where's the stuff?"

"It was all in the trunk," I answered, very scared of how she was going to respond. "I was about to leave and some guy shot the window."

"Why in the fuck did you put the bag in the trunk? I told you to keep it with you at all times!" She continued yelling at me. "Why are you so fucking stupid?"

"Should I call the police?" I wasn't sure what to do.

"No! What would you tell them? We don't need any more problems. Oh my God. I can't believe this happened. I'm on my way."

I told Tonya she should go home, and I stayed there alone waiting for mom to arrive. Soon after she got there, Marx and Theo also showed up in a separate car. Mom continued to yell at me, while Theo and Marx told her to settle down and explained that it wasn't my fault.

I was too scared to continue selling weed, and I never again let the Italian ice money out of my sight.

Looking back on this robbery now, as a parent myself, I can't believe that my family didn't seem very concerned about my safety. I was a 15-year-old who was luckily not shot and killed. Had I been able to get out that back door, I probably wouldn't be here today, because I would have walked right into what was happening and—being as stubborn as I know I am—I would have fought back and possibly been shot. But no one seemed that concerned about my welfare. Marx and Theo were instead occupied with calming mom's anger that she took out on me for losing all of that money. Theo was also expressing his thirst for revenge in the streets. Theo left the store walking up and down the streets around the store holding a large knife and yelling, "Come out, motherfuckers! I will find you!" My parents didn't seem to worry about him in that moment either.

Mom's weed business went on for close to two years before it ended, when her friendship with Danny was over and her connection through him to the wholesale supplier was gone up in smoke.

* ★ ☆ ★ *

Our Italian ice stores died after the summer of 1996. The library next to our first Italian ice store, the one mom ran, won their eminent domain case and bulldozed our store to make more parking for library patrons. Our second Italian ice store, the one I operated, was also bulldozed, not due to an eminent domain case, but because an investor bought our property after we lost it to business foreclosure. The land my Italian ice store was on now serves as a parking lot for the same Chinese restaurant where I ate most of my lunches and dinners when I worked next door. The Chinese restaurant has since expanded from a small space in the strip center to a huge stand-alone building. To complete the trifecta of loss, our sandwich stand caught fire, resulting in it being demolished. We should have gotten insurance money from that total loss, but some folks that my parents owed money to intervened, and they received the insurance payout instead. We lost our family's sources of income, and we would soon lose our home, too.

After our businesses were gone, I spent most of my time at home with the Kowalskis or on AOL in the chat rooms. I loved searching the internet and talking to random strangers.

Mom started waitressing full-time at a pizza place near our home. She was fast and efficient at her job, and the pizza managers loved her for her willingness to work 12-hour shifts. She would often bring us home leftover pizza that her customers didn't care to take home. I would squeeze as much leftover pizza as I could into my stomach, which had been stapled for nearly a year and half, as soon as she got home. I threw up most of it, but it sure did taste good going down. My weight was slowly climbing back up, with my weight up to about 250 pounds, although it didn't look like it since I am so tall.

Marx worked at various auto repair shops around the city. He wasn't licensed or formally trained, but he had a lot of experience fixing old cars that weren't as extensively computerized as they are today. In many ways, he was an asset to small neighborhood auto repair shops whose customer base had older vehicles that were not built with computer chips and electronic parts and were no longer covered by extended auto warranties. He could diagnose and repair a car built before the 1990s faster than those who went through certified mechanic training.

Theo was 18 and didn't care for the leftover pizza. He never craved food like I did. He was more interested in drinking and smoking weed. I'm not sure how he managed to graduate from high school, but he somehow did, maybe it was because the private high school he enrolled in was known for pushing students with behavioral issues through. The attorney that mom hired to represent him in his stabbing case had told us about the school, and had instructed us to immediately enroll Theo in it to show the court that he was a good kid who was committed to learning. But he wasn't. He was more interested in hanging out with his friends, who were always over doing drugs and drinking and God knows what else. Theo took over the primary bedroom in the house with his girlfriend, Angel, who moved in. Before that happened, it was my Papou and Yiayia's room for when they were visiting us for months at a time from Greece. Our house had four bedrooms, all on the second floor. One was Marx's. One was mine. And the third room used to be Theo's, but it stayed empty after he moved his bedroom set into the primary bedroom. Mom always slept downstairs in our TV room. Theo and his girlfriend rarely left their bedroom that had a TV and full bathroom. It was their very own crack den.

When I would sneak into their room on the rare occasion they would be gone, I would find rolled-up dollar bills on top of a tabletop mirror with white dust scattered all around. There were small piles of weed there too, alongside chunks of crack that looked like small pieces of dirty sidewalk chalk in plastic baggies, and overflowing ashtrays with cigarette butts everywhere. The beige carpeting had burn marks and holes throughout and was as dirty as the moldy and mildewy shower floor. It was fucking disgusting. While I could hear their loud music and sex when I was in my room next door, I was thankful the smell was contained to their space.

One time when I was snooping around their room, I couldn't control myself and started cleaning it, beginning with opening all of the windows so it could air out. I filled up two large garbage bags with empty beer cans and bottles, ashes and cigarettes butts, and whatever other trash I was willing to touch. I knew better than to put my hands on their crack or weed, so I left that shit alone. I even attempted to clean their toilet by filling it up with bleach hoping the bowl that was stained black would clean itself. And I sprinkled Ajax all over their shower and did my best to scrub it without directly touching the surface.

When they got back, Theo didn't embrace his somewhat cleaner crack den. He lost his shit instead, yelling, "Keep the fuck out of my room, you fat fucking bitch!"

From downstairs, I yelled back. "You're fucking disgusting, you crackhead! Clean your shit, asshole!" I knew Angel was with him, so I made sure to let her have it, too. "You and your fucking crack whore disgust me! Get the fuck out of my house you pieces of shit!"

I was cleaning the kitchen, which they used, while we were screaming back and forth at one another, when I came across a cup containing what I assume to be crack that they were "fixing"—or is it "cooking"? I don't even know how to describe the process of preparing crack.

"Hey, crackhead, I think you left your crack in the microwave!" I was screaming at the top of my lungs. "I'm going to throw it away, you pieces of shit!"

Theo ran downstairs and grabbed a knife from a drawer before tackling me to the ground.

Sitting on top of me and holding the knife at my neck, our eyes locked when he said, "I will slit your throat right now, you fat fucking bitch."

I knew he wouldn't do it.

"Do it motherfucker! Do it!" I screamed. "You belong in jail, you piece of shit!"

He got up, grabbed the crack I threatened to throw away, and ran back upstairs like nothing happened. They turned the music up, and I went back to cleaning the house the best I could while muttering under my breath that I was going to do whatever it took to lead a different life.

When I was 16 years old, in 1997, I landed a prestigious job. Aunt Maria got me, a seventh-grade dropout, a job in the Radiology Department at the Community Hospital where she worked. She had been working as a critical care nurse in the hospital for more than a decade. I realize now that this was nepotism, and essentially the kind of "affirmative action" that conservatives complain only people of color get, through diversity, equity, and inclusion initiatives. JD Vance even claimed on social media that "DEI is racism, plain and simple."[1] But here I was, a white teenaged middle school dropout, getting a "real job" that I was unqualified for because I knew someone who could get me in.[2]

I was a radiology service assistant making about $8.00 an hour in 1997, well over the federal minimum wage at the time, without even a middle school diploma. I did everything from greeting patients to hanging x-rays, which required that I learn about human anatomy in order to know how to display, for example, a chest x-ray, or being able to distinguish, and correctly hang, a left from right hip x-ray or the many x-ray films that would be produced from a colonoscopy. When asked, I lied and told the other assistants—as well as the technologists and doctors I worked for—that I was homeschooled. They had no reason to not believe me.

When I got my first paycheck from Community Hospital, it was about $500 of take-home money for two weeks of full-time work, I held the paper check in my hand and said to mom and Aunt Athena (who was over), "Look at this! Can you believe it?" I then kissed my check with a big smile, to which mom responded, "It's not even that much. You act like you've never seen money before." Her words hurt me more than I can describe, especially because I turned the check over to Aunt Athena for her to cash for us because I didn't have a bank account and the bank had closed mom's. We used my money to help pay our utility bills. We were on the verge of eviction, and we all knew it, but at least my paycheck was helping us keep the lights, heat, and water on.

I don't know why I spent so much time cleaning our home that I knew was in the foreclosure process. I was the only one who seemed to care, and was always cleaning up after others. I would dramatically cry while vacuuming the stairs and mopping the floors, yelling, "Don't you all care? How can you live like this?" Maybe keeping our home clean was my way of not wanting to let it go, or maybe it was my way of feeling like I had some sort of control over the situation.[3] Given how I am today, I think it was the latter.

I was working in radiology one day when my co-worker transferred mom's call to me.

"Good afternoon, Radiology," I answered, as I always did. "This is Missy."

"Come home right away." I could hear the stress in mom's voice. "The police are here and they are throwing us out."

My heart sunk. "Okay, I will be right there."

I told my co-workers that there was an emergency and that I was sorry I had to leave them on their own. They understood, and I quickly ran to my monkey shit green car in the employee parking lot.

I sobbed the entire way home, trying to think about where we could go and what we were going to do. When I pulled up to our home, I saw several cop cars. A white man in a suit, who I would soon learn was from the bank, was standing outside our home surrounded by several white uniformed state police officers. Two men were carrying out our things and placing them in the street. There were no boxes or packing involved. They were just hauling out our stuff as quickly as they could. When I approached the banker and cops, still in hospital scrubs—white pants and a fuchsia top—I asked in tears, "What are you doing? You can't do this!" They pointed to a legal notice they taped on our front door and told me that I had to immediately leave the premises. I said, "What about my stuff?"[4] The cops said that everything would be placed on the street. I somehow convinced them to allow me inside the home to find mom, who was allowed just a few more minutes to collect her personal belongings.

"Get the dogs and put them in your car before they run away," mom said to me, distraught, as she was shuffling through paperwork in the TV room.

We had four dogs at the time. There was Jack, a mixed breed that looked like a yellow lab; Blackie and Scruffy, both miniature schnauzers; and Whitey, a shih tzu. They were all in the outside dog run, which they lived in, because they weren't house-trained. It was attached to our house and even had a temperature-controlled doghouse that matched our home's exterior.

"Can they do this?" I asked. "What the fuck."

"I don't know," she said, frantically gathering paperwork in our TV room, which she also used as her bedroom.

"Where is Theo?" I wanted to know, still in tears.

"Missy, shut up, right now! He went with Marx to get a U-Haul."

I went up to my room to grab out of my dresser a Greek cross that my grandparents had given me for one of my birthdays. I kept it on top of a hundred-dollar bill they'd also given me, and that was sentimental to me. My room was already naked. Most of my bedroom furniture and clothes were in the street. The dresser was still there, but my Greek cross and hundred-dollar bill were gone.

"My cross and money are gone!" I yelled as I ran down the steps to the cops.

"There is nothing we can do about that," one cop said. "You need to leave the house now."

"I'm not going to leave until I get my cross back! Where the fuck is my cross?" I kept shouting.

"If you don't leave the home," the cop warned me, "we will arrest you for trespassing."

I gathered the dogs and put them in my car, letting my car run with the A/C on. Out of the corner of my eye, I saw many of our neighbors peering from their windows. Timothy was riding his bicycle in their driveway, staring at the commotion. I wish this would have happened in the middle of the night to save us face.

Timothy peddled over and asked, "What's going on?"

"The bank made a mistake and we have to leave," I told him, genuinely believing much of what I was saying. "It will get fixed soon and we will be back."

He nodded and continued slowly circling his bike on his driveway, not taking his eyes off of the action.

When the banker, escorted by the cops, was in our house but out of sight, I went to our backyard and turned on the filter system that was connected to our in-ground pool. I then proceeded to close all of the water flow valves, remembering that the pool guy told me to always make sure one valve was open or the filter system would completely malfunction. I wanted to fuck up our house so the bank couldn't sell it and we'd have a chance at getting it back. I then walked back to the front of our house and punched the dining room double-pane window as hard as I could. Glass shattered everywhere. The banker and cops heard the noise and came outside to see what was going on.

"What happened to this window?" a cop asked me.

"It was broken for years," I lied, with my right hand red and slightly cut up.

He looked at my hand, shook his head, and walked away. Had I been a young Black or Brown girl, would that have been his reaction? Hard to know. But those evicting us also overlooked my brother's leftover blunts and whatever other drug shit he had scattered around his bedroom.

"Go sit in your car," a cop said, empathetically warning me as he watched me walk to my car, "And please stay away from the house."

Marx and Theo eventually pulled up with a large U-Haul. They started removing our stuff from the street and into the truck, not nearly as fast as our belongings were being thrown in the street. When all of our stuff was out of our house, the banker's locksmith showed up and bolted padlocks on our front and back doors. The cops watched us get our stuff off the street and into the U-Haul. Mom got into my monkey shit green car and we drove to a dog boarding facility, where I decided we should leave our dogs until we found a place to live.

All of our stuff stayed in the U-Haul for days as we jumped around between Aunt Maria's house and Aunt Athena's house. Eventually, neither of them would let us stay any longer. They had their own troubles and they didn't want to deal with ours. When we had to bring the U-Haul back, we rented a storage space and unloaded all of our stuff into it. I never found my cross nor the sentimental hundred-dollar bill from my grandparents.

The eviction split up our family. Mom wouldn't let Marx live with us after the eviction, and even blamed him for it. She told him we wouldn't be in the position we were in if he was a "real man" and supported his family. He ended up in a homeless shelter outside of Chicago, while mom, Theo, and I spent the next few weeks staying at motels all around Chicagoland.[5] I used my hospital paychecks to cover the motel charges, because mom quit waitressing at the pizza restaurant in an attempt to focus on where we were going to go, and what we were going to do with our dogs. Theo and his girlfriend broke up after the eviction, but not much else changed for him. He kept doing drugs. He kept drinking. He never considered getting a job. He just stayed in the motel, ignoring the housing crisis we were in. He didn't care when mom and I yelled at him out of frustration. It just made things worse between us all, so we just let it be.

When the dog boarding facility called us and told us they were going to turn our dogs over to animal control because we had abandoned them, we picked them up with one of mom's bad checks that we knew was going to bounce. We snuck all four of our dogs into our motel room until we got caught. And then we moved on to a new motel until getting caught again. This continued for a while, until Aunt Athena rented an apartment for us in her name. Mom couldn't use her name because her credit was shot, and I was only 16 years old so no one would rent to me. Theo wasn't able to help either, because aside from having bad credit, he didn't have a job. We moved into a two-bedroom apartment in a large corporate apartment complex not far from the hospital where I worked. The apartment complex had a two-pet limit, but we snuck in all four dogs.

* * ✳ * *

Not long after we moved into our apartment, the hospital where I worked hired an external consultant to offer feedback on how our department could use our resources more efficiently. The consultant spent two weeks in our department taking notes as we went about our business, having been told to ignore her presence. A few weeks after she left, Julie, a white woman and Director of Radiology at the hospital, called me into her office.

"Come on in and take a seat, Missy," she cheerfully directed my 16-year-old self. After exchanging pleasantries, she proceeded.

"The consultant and I agree that we need leadership in the film room. And based on her recommendation, I want to offer you a new position of 'clerical supervisor,' which we will create and move you from an hourly rate of $8.00 to a salary position that comes to $13.70."

"Oh my God," I blurted. "Seriously?"

"Yes, you would start in your new role next week, and you would work 8am to 4:30pm like the rest of the leadership in the

Radiology Department. You will be responsible for scheduling the staff, employee relations including annual evaluations and disciplinary actions, as well as hiring. Our leadership team will train you." She continued, "You will be salaried, though. Do you know what that means?"

"No, I'm not sure," I answered, still stuck on the fact that I would soon be making nearly $14.00 an hour, in 1997, as a 16-year-old seventh grade dropout.

"It means that your pay will be fixed. You will not be eligible for overtime, evening, or weekend differential. But you will be the highest paid clerical employee in the Radiology Department and will be the new 'clerical supervisor.'"

"That's fine," I answered her. "With that pay, I won't need overtime."

Julie laughed as I enthusiastically looked forward to being the new "clerical supervisor." Most of the folks I would be supervising were more than triple my age. I was by far the youngest in the department, but I managed to smoothly transition into my new role without any animosity from those I worked with. I didn't have the language at the time, but now I know that my leadership style is best described as pacesetting and supportive. I floated from the lab check-in desk, to scheduling, to hanging x-rays, to wherever there was a backlog. And I was almost always in the department working across shifts to keep everything flowing.

The one big mistake I made that is laughable today because I am gender scholar is that I agreed with the external consultant's recommendation to move all of our x-ray files from a numerical filing system by medical record number to an alphabetical system by a patient's last name—segregated by, of all things, sex. All male patients had their x-rays filed in large blue folders, whereas all female patients had theirs in large pink folders. Today, as a gender scholar, I ask, and laugh, in embarrassment: what the fuck was I thinking to forcefully categorize people's medical records into either a pink or blue folder depending on their genitalia? We had thousands and thousands of folders in our film room and many more in a locked storage space in the hospital's basement and even more in off-site storage. Aside from the problems that can surface by depending upon people's ability to correctly alphabetize patient records, I upheld a sex binary that decades later I would teach my students is not only deeply flawed but also incredibly dangerous.[6]

One late evening after work, as I walked up to my monkey shit green car in the nearly empty employee parking lot, I saw something on my windshield. Thinking it was a repo notice of some kind, I panicked, despite knowing that I made every car payment on time if not early. What I found was an envelope that held a handwritten note from Jan Kowalski:

> *"Hi Missy!! We all miss you and hope you're doing okay. We drove around the hospital parking lot looking for your car which wasn't hard to find. Please come by and say hello if you can. Or call me. You know the number. Love you always, Jan"*

Soon after I turned 17 years old, I made an appointment to see Dr. Walter Lane, a gynecologist at Community Hospital where I worked. I had believed the endocrinologist I saw years earlier when he told me that I wouldn't die from ovarian cancer as long as I had my premalignant ovaries removed before I turned 18 years old. I wanted to live, and I trusted Dr. Lane to make sure I did.

Dr. Lane was one of the friendliest doctors I interacted with at the hospital in my capacity as clerical supervisor for the Radiology Department. Before medical imaging was digital, x-ray techs would take medical pictures of patients and deliver hard copies of the images to the film room, where clerical workers like me would hang them for radiologists, doctors who specialize in interpretating medical imaging, such as x-rays, MRIs, CT scans, and ultrasounds to diagnose, treat, and sometimes help prevent medical conditions. Other doctors, be it in family medicine, emergency medicine, obstetrics and gynecology, or any other specialty, would be the ordering physician of the medical imaging tests. If the ordering doctor wanted to see for themselves the films that the radiologist had interpreted, they would go to the film room on their hospital rounds. They would step into our office and give us a patient name, and we would retrieve the folder. They would then shuffle through the folder filled with the patient's films and transcribed reports. When they located the images they wanted, they would step into the dark room and attach them to the film viewer box. They would do their doctor thing and then sloppily stuff everything back in the folder and go about their day. Most doctors would snicker under their breath if we, the film room staff, couldn't immediately locate the patient folder that they were looking for—and the complaints would be louder and more condescending if the employee trying to locate the temporarily missing folder was one of the few Black folks who worked in our office.[1] But not Dr. Lane, who always had a welcoming smile. He was always understanding when we were busy or a folder was temporarily lost, often telling us not to worry and that he would be back in a couple of hours. He was a tall white man with neatly kept parted white hair, who always wore a long grey lab coat over a white dress shirt, tie, suit pants, and black leather loafers with tassels.

When I was deciding on which gynecologist to see to address my premalignant ovaries, Dr. Lane was a no-brainer. I asked mom to join me at the consultation, where we told Dr. Lane about my medical history, including what brought us to the urgent care center years earlier and all of the testing and specialist visits that followed.

After learning I had lost more than 100 pounds, Dr. Lane complimented me on my successful bariatric surgery. If he had asked for more details about my weight loss, he would have learned that I struggled with heart burn and could only eat food that was mashed-potato consistency and easily dissolved in my mouth. I couldn't tolerate most fruit—too acidic—nor many vegetables—too fibrous. I found most food difficult to chew down to a consistency my stomach could handle. Like most people, he focused on the pounds I lost, not the problems I gained. With his friendly smile, he proceeded to do an internal exam with mom sitting next to the exam room table. He advised us to proceed with what he called "exploratory surgery." He would schedule an operating room visit to take a more detailed look inside my body and remove the premalignant ovaries. He explained that he would try to do the procedure laparoscopically so that I wouldn't have a large surgical incision, but rather a few small ones for the surgical devices and medical camera that would be inserted into my abdomen to guide the procedure. However, because my stomach stapling was performed with an open incision, he forewarned me that the laparoscopic procedure might need to be converted to a traditional open laparotomy which would involve a horizontal incision along my lower abdomen. This decision would be made while I was under anesthesia on the operating table. He told me that it was very likely that the bariatric surgery had left lots of scar tissue that would make the laparoscopic procedure more difficult. I told Dr. Lane that I didn't care how my premalignant ovaries were removed, I just wanted them gone so I didn't die. He put a hand on my shoulder and confidently reassured me that he would take good care of me and that I would be back in the file room not long after the surgery, which he encouraged me to schedule as soon as possible. Because I was legally a minor, my mother had to sign the surgical consent form before my surgery was scheduled.

I had one question for Dr. Lane: "I'm not able to have kids, right?" He looked at me and answered, "I will have to see what I find during the surgery, but I don't think so. There is always adoption, though, and when the time comes, I will help you with that." He then vulnerably shared with me that he and his wife adopted four children because they, too, couldn't have biological children. In that very moment, my trust in Dr. Lane grew more than I ever thought was possible.[2] I respected his vulnerability, and I wasn't at all scared or anxious to undergo my second major surgery, which was scheduled for December 1997, just a few weeks after my consultation.

* ★ ☆ ★ *

As the nurses helped me slide over from the gurney to the operating room table, Dr. Lane was there waiting for me in powder blue operating scrubs that matched his eyes. Holding one of my hands while the anesthesiologist did his thing, Dr. Lane reassured me that he would take good care of me as I quickly drifted off into a deep sleep.

When I woke up, a nurse told me the surgery was successful and that Dr. Lane was able to remove my premalignant ovaries without any complications. He did have to open me up though, which didn't bother me aside from now having multiple small incisions from Dr. Lane's unsuccessful attempt to do the procedure laparoscopically in addition to a big one that he ended up making on my pelvis. My shoulders hurt like hell, too, apparently from the air or gas or whatever it is they use during the laparoscopy that was rising in my body after the surgery. Dr. Lane popped into the post-op room to see for himself how I was doing. I remember thinking I made the right decision asking him to perform this surgery, given that he was such a caring doctor with the perfect bedside manner. Dr. Lane explained to me that the big horizontal incision he made on my body was called a bikini cut because it was low enough on my pelvis that it wouldn't be visible if I wore a bikini. "A bikini?" I laughed so loud it hurt my cut-up abdomen, which jiggled from my breathing. Maybe I was loopy from the anesthesia wearing off, but I found the thought of my body in a bikini hilarious. "I would never ever wear a bikini and, besides, my flabby stomach rolls are covering the incision." Hell, I thought to myself, I wouldn't even wear bikini cut underwear. I much preferred granny panties, even though I was probably the only teenager who wore them. Before giving him a chance to respond, I asked him, "You will help me adopt kids when I'm ready, right?" He sat on my hospital bed and held my hand and answered me, "Missy, I will help you." He then pulled out his wallet and showed me a family photo. "These are my four kids with my wife and me. They are all adopted and you'd never know." I said, "Yeah, they look like you both! I can't believe it." I was relieved that I could still be a mother. When I was first diagnosed, motherhood wasn't on my mind. But that wasn't the case now, given that I was becoming an adult and thinking about wanting to someday get married and have a family of my own.

I was discharged after spending a few nights in the hospital. When I got home to our apartment, I was greeted with a mess of dog shit everywhere. I was so upset with mom and Theo, who promised me they would take care of our four dogs while I was in the hospital. But they didn't—at least they didn't to my liking. Our dogs weren't house-trained, which wasn't an issue in the home we were evicted from because they had an outdoor dog run that they lived in. I was ugly crying and angry yelling at them both as I walked around the apartment picking up dog shit with a plastic bag smooshing one pile of shit onto the next. I didn't even change from the pajamas I left the hospital in. I was the only one who walked our dogs and cleaned up after them. I should have known better. Theo went to his room, and mom laid on the couch passively watching the preview channel picking her lips telling me she will clean it and that I should go lay down in my bed. But I was stubborn and wouldn't let up. After I picked up all the shit and sprayed the shit stains with carpet cleaner, I left our apartment and went to the grocery store to rent a carpet cleaner. I was still in my pajamas. It took me a few hours to shampoo the carpet, and although most of the urine stains didn't come out, our apartment smelled better and felt cleaner. I was finally able to relax.

A few days into my recovery, I felt too sick and weak to get out of bed. I was getting worse and not better. When I got the strength to get up and go to the bathroom attached to my bedroom to pee, I noticed a really smelly and dark brown blood-looking fluid draining from my bikini cut, which was smothered under one of my fat rolls. It was late, and mom was working as a third-shift switchboard operator at the Community Hospital—a job that she got through Aunt Maria's connections. I called her at work and told her what was happening and that I was really scared. She panicked and told me to drive myself to the emergency room right away. But I was too weak to walk, let alone drive. I was so dizzy when I stood up that I thought I was going to pass out. It felt like the room was spinning and I had to lean on the wall as I walked to and from the toilet.

"Where's Theo?" she asked.

"I have no idea," I told her, "I haven't left my room."

"Theo!!!" I yelled, "Are you here? I'm dying!" I was being dramatic, sure, but I was really scared.

Messing with the incision made things worse. The smelly blood-like fluid was quickly oozing from under my fat roll onto my pajama pants and down my legs. Theo ran to my room and I immediately gave him the phone. He talked to mom for a few seconds and then proceeded to carry me down the flight of stairs in our apartment building to his car in the communal parking lot. He had recently acquired a beat-up brown car with leather seats. He put me in the back seat and told me to lay down. We only lived 10 or so minutes from Community Hospital, but the entire way he calmly reassured me that I would be fine before instructing me to stay down so I don't get blood all over his car. "Fuck you, man!" I laughed at his humor, which did a great job at calming me down.

We pulled up to the ER entrance and he immediately went in and got me a wheelchair. He knew the routine because he had been working in the ER as a security guard for a few months—a job Aunt Maria also helped him get, marking what I remember being his first legal job. It hadn't even been a year since we were evicted, and now all three of us had hospital jobs with great benefits.[3] Theo helped me get into the wheelchair before rolling me over to triage. He told me he was going to go back home and that I should call him if I needed anything. I begged him to please take care of the dogs, and he told me he would and that I shouldn't worry.

The ER paged Dr. Lane, who eventually met me in the ER. He pushed several long cotton swabs into my bikini cut, which was already ripping open. The smell was horrendous, but as the incision oozed even more with it being stretched open, I started to almost immediately feel better. He explained to me that I probably had a staph infection, which I thought meant that the hospital s-t-a-f-f didn't properly scrub up before my surgery.

I didn't know s-t-a-p-h was short for staphylococcus bacteria, and that I likely brought it upon myself by cleaning up all of the dog shit when I got home from the hospital. He told me he was going to admit me for a night or two so that he could run an IV antibiotic cycle, and that I would be better before I knew it.

However, as the hours went by, it was clear that the IV antibiotic wasn't working. I was still feeling weak, and the fever wasn't reducing. Dr. Lane ordered a CT scan, which revealed a grapefruit-sized mass in my pelvis—an infectious abscess—that wasn't responding to the IV antibiotics dripping into my body. He told me I was going to have to go back to surgery, and that he was going to bring in a general surgical specialist, Dr. Samuel Blue, to assist him with the emergency surgery. The surgery was long, but the recovery was even longer. I had to stay in the hospital for more than a week. Dr. Blue cleared out the abscess but then left my incision open and packed with some sort of gauze-soaked antiseptic. Twice a day, a nurse would change my dressing, removing the old antiseptic-soaked gauze that was dried up and stuck to my insides and replace it with a fresh pile of antiseptic-soaked gauze that was cold and burned inside my body. I dreaded the dressing changes.

When I was discharged for the second time, I came home to a clean enough apartment. Mom and Theo took care of our dogs this time, and while our apartment was still messy, it was nothing like it was before. Thank God.

* * * * *

Mom was working second shift at a greasy spoon diner. Before heading to the hospital for her third shift job, she'd stop at home to change out of her waitress uniform and into hospital scrubs. She'd leave leftover food in the fridge for my brother to eat. I hate reheated food, so I never touched it. Like so many other diners in America, the diner mom worked at was owned by Greeks whose immigration story started in a kitchen, where they worked long hours and saved up enough money to eventually open their own place.[4] Mom told many of the regular customers that she was related to the owners, to ease her embarrassment about waitressing. The owners loved my mom, so they didn't care and they even appreciated the Greek superiority that surrounded her lie. She was a hard and efficient worker who would gossip with her bosses in Greek about other employees and customers.

My staph infection resulted in another 30 pounds weight loss in seven or so weeks, bringing my total weight loss since the bariatric surgery to almost 150 pounds. For the first time in a long time, my weight was hovering around the low 220s. I was 17 years old, nearly 6 feet tall, and felt hot as fuck.

I would put mousse through my shoulder-length hair and then sit on the closed toilet to blow dry it. I would flip my head upside down and allow the hot air from the blow dryer to do its thing, blowing my hair up towards the ceiling. This was the late 90s and big hair was in. After mom dyed my black hair a deep auburn brown, she taught me this technique in order to give my thick hair even more volume. After my hair was "bone dry"—a phrase she used—I would cover it with hair spray before using my hands to scrunch my hair up one handful at a time. She also taught me how to use lip liner pencil to outline my lips before filling it in with a lipstick. I gravitated toward a really deep chocolate brown lipstick and an even darker lip liner. My lips popped. According to her, my skin was perfect. I just needed to dress my lips.

Before we lost the Italian ice stores, I had hired Kelly and Ramona to work at my store. I was 14 years old when I hired them, and they were 16. Kelly, a white soft-spoken girl with dirty blond hair, went to a private Catholic all-girls high school nearby. Ramona, also white, had long black hair and went to the public high school down the road from the Italian ice store. She was loud and silly like me. We hung out in the fall and winter when my Italian ice store was closed. We did typical high schooler things. We went to the movies, shopped together, and would regularly meet up at Denny's or IHOP for midnight pancakes. We also gossiped about our crushes, with me bragging that I was the first to lose my virginity by sleeping with Chuck, the lanky white boy I hired who was 16 and a year older than me at the time.

Although we had lost our Italian ice stores, I stayed in touch with Kelly and Ramona. They both were away at different colleges, private Jesuit universities in the Midwest. One weekend, when I was 17, I took a Greyhound bus to visit Kelly on her college campus—which was in a city I'd never even been to. She was halfway through her first semester of college and wanted to show me around. I stayed with her and her roommate in their small dorm room, sleeping on the floor in between their beds that they had lofted above their desks. We went to a house party where a bunch of white college kids filled a dark basement with The Notorious B.I.G. and Snoop Dogg on loop. I paid the entrance fee and received a plastic cup that I filled with cheap beer so I wouldn't stand out. But I didn't drink even a sip of it, because I hate the taste of alcohol.

This is it, I thought. This is what I want to do. I decided then that I would figure out what I needed to do to get my GED and chase this dream.

* * * * *

I had a laptop that one of mom's friends gifted me, but I had only been using it to talk to people in chat rooms about mundane shit through a dial-up internet connection. After visiting Kelly at college, I started searching the internet for information about getting a GED in the State of Illinois. I learned that the test was offered at the local community college, but that I needed to be at least 18 before I could take it because of a minimum age requirement. Illinois, like many other states, instituted the requirement to discourage youth from using the GED as an educational shortcut, allowing them to drop out of traditional schooling.[1] In less than a year I could take the test, so I went to a bookstore and purchased a GED prep book and vowed to work through it in order to sit for the test as soon as I turned 18. I also received a schedule of classes guide in the mail from the College of DuPage, a community college in the west suburbs. The guide was sent to everyone in the area, I think, and came four times a year because the College of DuPage was on a quarter system. When I'd sit on the toilet to take a dump, I'd flip through it reading course descriptions. I couldn't wait to enroll.

I also was spending far more time in AOL chat rooms, mostly local rooms for people my age in and around Chicago. In the 1990s, the internet was still a strange way to meet people, but I was substantially younger than everyone I worked with at the hospital, and it was my only way to connect with people my age. My AOL screen name was "MissyLuce." I'd enter a chat room almost every night the same way:

> MissyLuce: Hi! I'm Missy and I live in the west suburbs!
> I work at a hospital and am homeschooled.

I didn't private chat with many people, but when I did, I would usually lie, like many other teenagers who lie about mundane things all the time. One study showed that high school students tell, on average, 4.1 lies every 24 hours—which is 75% higher than college students and 150% higher than a representative sample of adults.[2] My lies were usually about school. I would tell whichever new chat room friend I was IM'ing with that I was homeschooled and was going to go to DePaul University after I finished high school. My lie included DePaul for a number of reasons. It was in Chicago and one of the only universities I'd ever heard of in the city I grew up in— my brother, and many of his friends, would wear DePaul University apparel because its mascot is a Blue Demon. He and many of his friends were associated with either the Satan's Disciples—a street gang whose trademark was a devil—or the Gangster Disciples, whose one symbol featured pitchforks.[3] I also loved the school's colors—one of which I saw as a purplish blue. I also knew a couple of Italian ice store employees who ended up going to DePaul.

Because I'd worked in the hospital since I was 16, first as a radiology service assistant and then as a clerical supervisor, I had a lot of knowledge for a 17-year-old about the medical field. I had enough medical knowledge that I felt completely comfortable telling everyone I chatted with online that my mother was an emergency room medical resident—a newly minted doctor. I chose emergency medicine for my lie because she did in fact work third shift at the hospital. And what doctors work third shift? Emergency medicine was perfect. I also said she was a resident, because we were living in a two-bedroom apartment and didn't have any money. And I knew residents didn't start banking quite yet, so constructing her as a resident was quite convincing. I wouldn't have to lie about where I lived if that came up, or where my mom was at night. I would sometimes tell people my biological father, Marx, had passed away. After our eviction, mom had refused to allow Marx to live with us, and I was embarrassed that he was left homeless, living in Chicagoland shelters for the better part of a year. There was no way in hell that I was going to tell strangers on the internet the truth about my family.

* * ⋆ ⋆ *

One late cold winter evening I was in a chat room and began privately chatting with a guy whose screenname was "CharlieIsShy." I can't remember who initiated the chat, but I do know that I've always been extroverted, which is probably why I've always gravitated to people who were like my soft-spoken, reserved, and excellent listener friend Kelly. Quiet people didn't fight me for the microphone in conversations or gatherings. I also think, when I wasn't annoying them, I made them feel more comfortable, too, taking the spotlight off of them in group settings where they might have otherwise felt pressured to communicate in a way that didn't work for them.

I don't know what Charlie and I talked about when we initially connected, but I know I told him the same lies about my life that I told every other person I met in chat rooms. I was homeschooled with an acceptance from DePaul University, my mom was an ER medical resident, my dad was dead, and my brother was a typical college student. I also lied and told him I was 18 years old when I was, in fact, only a few months past my 17th birthday.

Charlie, who was 20 years old, told me that he was Jewish and lived in a North Shore suburb of Chicago, which meant nothing to me at the time, but I later learned that his neighborhood was among the wealthiest areas in the entire state. He said that after he graduated high school, he went to a state school but decided it wasn't for him for a variety of reasons and left, before continuing on full time at a community college in the north suburbs. His father was among the third generation who worked for their family business, and his mom was a home-maker. I learned he had a younger brother who was still in high school, and a family dog, a spoiled corgi, named Molly.

"Hey, what do you look like?" I asked Charlie, expecting a description, but he replied with a scanned picture.

"Do you play soccer?" He was wearing a long sleeve t-shirt that read "World Soccer." He had on a white hat with some sort of soccer logo on it, and glasses. I found his pronounced jawbone and half smile good looking.

"No, I don't," he typed, "I just like following both the women's and men's U.S. National Teams."

"I love sports. I used to have season tickets to the White Sox. I even met Frank Thomas and have his autograph. And I met Ken Griffey, Jr. from the Seattle Mariners. I used to collect baseball cards and autographs. Do you like baseball?"

"I used to be into the Cubs," he typed, "but I don't like traditional U.S. sports anymore. I read *Fever Pitch* by Nick Hornby, and the sport fascinated me because of its popularity in the rest of the world. I like rooting for underdogs and soccer is definitely an underdog sport here."

"That's cool. I don't know anything about soccer. Have you ever been to a game?"

"They are called matches. But, yes, I go to a lot of World Cup Qualifiers around the country, and I really love U.S. Women's Soccer and even drove to Atlanta in 1996 where the women's team won gold."

A memory popped into my head. The bag of Italian ice money, weed, and drug cash that was taken from my Neon's trunk was a purple and blue Atlanta Olympics duffle bag. I was never interested in the Olympics. I must have gotten that bag for free somewhere. I pushed the memory back down to wher-ever memories are stored.

"Oh, wow! That's awesome. Who did you go with?"

"I drove myself."

"How long did it take you? Were you scared driving by yourself?"

"Nah, I had a map. I used to work for a store that sold them so I'm comfortable driving long distance. And I checked in with my mom along the way. It was the best experience of my life seeing the Women's Team win gold."

"I've never seen soccer. Sounds cool. Hey, I think you're cute. You kind of look like Adam Sandler."

"I'm not funny like that guy."

"Are you shy? Is that why you have 'shy' in your screenname?"

"Yeah, I'm really shy."

"I'm not at all. I talk too much and don't shut up."

"That's a good thing. I wish I was more like you then."

He asked me what I looked like and if I had to picture to share. I didn't have a photo, so I did my best to describe myself to him.

"I'm a tomboy who loves sports. I have hair that goes to my shoulders. It's dark auburn brown and wavy. And I'm not skinny. But I'm not fat."

"You sound pretty, MissyLuce. Is that your name?"

"My name is Missy, but my mom jokingly calls me Luce, which is short for Lucifer. I drive a bright yellow-green Plymouth Neon that has 'Go Luce' personalized plates."

"Your car sounds fun. I drive a black Ford Escape. I would never want to stand out like you. Do you have a scanned picture?"

"No. I don't have a scanner."

"Do you live near a Kinko's? They will scan a photo for you for a small amount."

"I didn't know that. I will go check it out tomorrow after work. Will you be online tomorrow?"

"Yes, let's plan on meeting online. 9pm okay?"

"That works! Talk to you then!"

"Goodnight, MissyLuce."

"Haha. Just call me Missy."

"Alright, goodnight, Missy."

"Goodnight, Charlie."

I logged off and searched through some photos to find the perfect one to try to get scanned at the Kinko's down the road.

They were open 24 hours and I thought about heading over there before I slept, but it was late and I was tired and had to be at work at 8am. I found the perfect photo, though. I was wearing Gap overalls with an unbuttoned teal green Seattle Mariners Ken Griffey Jr. jersey. I bought the authentic jersey years earlier, but the biggest size they had was XL. I couldn't fit into it when I got it, but I still bought it in case I someday could, which happened after the staph infection revived the weight loss from my stomach stapling. I even got Ken Griffey Jr. to sign his name on the "4" of the "24"—his number on the back of the jersey—after paying to get his signature at a signing event. My hair was styled like mom taught me. And my lips were perfectly dressed and lined. I also had on a new pair of brown Doc Martens, which I saw were obviously in style on my trip to visit Kelly at college.

The next night around 9pm I dialed into AOL, where Charlie was waiting for me in a chat room. He immediately privately messaged me and I shared the photo. He told me I was gorgeous and looked like Candace Cameron, who played D. J. Tanner on the popular sitcom of our youth, *Full House*. I didn't see the resemblance at all, aside from the fact that we both have bigger heads with round face shapes. We chatted a lot on the computer that night. And even exchanged phone numbers the next night. We eventually met in person at a chain restaurant I chose not far from where I lived. We met in the parking lot by my car, which was easy for him to find given that my car always stood out. We walked into the restaurant together. I thought it was hilarious that he was wearing the same World Soccer shirt he had on in the photo he shared in our private online chat. I was wearing a horizontally-blue-and-white-striped long sleeve men's shirt and men's jeans that I got from the Gap. I had on my Doc Martens, and my hair and lips were done. I also sprayed lots of ck one, a bottle of Calvin Klein unisex fragrance, under my arms and on my chest before I got out of my car.

A few weeks into dating Charlie, we talked about sex. We both were inexperienced but not virgins. I told him that I wouldn't have sex with him without a condom because I didn't want to get pregnant. I knew damn well that I couldn't get pregnant, but I wanted him to think I was a good white teenage girl.

Charlie went into a gas station to purchase condoms while I waited in the car. He came back with them and he drove us to his home. It was late, and his parents were upstairs in their room watching TV or sleeping, while his brother was probably in his room studying for his AP classes. We went downstairs to their finished basement, which was almost as big as the apartment that mom, Theo, and I lived in. There was a huge comfortable Ethan Allen soft grey sectional against the wall. And a big-screen TV that was huge. In one of the corners there was an oversized office chair pushed up against a fancy looking desk with a new desktop computer, printer, and scanner on top of it.

As we were making out and got undressed, I was embarrassed that I had no hair around my vagina, so I lied and said that I shaved it. Charlie reassured me that he liked it, before we continued to fuck around. I wouldn't know the real reason I didn't have pubic hair, or underarm or leg hair for that matter, for several more years. While Charlie initially told me that he was turned on by my lack of pubic hair, later when we were married, he told me that my body was weirdly child-like because of it. When I brought up the fact that many people pay to have their pubic hair removed, he dismissingly laughed, "Not all of it!"

A month or two into dating, when things were getting serious with us sleeping together and falling in love, I decided it was time to start telling the truth about myself. As he was driving us to go to dinner before a movie, I told him that I needed to talk to him about some things that happened in my life and that I was really scared to share. He was calm and felt safe as I started crying. He held my hand and said that whatever it is it's fine.

I eventually blurted out, "I can't have kids. I had ovarian cancer. And I left school when I was young because of it."

Through my tears, he smiled and said, "That's it? I thought you were going to tell me you were on *America's Most Wanted* or something."

We laughed, and I shared what I knew about my reproductive organs. He wasn't sure if he wanted kids, and he certainly didn't seem bothered by the fact that we would have to adopt. After less than year of dating, he asked me to marry him and I said yes. While his mother wasn't pleased and didn't really take our engagement seriously, encouraging us to think of the ring as a promise ring, I considered myself his fiancée. While dropping out of school was far more complicated than I made it out to be during the "come clean" car ride, it was my way of trying to unravel at least some of my lies. I was extremely protective of my mother's reputation, so I never told him, or his family, that I lied about her being a doctor. And there was no way I was going to tell the truth about that either. Mom had no problem going along with the lie. We also talked a little bit about my brother, and how he got in a fight in school but that the charges were dismissed because it was self-defense. I don't remember if I shared the fact that a knife was involved.

One cold winter day, when Charlie and I were seriously dating but not yet living together, Theo got arrested. He was, and still is, always in and out of jail. He was in the Cook County Jail awaiting a court date, and mom was really worried that he was in a violent jail that had lots of gangs—as if he, himself, wasn't violent. I can't recall the bail amount, but it must have been substantial enough that mom and I didn't have it, so I asked Charlie if he would lend me the money. I said that mom, the supposed ER resident who went along with the lie I created about what she did at the hospital, would pay him back after she got paid. He agreed without any hesitation. This was probably the second time I realized that Charlie came from "old money." His family's wealth ran generations deep, and while you wouldn't know it by the Ford Escape he drove or the modest home on the North Shore he grew up in, he was rich. The first time I had realized this was when I asked him if I could see his family business. He told me it was a fabric store. I expected his family business to be a small retail store that sold yarn and crafts. But when we drove up to it, I realized I was way off. The business wasn't in a strip center like I imagined. It was a fucking warehouse, almost like a factory, with countless semi-trucks bays and a huge office at its front entrance. What the fuck, I remember thinking. Charlie is rich.

While Charlie was inside the Cook County Jail bailing out Theo, I waited in his parked car. I sat there with nothing to do, staring at the cars passing by for what felt like hours and hours. Before Charlie left the car to bail out Theo, we had decided that he would post the bond money, fill out whatever paperwork was needed, and then just leave. Theo would find his own way home because mom warned us that it takes a long time for an inmate to be released after posting the bond. Even longer than it took for Charlie to post my brother's bond.

* * ✮ * *

It had been nearly a year since we were evicted from our home. We were living in the two-bedroom apartment Aunt Athena rented for us in her name. Aside from Marx, who was living in and out of homeless shelters, things seemed to be working out for us. Mom, Theo, and I were all working at Community Hospital. And mom was working at a greasy-spoon Greek diner, too. I was seriously dating Charlie, and I spent a lot of time at his family home on weekends—after getting my hair blow dried and round-brush styled for $35 every Friday at Mario Tricoci, an upscale Chicagoland chain of salons. My hair could hold the blow dry and style the entire week, although by Wednesday night, it started to look flat and a bit messy. I first learned of Mario Tricoci while catching the credits of an episode of *The Oprah Winfrey Show*. The salon was thanked in the credits for doing hair for the guests or something like that, and I thought I wanted to check it out. With weekly blow dries and styles, I must have been to three or four Mario Tricoci salons throughout the city. I had my favorite stylists at each one, so if one stylist didn't have an opening, I would go on to the next, who was sometimes at a different location. I also got my hair cut and dyed and my eyebrows waxed. I encouraged every stylist to use me as their canvas and have fun. They tried zig zag parts, different highlights in my hair, and tried different arches with my eyebrows.

Every Friday, walking out of the salon, I strived to look like I was from old money, with clean-styled hair, unassuming and boring clothes that looked like they came from Ann Taylor Loft or Nordstrom, and a modest black handbag that Charlie's mom gifted me—a Prada bag that didn't have the logo blasted all over it.[4] Observing Charlie's family, I learned that old money folks don't wear or drive money to feel important. They invest it, unlike my five star white trash family and others like us who want to pretend they arrived with gaudy and flashy things.

Mom and I split the apartment rent. Theo didn't contribute, but he also got fired from his security job not too long after he started it. I was the one to physically make sure the rent got paid the first of every month, if not a few days earlier. I didn't trust mom to pay the rent on time, and I never wanted to deal with being evicted again. Near the end of our one-year-lease, I called the apartment office, pretending to be Aunt Athena because the lease was in her name, asking about a renewal. I mostly wanted to know how much our rent was going to go up so I could plan accordingly. I was shocked when they told me that they weren't going to renew our lease because of complaints that we were violating the two-pet maximum. I couldn't believe that someone in the complex would turn us in. I lied and said that we only had two dogs but sometimes watched our cousin's dogs. The white apartment manager was nice about it, but said we had until the end of the next month to leave. In that moment, I was so thankful that I reached out early about the renewal because at least now I had a little more than two months to find us a new place to live.

One day, driving home from work, I saw a "house for rent" sign and followed it. It was only about a mile from the apartment we were living in, but it was a house and on the way to the hospital. It was perfect. I called up the number on the sign and was excited to hear it was still available—and only $1300 a month. With mom and I splitting the rent, we could afford this three-bedroom house with one and a half bathrooms. I made an appointment to see it—and made sure mom and I both had scrubs on to project a powerful professional identity when we did—and almost immediately decided it was going to be our new home.[5] Mom thought the ranch home looked like shit. It was old and run-down, but it was bigger than our apartment and only a couple hundred dollars more per month to rent. It was in Hinsdale, an affluent suburb, but on the shittiest block in that west suburb. The best part about the house was that it had a full basement. It wasn't finished but it had some airflow and a few well-windows. I thought it was the perfect place for our dogs. Mom eventually caved, and we moved in. I put the lease in my name, changing my birth year from 1980 to 1979 on the rental application in case the landlord wouldn't rent to a 17-year-old. Mom's credit was still fucked from the eviction, so we knew any rental application in her name wouldn't be approved. When the prospective landlord inquired about why my mom, who we pretended was an ER resident, didn't want to fill out the rental application and put the lease in her name, we lied and said her credit was ruined because of a divorce. Since I had been working for over a year and half at the hospital, and managed to get a secured credit card in my name—I'm not sure how, given that I wasn't 18 yet—my credit wasn't extensive but it was excellent.

We also allowed Marx to move into our new home. He was so happy to have a place to sleep. He stayed in our basement with our dogs and Theo, who had a full bedroom set downstairs, a TV with cable, as well as a used couch and loveseat that our Aunt Athena gave us.

Every morning before I left for work, I would go downstairs and pick up all of the dog shit with a plastic bag smooshing each pile of shit on top of the next. I would then splash straight bleach from its container around the basement and mop it up with hot water and a yellow industrial mop bucket set I got from Walmart. Almost every morning, Theo, who was sleeping on his bed, and Marx, who was sleeping on the couch, would scream at me for using bleach. Their complaints were valid. My eyes would water and my lungs would burn when I was mopping. My throat would feel like I swallowed acid, but I couldn't stand the shit smell creeping up through the vents to the rest of the house. Mom joined them in yelling at me for using bleach. However, she would add that she was allergic and that I was getting her sick. Their collective complaints didn't stop me. I would repeat this cleaning process when I came home from work before heading off to the North Shore to meet Charlie for dinner, a movie, or to watch an episode or two of *Friends*, our favorite sitcom—which I'm embarrassed about today given the show's rampant racism, anti-fatness, and transphobia.[6] I went through two gallons of bleach a week, and sometimes if I didn't take off my scrubs before starting the process, I would fuck up and ruin them with bleach.

* * ☆ * *

On October 24, 1998, 12 days after I turned 18 years old—which was the minimum age requirement for the GED test in Illinois—I sat and took it. It was the first time the test was offered after I was eligible. When I walked into the community college lecture hall, which had about 50 seats, I immediately locked eyes with Tyrone, a handsome Black man with a gorgeous smile dressed to the nines. He was my brother's friend, and his presence in the room alone eased my test-taking anxiety. I sat in front of him.

"Hey, Missy!" He waved and smiled while asking, "What are you doing here?"

I laughed, "Um, taking the GED. I'm so scared."

He comforted me, telling me that he heard it was really easy and to just make sure I answered every question. I had been studying for the test on and off for about a year with the GED prep book I bought after visiting Kelly at college and deciding that I, too, wanted to go to college. I also took a GED prep course at a community college in the area, after seeing it advertised in a schedule of classes I found in our mailbox with other junk mail. I hadn't known that a GED prep course was even a thing. I immediately decided to enroll in the section that met once a week in the evening for 6 or so weeks. I filled out the paper application and drove to the college to drop it off at the registration office. I can't remember if there was a charge, but I would have paid whatever they wanted. The class required their own GED prep book, which I bought in cash from the instructor the first day of class.

As Tyrone and I sat in the room waiting to take the GED test, we talked about my brother, their mutual friends, and more until the proctor asked everyone to be quiet so that he could give us directions and administer the test. I finished the test before Tyrone, and waved goodbye as I walked to the front of the classroom to turn in my Scantron.

A few weeks later, after anxiously checking the mail every day after work, I received the results.

I passed.

I fucking passed.

My fucking God. I passed.

I got a 95th-percentile score in social studies, 78th-percentile score in literature and arts, 67th-percentile score in mathematics, 60th-percentile score in science, and 57th-percentile score in writing skills.

I couldn't believe it.

I fucking passed.

Even though I dropped out of school during the seventh grade, I still managed to pass the GED test the first time I sat for it. I'm not sure what that says about the test itself, high school education, and/or the benefits of reading the *Chicago Sun-Times* every day, as I loved doing.

Standing by the mailbox with the GED results in my hands, I jumped into my car and drove directly to the College of DuPage to register for classes. The registrar's office helped me fill out the paper application, and then directed me to a nearby office where I was required to take two placement tests: English and Mathematics. I wanted to start classes as soon as possible and the new quarter was not far away, so I took both tests right then so that I could register for course sections that didn't interfere with my work schedule.

The tests—which research has since shown can't reliably predict success in college classes—were computerized and scored almost immediately.[7] I placed in remedial math and remedial English. I didn't care that my college career was going to begin with 089-level classes. I wanted to get the ball moving, so I enrolled in both a remedial English class and a remedial math class. My math score was much lower than my English score, so I was told I was going to have to take not one but two remedial math courses before being allowed to enroll in College Algebra.

The first week of classes was exciting. I had my paper schedule in hand. New folders and pencils, and the required texts from the bookstore. The campus felt huge, but I knew where to go because Charlie went to campus with me the weekend before classes started to help me find my classrooms and pick up the required books from the bookstore. I had no idea that colleges had their own bookstore. Although Charlie went to a community college in the north suburbs, and I was going to start at one in the west suburbs, he shared everything he knew about being successful in college, including what a syllabus was, to ask the professor if you have questions, the best way to take notes, and more.

During the second week of the quarter, my English professor, a white woman who looked like a stereotypical soccer mom, asked to meet with me for a few minutes after class. I was one of very few white students in the remedial English class. Most of my peers were Latinx and/or Black. I feared that the paper I had turned in the last time we met was horrible, but I was wrong. After class she asked me about my educational background, to which I lied and told her I was homeschooled instead of telling her that I dropped out of the seventh grade. She went on to say that she was really impressed with my work and curious about why I was in the remedial English class. At the time, I didn't think that it was probably my whiteness that stood out to her and not so much my writing.

"You don't happen to have your English placement results with you, do you?" she asked.

"I do," I said as I reached into my English folder to grab them. I kept the results behind the syllabus.

"Can I see them for a minute?"

After handing the golden yellow form with my results on it to her, she said, "This makes sense now. It looks like you were only a few points away from testing out of remedial English. I don't think this is the best class for you. Have you thought about taking the test again? I bet if you were more relaxed you could test out of this section and get into English 101."

"You think? But I already paid for this class."

"Yes, I'm confident you could pass out of remedial English. Did you know you could take the test more than once?"

"No, I had no idea."

"And you can transfer out of remedial English and enroll in English 101. You won't lose any money." She continued, "Do you have time this evening to take it again? Do you want me to walk you over to the testing center?"

"Sure," I said, thankful for her help.

As my professor walked me to the testing center, she explained that she also taught English 101, on a different night of the week, and that it was early enough in the quarter that I could enroll in that section if I placed out of remedial English. She gave me all of the information I needed to enroll in her section if I did indeed qualify. If I didn't, she said, she'd see me in the English 089 class the following week. I scored substantially higher the second time around on the English placement test, so I followed her directions, dropped English 089, and enrolled in her section of English 101. Fortunately, my English professor's section of English 101 was offered on a different night of the week than the remedial math class I was also taking. I didn't try to take the math placement test again, because everything I was learning in the class was new to me and I was struggling to pass.

* * * * *

As I was working through my first quarter at the College of DuPage, I was thinking about what I wanted to study. When I was younger, I loved playing teacher with my stuffed animals, so I thought maybe I would plan to study elementary education. But since I was also quite experienced in the workings of radiology, applying for the community college's x-ray program was also on my mind. I had to take a few general ed classes before I could apply to the x-ray program, so in future quarters, I took an Introduction to Education class, along with a basic biology class, a typing class, and a religious studies class. My options were limited to the course offerings that didn't interfere with my work schedule. I also enrolled in a bunch of other classes, including political science, geography, and history, that I ended up dropping early for a variety of reasons, ranging from not having enough time to study the material (which was all new to me) to finding the readings incredibly boring. But since I didn't drop the courses early enough into their quarters, I ended up with a lot of Ws for "withdrawal" up and down my transcript.

During one registration cycle, Charlie told me that I should check out sociology. He had taken a few sociology classes, and eventually even minored in it, and told me that he thought I'd really like the readings and class discussions. I'd never heard of sociology, but it sounded interesting and I trusted him. I enrolled in Introduction to Sociology the same semester I was accepted into the College of DuPage's x-ray program.

The Introduction to Radiography class I was taking was so basic that I remember thinking I could have taught it. Having worked in a hospital's radiology department full-time for a couple of years already, I knew all of the medical lingo the professor was writing on the board and explaining to us: phlebotomist, catheter, medical imaging, computerized tomography, barium, blah, blah, blah. The class was so boring, and nothing like my Introduction to Sociology class, which sort of resembled the newspapers I loved to read. We discussed social problems, world events, and ways to understand life circumstances. The class was engaged in a discussion, not lectured to as if we didn't bring any knowledge into the room. I also learned in the Intro to Soc class that my experience with inequalities was not unique. We talked about the Columbine High School massacre (which had just happened), Rodney King, drug dealing, and more. I was hooked.

I came across a table in our Introduction to Sociology textbook about the likelihood of completing college, a master's degree, etc. There were different numbers for different sample students: the community college student, the four-year university student, and more. I don't recall if the statistics were broken down by race and gender or things like that, but I doubt it. A 2024 report from the Community College Resource Center revealed that about 80% of community college students wish to eventually transfer to a four-year college or university, but only a third of them actually do.[8] And of those who do transfer, roughly one out of two never earn their bachelor's degree. And these rates are far lower for Black students, older students, and low-income students. As a community college student reading these statistics, I was so discouraged, and quite frankly scared. Community college students, like me, were very unlikely to ever earn an associate's degree, let alone a bachelor's degree. When I brought this up in class, the sociology professor guided us into a discussion on various forms of capital and outcomes. She also told us that there were outliers in all models, and explained that an outlier is someone who goes far outside of what is expected based on statistical patterns.

I wanted to be an outlier in the community college model.

I wanted to transform my outward lies—especially the acceptance to DePaul—into inward reality. Working at the hospital gave me a taste of what a prestigious job felt like. I was treated differently when I wore scrubs at the grocery store, or when filling out the housing application for the home I rented for our family. I could feel the prestige I benefited from, even though I didn't really understand it. It was then that I decided to drop out of the x-ray program, despite the prestige my scrubs afforded, and instead focus on finishing my associate's degree so that I could transfer to a four-year college to study sociology. My goal was to earn a master's degree in sociology so that I could teach sociology at a community college—like my professor, who had her master's from DePaul University.

I wanted to be the outlier in my family.

While my family was determined to chase a flashy lifestyle at any cost, including breaking the law, I wanted to chase stability and financial security through education. And while education is considered to be one of the most realistic vehicles to get ahead in life, the ride is smoother when you're white.[9] I always assumed that the Intro to Soc course changed my life. And it did. But so did my whiteness. White folks who sit for the GED are, in fact, far more likely to pass the raced and classed exam than Black or Latinx people.[10] And professors, like the white woman who was determined to help me jump out of the remedial English line, are far more likely to mentor white students, especially men, than they are their racially marginalized peers.[11] And it was Aunt Maria's white network that landed me a job at the hospital, not my nonexistent interview skills as a seventh-grade dropout.[12] And I have no doubt now that it was my whiteness in the online dating pool that brought Charlie, and his old money, intellect, modest style, and other upper-middle-class behaviors to my world, but most importantly, his forgiveness of my lies.[13] These facts do not take away from the resiliency I displayed and the tears that I shed over the years. They just offer some insight into why my hard work was amplified.[14]

I had seen plenty of doctors after my abdominal pain brought me to urgent care the summer after I completed the sixth grade. From 11 years old until I was 19 years old, I had seen endocrinologists, gynecologists, urologists, and psychiatrists all over Chicagoland. I had been told that I had premalignant ovarian cancer and was, by medical definition, "morbidly obese," so the countless medical visits to a wide range of specialists made sense.

Now, because I had different health insurance and had moved into a one-bedroom apartment that Charlie and I rented together in a north suburb, I knew I needed to establish medical care with a new family practice office. I did minimal research to find a provider who took my insurance, was accepting new patients, and whose office was close to my home. I decided to schedule an appointment for a physical as a way to start the provider-and-patient relationship. I figured it would be helpful to be an active patient of a practice should I come down with a sore throat, the flu, or some other seasonal illness. When making the appointment, the office staff asked me to collect my medical records from my previous providers and bring them to my first appointment. Working in a medical setting, I expected the request and was already on it. I was afraid to reach out to some of my childhood medical providers, including the bariatric surgeon who stapled my stomach, because I knew we owed them money—or rather my parents did, because I was a minor and couldn't legally be held responsible for the costs of their services—and I didn't want to rattle the snake's cage, so to speak, and start their collection process again. I decided to focus on getting my records from Dr. Walter Lane's office. Because I had health insurance when he operated on me and I always paid my co-pays, I knew I didn't owe him, or the consulting surgeon brought in for the emergency surgery due to the staph infection, anything. Dr. Lane's office asked me to give them a week's time to photocopy my medical file. My records, I was told, would be waiting for me a week later in a sealed envelope at their front desk.

As I stepped out of their office and made my way down the hall to the elevators, I didn't think much of what was in the large, sealed manila envelope I clutched in my arm. I was a bit curious, I suppose, but having worked with medical records, my curiosity was minimal. I figured I would be inundated with boring lab results, provider notes, and consult summaries.

Sitting in my monkey shit green car in Dr. Lane's office parking lot, I opened the sealed envelope and pulled out a stack of papers about two inches thick.

Boring lab results.

Boring lab results.

More boring lab results.

There were so many fucking boring lab results.

But then I came across a surgical pathology report. It was only one and half pages. And parts of it were redacted with a black sharpie marker.

Hmm, I thought. This looks interesting.

It read:

GROSS AND MICROSCOPIC DIAGNOSIS:
A&B. Gonads, right and left, excision:

SERTOLI CELL HYPERPLASIA arising in bilateral REDACTED of androgen insensitivity syndrome (REDACTED feminization). See microscopic description.

CLINICAL HISTORY:
Absent uterus and bilateral gonads. Genotype 46 XY

SPECIMEN:
A Right gonad
B Left gonad

When I read this report, I was a seventh-grade dropout who had only recently passed the GED exam. I had barely tested into English 101, yet there I was in my doctor's parking lot left to comprehend my medical history, and the lies that surrounded it, all on my own. I read on:

GROSS DESCRIPTION
A. Specimen, submitted in formalin, labeled "right gonad," consists of a piece of partially peritonealized testis measuring 6 x 1.9 x 1.9 cm. The specimen is serially sectioned and consists of two grossly distinct areas. One area measures 3.5 cm in length and consists of a soft tan brown tissue with a few well defined tan nodules within it. The largest nodule measures 1.1 cm. The remainder of the specimen consists of pink white non-descript soft tissue. A 0.5 cm thin walled cyst is also identified. The largest nodule is submitted in cassette A1 and A2; other nodules and surrounding tan-brown tissue in cassettes A3 through A5; representative portions of the cyst and remaining soft tissue in cassette A6. AAH
B. Specimen, submitted in formalin, labeled "left gonad," consists of a partially peritonealized testis measuring 5 x 3.3 x 2.5 cm. A few thin walled cysts in aggregate measuring 1.8 cm in greatest dimension are attached. The specimen is serially sectioned and contains a small amount of brown gray tissue. The majority of the gonad is replaced

by a fish-fleshy well circumscribed nodule measuring 4cm in length and 2.5 cm in diameter. Touch preparations are prepared. Representative portions of the nodule are submitted in cassettes B1 through B4; and gray brown area in cassettes B5 and B6. AAH

MICROSCOPIC DESCRIPTION:

Sections show a bi-phasic architectural pattern. The histology corresponding to the well circumscribed tan white nodules consists of closely packed seminiferous tubules composed only of Sertoli cells. In these areas no intervening leydig cells are identified. The histology corresponding to the tan brown areas outside of the well circumscribed white nodules is composed of closely packed tubules lined by sertoli cells with numerous intervening leydig cells. No mitoses, pleomorphism, vascular invasion, or necrosis is identified. The terminology used to identify testicular lesions in androgen insensitivity syndromes interchangeably employs the terminology sertoli cell hamartoma and adenoma to describe a benign proliferation of seroti cells. No malignancy is identified either gonad.[1]

What the fuck is all of this?
My heart dropped.
What the fuck am I reading?
No malignancy identified?
No cancer?
What the fuck are gonads?
46 XY?
What does that even mean?
Who am I?
What am I?
The questions kept coming. I felt my body heat up and my heart pacing, much like your body reacts when you come close to getting in a car accident. I started quickly flipping through the papers, scanning everything as quickly as I could. I was

searching for answers. The papers that were once neatly organized in an envelope were scattered all over my lap and passenger seat. I picked up the pathology report and held it up to the
sun to try to read through the redaction.

It worked.

"TESTES." Why is the word "testes" blacked out? Wait,
are testes the same as balls? My fucking God. Am I a man?
What the fuck is going on? I read another redacted word:
"TESTICULAR." Oh my God. I'm a man. Holy shit. I'm a
man. I started crying. What the fuck is Charlie going to say? I
just knew he would call off our marriage. I felt like a fucking
circus freak. I felt like my life, the one I wanted so badly, was
crashing down.

I then came across a clinical encounter note with Dr. Lane.
It read:

> "After extensive discussion I feel pt [patient] needs surgery
> to have gonads removed. She is not aware of any chromo-
> somal studies and most literature agrees it best she not be
> aware of the chromosome studies. She has been told she
> is missing her uterus, she does have a vagina. She has no
> tubes. She has been told she may have streaked ovaries
> and they should be removed because of the possibility of
> developing gonadal cancer."[2]

Dr. Lane, the doctor I trusted and admired for his bedside manner, lied to me.[3] He lied. Did my mother know?

As I drove to my apartment as quickly as I could, swerv-
ing in and out of tollway traffic, I felt my mind moving faster
than my car. Maybe I just don't understand what I'm reading?
Maybe XY chromosomes are female, and I'm remembering the
wrong thing? I needed to get home so I could dial in to the internet in order to search on Yahoo! everything I was reading. I
needed definitions of words I didn't understand, and I hoped
they would give me clarity. I also didn't have a whole lot of
time to get answers. Charlie and I had only recently moved into
our one-bedroom apartment together, and I didn't want him to

come home from work and ask what I was doing on the internet, or worse, ask to see my records.

With each internet search I did, I'd unravel another lie.[4] Only this time, I was on the receiving end of the lies, not about my age or my family background, but about my body and my entire identity. It was clear from what I was reading that I was a "hermaphrodite"—the term then in use that describes a person born with both male and female genitalia. Today, "hermaphrodite" is considered a derogatory term by some, but not all, people with bodies similar to mine. The word "intersex" has mostly replaced "hermaphrodite" as the preferred term and is more widely used by intersex people.[5]

I never had cancer. Dr. Lane didn't remove cancerous ovaries. He took out my balls. I was a fucking freak with a vagina on the outside and balls on the inside.

No wonder psychiatrists asked me if I had crushes on boys or girls. I'm a freak. I'm a man and a woman. Oh my God. Does this mean I'm gay? Am I a fag because I love Charlie? Did I have a dick? Did they take that, too? Oh my God. Why did my mom lie to me? My aunts? Do they all know I'm a fucking freak? How could Dr. Lane have lied to me? Charlie is going to break up with me and kick me out if he finds out I'm a fucking freak.

I looked at the clock. Shit. Charlie's going to be home from work any minute now. I deleted my browsing history the best I could without clearing the whole thing. I then stuffed all of the papers back into the manilla envelope, left our apartment, and ran down the stairs as fast as I could. As I made my way to the huge trash dumpster where all of us tenants in the area threw away our trash, I sobbed as I flung the envelope into the pile. I ran back into the apartment wiping away my tears, comforting myself by the fact that I got rid of what I learned.

Afraid of learning more things that would scare me, I protected myself and didn't search for clarity. I didn't ask my family for answers. Instead, I promised myself I'd take these secrets to my grave. I canceled the appointment I had scheduled with what would have been my new family practice doctor. I wasn't ready to tell their office that I was born with both a vagina and balls. I wasn't ready to publicly deal with the medical lies. Despite having health insurance, I wouldn't see a doctor for years because I couldn't face the truth about my body and what doctors had done to me. I stuck to regular dental cleanings, though all the while thankful that I didn't need to be treated in my early twenties for anything that an over-the-counter medicine couldn't treat. And while my weight got up to the 280s with my ability to eat more food than ever, I was more occupied with the numbers on the scale than I was worried about the likelihood that my stapled stomach was stretching.

Charlie and I got married the day after my 21st birthday. A few weeks before the wedding, we went to the county clerk's office to get our marriage license. We each filled out our portion of the application and submitted it to a woman behind the desk, who entered our application into the system and printed it out for us to review. She handed a document to us, asking us to make sure all of our information was correct. My heart dropped. Because it was a legal document, I wrote my real birthday, October 12, 1980, on the application. I thought about listing my birth year as 1979, as I did on HR documents at Charlie's family's business (where I now worked), but the woman also needed to see a government-issued ID and I would have gotten caught. I had never come clean to Charlie about being a year younger than I said I was when we first chatted online three and a half years earlier. Charlie, being meticulous as he was, circled the 1980 that was listed near my name in red pen.

"Everything looks fine," Charlie said to the woman who was waiting for us to confirm the accuracy of the information on the printed document, "but Georgiann's birth year is 1979 not 1980."

"No, it's correct," I said with my face turning red and my body shaking.

"What?" Charlie looked at me clearly confused. "1980?"

"Yes," I told him. "I will explain later."

Charlie smirked, still looking confused, as he returned the application saying everything was correct. As we walked out of the office building, I started crying and apologizing for lying. Charlie wasn't bothered, but he wanted to know why I lied. I told him that I was under 18 when we met in the chat room and told everyone that I was year older than I was so that they would feel comfortable speaking with me. I went on to explain that I wanted to tell him the truth, but I didn't know how. I told him we could call off the wedding, which he laughed at and said I was being ridiculous. He reassured me that it wasn't a big deal, and then went on to joke with me for weeks up to and including on our wedding day that he was going to make a big speech about how I had lied to him and that I was an underage bride.

I fell victim to the wedding-industrial complex, inviting around 150 people to our wedding at a decent enough country club on Chicago's North Shore.[1] Our wedding cost me, because of my five star white trash ways, about $15,000 in credit card debt. To save my family's face, I told Charlie's family that my mom covered it all. The entire wealthy, white, and mostly Jewish family from the North Shore of Chicago believed me when I said my mom was an emergency room doctor and that Marx owned an auto repair shop. Because I'd told Charlie my real dad was dead, I just lied and told his entire family that Marx was my stepdad. As I counted on, I made most of the money I spent on the wedding back with the cash gifts we received from our guests—and that was after Charlie and I evenly divided our wedding money. Charlie assumed I put my share of the wedding money in my personal savings account like he did with his, but I used the money to pay down my credit card. There was no way I was going to ruin the strong credit I was building, so I was beyond relieved to repay my credit card loans.

The day after our wedding, Charlie and I flew to London for our honeymoon. Mom said if I paid for the honeymoon, she'd pay me back. The trip was a shower gift from her, and I didn't expect, nor believe, she would be able to repay me. The desire to do such a thing was more than enough for me. At the shower she presented us with a luggage set, with the largest bag holding a smaller one and so on until you got to a cosmetics bag that had the travel itinerary in it. I could have gotten an Academy Award for the surprise on my face reading the itinerary aloud in front of the women in our families, who gasped in awe at the generous gift that cost me a couple thousand dollars. I handed off the itinerary to mom two hours before everyone else arrived for our shower, in the parking lot of the Greek Islands restaurant, and watched her stuff it into the cosmetics bag.

Marriage didn't feel different. We had been living together for a year and half when we got married, at a time in America's history when the rate of cohabitation before marriage was on an upswing.[2] We went to Dave Matthews Band concerts like many other middle-class white college students, and we attended as many professional soccer matches as we could.[3] Charlie did keep asking me about my last name, and if I was ever going to change it to his. I did like the simplicity of Davis, but Markozis was obviously Greek, which was a big part of my family's history. I also didn't want to deal with the hassle of getting my last name changed on all of my official documents. However, I eventually agreed to claim Davis as my own, and did so uneventfully, even getting a new driver's license, social security card, and passport all before I graduated from community college with my associate's degree in 2002. I would enter Northeastern Illinois University that same year as Georgiann Davis, with Charlie and his family's money covering all of my tuition. I was officially a Davis. And that was when I retired Markozis as my last name.

* ★ ☆ ★ *

About a year after our marriage, and for the first time since I dropped out of the seventh grade, I was focusing exclusively on school and not bringing in any money. Being unemployed wasn't in my larger plan. But I resigned from Charlie's family business after he assured me that he would cover all of my expenses, not only my university tuition, so that I could focus on school. He even paid off my car.

We grew apart almost as quickly as we got serious, which I suppose is not surprising given how young we were when we got married. And, in the spring of 2004, we officially separated when I moved into an extended stay hotel. I was almost certain that I wanted a divorce at that point, and he generously agreed to pay for my long-term hotel room, which even had a decent enough kitchen in it, until I made up my mind.

I loved Charlie. And I know he loved me, too. But our relationship was falling apart. I admit I wasn't understanding of the stuff going on his life, but he wasn't emotionally available to me in ways that I needed either. We fought a lot and said nasty things about each other when we did, forgetting that we were once in love.

We tried to make it work.

"Missy," Charlie said, "a letter from Northwestern came today. Do you want me to open it?"

"Yes! What does it say?"

As he opened the letter, I imagined what it'd be like to be a Northwestern PhD student. The hoodies with Northwestern written in purple on them, classes in Evanston with some of the best sociologists in the world, and just the overall prestige of being at Northwestern—a private school with a shitload of resources. I had applied to several other graduate programs but I was set on Northwestern. Maybe it was my five star white trash upbringing, but I couldn't resist the prestige. I had been checking my mail every day for admission decisions.

"I'm sorry," he said, "You didn't get in."

"What? Are you serious?"

"Yeah, but don't feel bad. It would have been like going from the indoor soccer league to the English Premier League."

"What the fuck. I am English Premier League. Dude, that's so fucking rude of you to say."

In retrospect, I shouldn't have been surprised that an elitist department like Northwestern rejected my application. Although I had a 4.0 GPA at Northeastern Illinois University, I'm sure they saw the school as "North Easy" like Charlie did. And they required GRE exam scores—a fucked-up exam that is supposed to predict one's success in graduate school—as part of one's application for admission. In 2021, almost 20 years later, the American Sociological Association issued a statement, endorsed by the American Anthropological Association, recommending that graduate departments not only stop requiring GRE scores for admission consideration but also to not even allows students the option to submit them.[1] These recommendations were made in consultation with more than 40 scholarly sources referenced in the statement. I have no doubt that Northwestern used my low GRE scores in 2004 to justify why they rejected my application for admission, because I've witnessed faculty do that very thing on the various graduate committees I've been on across different, far less prestigious, universities since 2011. And, even as recently as 2022, I continued to witness sociology graduate departments debate the value of GRE scores as a tool to predict graduate student success.

I was still waiting to hear from the sociology PhD programs at Loyola University Chicago and University of Illinois at Chicago. As well as the sociology MA programs at the University of Wisconsin, Milwaukee and DePaul University. I was rejected from all three PhD programs that I applied to, but thankful that I was offered admission and funding to join the sociology master's program at the University of Wisconsin-Milwaukee several months before I was set to graduate from Northeastern Illinois with my bachelor's degree.

Claire, a white 20-something-year-old beautiful woman, was a stylish dresser with sassy hair and an even sharper mouth. We were undergrads together at Northeastern Illinois. In class, she would openly critique our instructors for the readings they assigned, pointing out how they were white and elitist and disconnected from our student body, which was predominantly first-gen and people of color. At the 2004 American Sociological Association Annual Meeting in San Francisco, she confronted a senior white, male sociologist who had published bestselling books in the field. While he was sitting at his publisher's exhibition booth while his editors celebrated the new edition's publication, she walked right up to him and loudly asked him how he could live with himself profiting off of his dumbed-down interpretation of social theory at the expense of marginalized students. There was no way, she informed him, that students at elite institutions were using his textbook and being taught *what* to think about social theory instead of *how* to think about it. He looked like a deer in the headlights as Claire and I stormed out of the exhibition hall.

I was in awe of Claire and found myself in all sorts of love with her. We had been developing a deep level of intimacy—the kind unique to queer couples—since the spring of 2004 despite my marriage to Charlie, which was rapidly deteriorating.[2] When we first started hanging out, she had recently gotten out of a long-term relationship with Amy, a white woman and friend of hers from high school, who was in business school in Milwaukee. With Claire, I had an emotional intimacy that I never knew was possible in a romantic relationship. We talked about our ideas and academic plans, and we argued about them, too. I even briefly shared a little bit of my medical history with her. Although she was supportive, I avoided talking about it as much as I could. I wasn't ready to further explore what it all meant.

I eventually told Charlie, while I was still living in the long-term hotel room that he was paying for, that I wanted to proceed with a divorce. He agreed. I didn't want to unnecessarily hurt him, so I didn't tell him that I had fallen in love with Claire. Together we scheduled a consultation with a divorce attorney to figure out how to proceed. The divorce was uneventful and amicable. During our separation, Charlie and I flew to a soccer match together as friends, and in the air on the way home, I asked him if he would be willing to give me some money so that I could pursue my dream of getting a graduate degree and not have to worry about paying rent or buying food. He asked me for details about my University of Wisconsin-Milwaukee admissions package, which I shared. He couldn't believe the teaching assistantship I was offered came with so little money. He offered to give me $15,000 a year for three years to supplement the yearly stipend the university offered me, which I believe was under $10,000. He also agreed to buy me out of the townhome we bought together a few years earlier. I thought the terms he agreed to were really generous and enough to get me through my master's degree—and maybe even get me through a year or two of whatever PhD program I could get into after the University of Wisconsin-Milwaukee.

When our meeting with the divorce attorney came, the middle-aged balding white man, who looked like a stereotypical Italian, listened to the terms we had agreed on before telling us that he could only represent one of us. Charlie asked me what I wanted to do, and I said I wanted to be represented by the attorney. Charlie was fine with it, so the attorney instructed him to leave the office, and he waited in his car while I finished my meeting.

"This is a great deal for you. If I was representing him, I'd tell him the same thing and encourage him not to proceed with the agreement." He continued, "Alimony just doesn't exist like this anymore, especially since you have only been married for a few years and don't have any kids."

"Okay," I nodded.

"This money that he is agreeing to give you will be taxed. Are you alright with that?"

"Yeah, that's fine."

"How did you get him to agree to this? Does he have the money?"

"He is rich. His family is really rich and he gets a lot of money from his family business."

I shared what I knew about the business, emphasizing Charlie's stake in it.

"Oh," the attorney said, looking shocked, "well then we might want to reassess that the agreement is in fact in your best interest."

"The agreement works for both of us," I said, "and I just want to proceed with it."

Aside from meeting the attorney at the courthouse a few weeks later, where I answered a couple of questions the judge had about our uncontested divorce, I never saw him again. The judge, a woman, asked a couple of clarification questions about the agreement. She wanted to know why Charlie, who didn't have to be present so decided not to come, agreed to these generous terms. I explained, in better terms, that Charlie was old money, to which the judge replied, "I'm happy to hear that you came up with a mutual agreement that works for both of you." And that was the end of our marriage. I walked out of the courthouse and into my car, where I cried harder than I ever remembered. I called mom while I was sobbing, and she told me that she thought this is what I wanted and if that she knew I would be this upset, she would have been there with me. I explained that it is what I wanted but that I was just sad. After our conversation, I drove over to Charlie's family business. We agreed to meet there and drive together to lunch to celebrate the divorce. We went to a steakhouse and vowed to stay friends, which we did for a number of years, especially while Cactus and Dingle, our rescued greyhounds, were still alive. After they passed on, though, we drifted apart and haven't spoken for nearly a decade aside from the occasional email here or there.

* * * * *

I graduated summa cum laude from Northeastern Illinois University with a bachelor's degree in sociology and a minor in communication. The ceremony was outside on a beautiful spring day in Chicago. Mom and Andrew, her new husband, a white guy about a decade younger than her, and Claire all sat together and cheered for me when my name was announced. It will forever be one of the happiest days of my life. I was a college graduate and set to begin my graduate studies at the University of Wisconsin-Milwaukee.

I moved in with Claire, and her roommate Cathy who was her college friend. I lived with them the summer before moving into a one-bedroom apartment in Milwaukee near my new university. Claire ended up splitting her time between Chicago and Milwaukee so that she could finish up her last year of undergraduate while applying for graduate programs. So, when she wasn't in class at Northeastern Illinois, we were living together in Milwaukee.

I was a teaching assistant (TA) for a large section of Introduction to Sociology during my first semester at the University of Wisconsin-Milwaukee. Amy, Claire's ex, had transferred from her business university to UWM and had enrolled in the class that I was TAing along with four other graduate students. Claire had introduced us, and Amy and I started spending time alone together when Claire was in Chicago. I started fucking around with Amy, which brought an end to the serious relationship Claire and I had been in for more than a year. It was a nasty breakup, and I was a real asshole and remain deeply regretful for how it all went down. Amy and I ended up staying together for about five years, through her admission and subsequent withdrawal from a graduate program, and my completion of a master's degree and most of my PhD pursuit at the University of Illinois at Chicago, where I continued my sociology studies after finishing my master's at UWM.

11

I had my first panic attack in the middle of a lecture. As I sat in the front row taking notes, the professor was discussing wealth accumulation. He explained that for most Americans, the only way to accumulate wealth was through home ownership.

The day before this wealth accumulation lecture, a sheriff was standing at my front door with foreclosure paperwork. He asked for "Georgiann Markozis," and when I explained that my last name was "Davis" and no longer "Markozis," he confirmed my birthdate. As he read "October 12, 1980," my heart dropped and my entire body got red.

"That's me," I said, "but I don't own a house."

He continued, "Well it says here that you are the property owner of . . ." he rattled off an address. "Have you ever lived at the property?"

"No, my mom lives there. She is renting it."

The sheriff looked as confused as I was.

"I don't know what to tell you. I have to deliver this paperwork to you. You have to be in court down in Chicago on the date listed here."

"But this isn't me. I don't own anything. It must be a mistake. Maybe you are looking for my mom, her name is Ann Markozis and my name was Georgiann Markozis before I got married and changed my last name to Davis."

"If I were you," he said, "I would find an attorney to figure out what is going on."

I signed for the pile of papers and started flipping through them. I saw my birthdate and social security number on a loan application as well as my mom's signature and initials on nearly every page. She has sloppy handwriting that I know very well.

I immediately called mom at the restaurant she worked at to find out what was going on, to which she told me that there must have been some sort of mistake and that our credit reports crossed or something because our names were so similar. But I knew that was a fucking lie. I saw her signature and my social security number and birthdate on the documents. She even wrote my birth date next to her signature. I started sobbing and screaming at her. She yelled into the phone before hanging up on me, "It's busy here. I can't talk. Don't call back." I sat there as the landline phone started beeping in my ear. I got into my car and drove about two hours from Milwaukee to the restaurant mom was at.

"What the fuck are you doing here?" she said to me with fear on her face as I walked into the restaurant with the huge pile of papers I had been served a few hours earlier. "You're going to get me fired," she mumbled under her breath while holding a large tray filled with plates of food that she was about to deliver to one of her tables.

"I don't give a fuck!" I shouted with tears pouring down my face. With everyone in the restaurant staring at me, I asked, "What the fuck did you do?"

"Get the fuck out of here before you get me fired! Please, please leave! Please!"

She promised me that she'd call me at night when she left the restaurant and got to the hospital. She was the only one who worked the switchboard on the third shift, so she could get away with making personal phone calls.

Pissed off, I left the restaurant and drove back to Milwaukee. I was devastated and didn't know what the fuck was going on. That night she confessed. She bought the home she was renting with Andrew using my social security number and birthdate instead of hers. She was able to get away with it because my birth name was so similar to hers. She explained to me that her landlord had decided to sell the house she was renting, and she knew that with her bad credit she couldn't buy it in her name. So she used my identity. She assured me that she had the money to pay the mortgage but that the home was currently in eviction because of some sort of "mess up" on the bank's end. I decided to fix it myself. I would take over the mortgage (she'd never make payments on time) and she promised to send me a money order every month. I needed my credit for my future, and I lied and told her that the university wouldn't let me TA for them if I was in collections or had judgments in my name. I was angry but I wanted to move forward, I convinced myself that I could be her landlord. She needed a place to live. But with a mortgage that was nearly two thousand dollars a month, I had no idea how I'd be able to cover it on a TA stipend if she didn't give me the money as she promised she would. I didn't trust her, so my mind played worst-case scenarios over and over again. Would I go to jail if she didn't pay the mortgage? Would I ever be able to buy a house on my own? What if I needed to take out a student loan? How bad has she already fucked up my credit? What else is she lying to me about?

I couldn't sleep all night, despite being mentally drained from the mess and physically exhausted from driving, in traffic, from Milwaukee to Chicago and then back to Milwaukee. My head hurt. My eyes were sore from all of the crying, and my voice was gone from the screaming. But I somehow managed to show up for my TA duties the next day, where the professor coincidentally had planned a lecture on the relationship between wealth accumulation and home ownership. I silently had a panic attack and did all I could to hold back my tears, not knowing that this was just the beginning of my identity theft nightmare. While I always feared, like so many of us, the stranger searching my trash for a document with sensitive information on it that I was too lazy to shred, I've since learned that one in five identity theft victims are related to their offender.[1]

And my mom was mine.

I became a landlord-of-sorts in my first year of graduate school. But not to my mother. I managed a multifamily 36-unit apartment complex about two miles away from campus. I wasn't looking for an extra job—being a full-time graduate student and teaching assistant was more than enough to keep me busy—but when the owners said that the compensation was a $250 rent reduction, it was hard to turn down. While the position was titled "manager," I was more like the complex "custodian" because I didn't handle any of the finances. I was mostly responsible for vacuuming the hallways, keeping the entry ways and laundry room clean, and an annual smoke detector check in all 36 apartments. If the owners—a white couple in their fifties—were at one of their other properties, they would sometimes ask me to show a vacant apartment and give the applicant a rental interest form to fill out. After each showing that I did, the owners would pick up the completed form from me and ask if the applicant "looked good." The first time they asked, I clarified what they meant, and they'd asked, "Would you want to live next to them? Would they fit in here?"[1] I read between the lines when I witnessed them tell a Black college student interested in living there that the building was not ideal for college students. While it was true that most of the tenants were not affiliated with the university, I certainly was. And so was the white woman who moved into my unit, after I left for a pet friendly place that would allow Cactus and Dingle, the rescued greyhounds Charlie and I adopted when we were married, to move in with me after he was no longer able to care for them because of a busy work schedule.

* * ⋆ * *

Soon after mom told me she bought a home in my name, I decided to run my credit to see just how bad she messed it up. It was then that I learned that mom didn't just take out one home loan in my name, but eight of them totaling to approximately 1.5 million dollars. One-and-half-million dollars.

How could she? My anxiety went soaring through the roofs I didn't even know that I owned.

I placed a plastic grocery bag over my head and sealed the opening around my neck with duct tape. I placed a second grocery bag over the first, and taped it the same way in case the first bag wasn't thick enough to keep air out. Moments before, I wrote a few letters—to mom, expressing anger for causing me so much pain but also expressing my love for her because I didn't want her to hurt when I was gone; to Claire for her unconditional love and support in life and school; and to Charlie, thanking him for everything and begging him to find Cactus and Dingle a good home.

As I laid on my bed with my breathing rapidly moving the now fogged up bags in and out of my mouth as tears streamed down my cheeks, I held on to Cactus and Dingle as tightly as I could. I kept trying to convince myself, through my tears, that death would make the extraordinary pain I was feeling go away.

With my breathing getting heavier alongside my fear of death growing, I freaked out and started yelling out loud to myself as I tried to get the bags off of my head: "What the fuck did I do?!?" "God, please help me!" "Help me, please!" The tape wouldn't budge, which resulted in more panic. I tried to rip open the bags with my fingers, but being a long-time nail biter, I couldn't. Cactus and Dingle were moving their lanky bodies around restlessly on my bed as I kept crying and panicking. I jumped off the bed and made my way to the kitchen and grabbed a knife from the drawer and cut a hole in the bags and then ripped them off of my head.[2]

I phoned Claire, who was in Chicago, and told her I wanted to kill myself. I did not tell her that I had just taped two plastic bags over my head and written suicide notes. The next thing I know, Amy, Claire's ex, was at my back door knocking and calling out my name. She ran from UWM to my place and was breathing hard, not from the mile distance but from the speed at which she ran. I was out of tears the rest of the night but didn't need them because I had Claire and Amy's support.

* ★ ☆ ★ *

The next day I took action. I called each mortgage company listed on my credit report and explained to them that I was a victim of identity theft.[3] These calls mostly went the same way. I would wait on hold for some time before eventually getting through to a live person, only to be transferred to a fraud department. From there, a representative would take down my information and tell me where to send a notarized statement, photocopies of my government-issued IDs, and whatever else they needed. To keep track of everything, I took meticulous notes with each phone call. The number I called. The name of the person, or persons, I spoke with. The date and time of our conversations. The loan number or numbers as applicable. The amounts of each loan. I recorded everything and anything I uncovered. I didn't know what I was going to do with all of the information I collected, but I found compiling the large file therapeutic because it gave me some sense of control over the situation.

The one thing each bank needed was a police report. Without it, their fraud department wouldn't proceed with my claim. I would have to call the police and report that my mom was a criminal. I didn't want to turn mom in. But I also didn't know how else to try to crawl my way out of the mess she created. She may have been the first to victimize me in this mess. But the banks revictimized me by making me go through the legal system before taking my situation seriously.[4]

I reached out to my Aunts Maria and Athena for help and their approval to proceed with notifying the police. But they stood in support of their sister. They agreed that she was wrong for what she had done to me, but they kept saying over and over again that "She is your mother, Missy" and "You can't put her in jail."[5] When I told them that I had no choice if I wanted to clear my name, they pulled back from me and said in similar words, "Well you have to do what you have to do. Just don't forget she's your mother and you will have to live with whatever happens to her."

It felt like my aunts were blaming me. But my Yiayia's reaction was worse. Although she said many of the same things as my aunts when I phoned her at her home in Greece—"I know, but she's your mother"—the words hurt more coming from her. My Papou, my mom's dad, was the only one of my mother's relatives to express the level of anger and disappointment that I did. He would tell me that she was a horrible mother who deserved to be in jail and that if it was up to him, he'd never see her again for what she did to me.

As the week went on, I kept collecting information from the banks, from which I learned that the properties were each in foreclosure or about to be. I genuinely felt my dreams would be over if I didn't do something, and quick. I kept in touch with mom as I struggled with what to do, but on each call, I would scream and yell at her for what she had done. She would tell me to calm down and that she did it all for me and my brother. She bought the homes, she said, with the intent to have Andrew, her new husband, fix them up and resell them for a profit— money she said she was going to give to me and Theo.[6] I would yell back that I didn't fucking want her money. I just wanted to be left alone. I told her that she had ruined my life, which she brushed off, saying everything she does is for me and Theo.

I couldn't understand how mom was able to fool all of these banks. I had bought a townhome with Charlie, and the funder wanted all sorts of information from us beyond just our social security numbers. Photo IDs, paystubs, bank statements, and more. I mean, what the serious fuck? I just didn't get it. As I was reading through the loan documents that were included in the foreclosure paperwork that I was served by the sheriff days earlier, I came across the name Bryan Lahbo. He was a mortgage broker and had an office in a western suburb of Chicago. I found his phone number on the internet and decided to confront him on a call. He answered on the second ring. When I calmly explained my situation and asked him how in the hell this could happen, how he even believed that my mother, who was then in her late forties/early fifties, was born in 1980 and was supposed to be in her early twenties, he laughed.

"I had my doubts," he said.

"Did you not see an ID?" I asked him through my tears. "A paystub? I just can't believe this."

"This is clearly between you and your mother."

Click. He hung up. I kept calling him back, but I could only get his voicemail. Although I never spoke with him again, I will never forget his real name, which I'm not sharing here to ease my fears of legal repercussions rather than to protect his privacy.

After being ignored by the fraudulent mortgage broker, who clearly had an active role in the predatory lender game, I was left with no choice but to go to the police.[7] I hoped they'd somehow hold Bryan Lahbo more accountable than my mother. I mean mom wouldn't have been able to take out the eight loans without him violating all sorts of lending laws. I was sure of it.

Although the local Wisconsin police department near my home filed a report for me, they said that because the loans were all for Illinois properties that I also needed to contact an Illinois precinct that covers at least one of the properties she illegally bought in my name. I don't know if it was the adrenaline anger rush that I felt from speaking with the mortgage broker or if it was the limited time I had navigating graduate school as a TA, but I left the Wisconsin police station and immediately drove to the western suburbs of Chicago. I filed a police report in the State of Illinois at a precinct near one of the properties.

I met Donald Jurgun that same afternoon. He was a Detective in the police department's investigation division. He was your typical balding white middle-aged cop type who wore a white polo and khakis pants. I saw a police badge on his belt, and I figured he had a gun somewhere on him, too. He sat down across from me at a table, taking notes and expressing shock and disgust about everything I was telling him. I was in tears for most of our meeting, but I also explained to Detective Jurgun that I didn't want my mom to go to jail. I just wanted to get out of this mess and for her to leave me alone. I remember him saying that he was a newish father and that he couldn't ever imagine doing something like this to his child. He was as empathetic as he was angry. It was comforting knowing that he shared my emotions and understood the complexity of the position my mother put me in. We only met in person once, but we exchanged many phone calls and emails over the course of the investigation.

After meeting with the detective, I drove to mom's house—really, my house, one of the many properties she bought in my name—and told her that I filed a report. I don't know what I hoped to get out of telling her in person, but I think I wanted forgiveness. Screaming through tears at her doorstep, I told her that she made me do this and that she was a horrible mother to put me in this position. She just yelled back at me, "Okay, you made your point. What else do you want from me? Please leave me alone." I didn't leave until Andrew came to the door with a phone in his hand threatening to get me arrested. "Fuck you!" I screamed back at him pulling out the detective's card. "Call him, motherfucker! You both are going to jail! What are you going to do, get me arrested for being at MY home you stupid motherfuckers?!?" He proceeded to call the police, so I got in my car and drove back to Milwaukee.

I wouldn't talk to mom, nor her sisters Maria or Athena, again for four years. I saw them briefly in May 2006, at my

Papou Theo's funeral, which I (in therapy) contemplated not going to, but decided I should go and just not speak to any of them. My mom and her sisters paid an extraordinary amount of money to have their father's body flown from a small city in Greece to Chicago in order to bury him at a gravesite they could all regularly visit. At the funeral, Marx and Amy sat by me. Amy moved into the duplex I was renting not long after Claire and I broke up. Claire wanted nothing to do with either of us anymore, and I couldn't blame her. I was an asshole who, at the time, didn't realize how inconsiderate and selfish it was of me to pursue her ex, Amy, while Claire and I were still dating. Claire wouldn't take my calls or return my emails for about a year and a half. If I happened to run into her somewhere, she would vanish more quickly than she appeared. Claire eventually agreed to meet with me and allowed me to apologize in person for what I had done, and somehow, she thankfully agreed to give the possibility of a friendship a chance. We've remained close friends ever since.

I avoided mom and the rest of her family at all costs at Papou Theo's funeral. Although I wanted to talk to them and it pained me not to, given how close we all once were, I couldn't. I needed to protect myself. The space I created between us helped me ease the tremendous guilt I was feeling from pursuing legal charges. But they also didn't try to reach out to me either. Instead, mom, her sisters, and Yiayia framed me as the selfish one for turning my mom in. A therapist once told me that my situation reminded her a lot of what happens in familial sexual abuse cases. She explained that it is often the case that when a person is sexually assaulted by a family member, the rest of the family empathizes but discourages the victim from pressing charges.[8] In turn, the victim is left to feel alone, unsupported, and guilty while the predator's actions appear to be forgiven.

Earlier in 2006, about six months after I filed the Illinois report, I got an email from Detective Jurgun. He let me know that the United States Secret Service was assisting him with the investigation, and that they were going to charge mom on the federal level with bank fraud and identity theft. On the federal level, the U.S. Secret Service would have jurisdiction over "all the banks and mortgage companies that will take a loss from the loans." He then continued, "I will still charge your mom with all the crimes I can tie to [my jurisdiction]."

The severity of the charges against my mom gave me pause, but I also was annoyed that the banks were being framed as the primary victims. I saw it differently. I didn't understand why the investigation wasn't focusing in on the mortgage broker for his role in the theft of my identity. I never saw the banks as victims. I was the only victim in this case, a plea I would later publicly make in federal court.

* * * * *

While navigating the identity theft mess, I was rapidly losing weight. Although I'm sure mom's actions didn't help, it wasn't what prevented me from being able to eat. I was experiencing severe complications from the stomach stapling surgery I had a decade earlier. I wasn't able to eat any food without becoming sick and needing to vomit. Even water made me sick. I would get a horrible burning sensation in my stomach that would travel up into my throat. The only thing that would ease the burn would be to vomit up a foam-like white substance that looked like pure stomach acid. I tried everything from Rolaids to TUMS to make the pain go away. Nothing helped what I can only describe as my medically induced bulimia.[9] But because everyone routinely complimented my weight loss, telling me I looked "happy" and "healthy," I dismissed the severity of the health crisis I was in despite running to the bathroom multiple times each day to throw up whatever I had just tried to consume. Sadly, looking back, I was also happy with my weight loss even though I was in physical pain. The compliments felt amazing. I got down to 215 pounds, at five feet ten inches, and loved the ease of being able to shop for new clothes in "normal" places like Old Navy before they experimented with carrying extended sizes in some stores. I could fit into chairs with arms, something I always avoided. Movie theater seats, classroom chairs, and airplane seats were no longer my enemies.

But eventually the physical pain was too much to handle. Not being able to keep food or fluids down, I was getting weaker by the day. I even came close to fainting in a grocery store. I decided to use the health insurance provided by UWM to see a primary care physician about my stomach problems. Because I wasn't comfortable discussing my intersex body, I just filled out the new patient forms without mentioning that. The middle-aged white female physician, surprisingly, didn't ask many questions about the cancerous ovaries I supposedly had, but maybe that was because my 15-minute visit was centered on the stomach stapling complications that I was experiencing. She somehow happily observed that the weight loss surgery was successful, given my weight was in the low 200s, as if that's all that mattered. She referred me to a bariatric surgeon, telling me that he would be best suited to tend to my complications.

* * ☆ * *

The bariatric surgeon measured the percentage of my body fat on a fancy scale and, like my primary care physician, applauded how successful the stomach stapling had been for me. I explained to him that I wasn't able to keep any food or fluids down without getting a severe burning sensation in my stomach that traveled up through my throat. I also explained that I felt like I was always full. He ordered an "upper GI," an x-ray of the stomach and esophagus that is taken while a patient drinks barium that coats the lining of these organs and highlights them on x-ray images. Later, during my second visit at the weight loss clinic, I learned that the surgeon had determined I was suffering from an esophageal stricture: the production of acid in my stomach was so severe that my esophagus was narrowing in an attempt to keep the acid from traveling up through my esophagus into my mouth. The surgeon recommended that I immediately take prescription antacids to reduce acid production while he scheduled me for an esophageal dilation, which involves inserting a balloon-like device down the esophagus to stretch and enlarge the narrowed area to make it easier to swallow food and fluids.

He also referred me to his weight loss clinic's psychologist, Elaine Blake, for a consultation before proceeding with any sort of necessary surgical revision. My initial visit with Elaine quickly turned into a much-needed therapy session about my identity theft case, about which she encouraged me to continue to see her in her private practice outside of the weight loss clinic, which I did on an almost weekly basis for years.

Because the prescription antacids worked almost immediately, I ended up not needing the esophageal dilation. I was able to eat normally again. My stomach had stretched but the stapling was still intact. I was able to eat more than ever, and the acid reflux was mostly gone. I never went back to that weight loss clinic. Another decade would pass, and I would gain more than 150 pounds, bringing me back to nearly 400 pounds before I would feel the need to see another weight loss surgeon.

* * ⁂ * *

I found an attorney in Milwaukee who agreed to meet with me to discuss my stolen identity. Marx and Amy were there to support me at that meeting. I remember the attorney saying that he couldn't help me because the properties were all in Illinois, but I don't remember if I had to pay him for the consultation. I eventually found an attorney in downtown Chicago whom I retained for a couple of thousand dollars, using a chunk of the alimony money Charlie gave me to help get me through graduate school. I only met the attorney once and never heard from him again. I don't know what happened to my retainer fee nor do I think he did anything for me. I was the one who was in constant contact with Detective Jurgun and the banks, sending notarized documents, photocopies of IDs, and whatever else they requested for their fraud departments. A few months after we met, I did call his office asking for a refund of my retainer fee, but my call was never returned. I gave up and just accepted that the retainer fee I shelled out was an expensive mistake. I also spent thousands and thousands of dollars seeing therapists over the years to work through the guilt I felt for reporting my mother to the police.

* ★ ✮ ★ *

For the nearly four years I didn't speak to anyone in my maternal family, I remained focused on my graduate studies. I graduated from UWM with my master's degree in sociology, and started immediately after in the University of Illinois at Chicago's sociology doctoral program. The second time applying to PhD programs, I was admitted to two doctoral programs fully funded, which meant that, in exchange for being a graduate assistant helping professors with either grading or their research, my tuition would be covered and I would receive a small monthly stipend for nine months of the academic calendar. With Charlie and me divorced, I no longer felt confined to the Midwest, which enabled me to cast a wider net, including applying to PhD programs on the East Coast. But of the two programs I did get into, UIC was a better choice given their program's broad area of expertise. I was reluctant to continue my studies in Chicago because that's where my family lived, but I was able to work through my reservations in therapy and decided to join UIC and just live on the north side of the city to be as far away from them as possible.

I was also offered a part-time teaching position at my alma mater, Northeastern Illinois University—while adjunct pay is not good, it would help me gain teaching experience while supplementing my graduate assistantship stipend.[10] I taught two sociology courses a semester at NEIU in addition to whatever my TA obligations at UIC required for the entirety of the five years I spent in my doctoral program. Between my graduate assistantship stipend and part-time teaching at NEIU, I was able to gross about $38,000 a year, which wasn't a lot—especially in Chicago—but it was enough to cover rent in a one-bedroom attic apartment, make my car payment, and pay for any books I needed and still have enough left over to spend on pets I rescued, restaurant meals, and decent enough clothes. I was even able to financially support Amy for the majority of the time we were together. She was dealing with issues of her own after dropping out of graduate school, before working her way through prerequisites required for admission into a library sciences program at a community college. I made sure she had a reliable car—a used one Marx helped us get—to drive to and from school, and even helped her decide on the best career path given her personality and interests. After about a half a year of unemployment, Amy started working part-time at a jewelry store, where she was still working when we broke up in the summer of 2010 after about five years of dating.

Marx would treat Amy and me to dinner almost every weekend. He always covered the check in cash, as he was paid under the table at the auto repair shop he worked at. We also loved going with him to the casino. He and I would play table blackjack with his money, as Amy stood behind us and cheered us on. If we were down more than a couple of hundred dollars, I would make us leave. I would also do the same when we were up a couple of hundred dollars, despite Marx's pleas with us to stay longer, hoping we could win more. But he would never put up much of a fight, especially as I divided up the winnings evenly between the three of us and he saw the smiles on Amy's and my faces. To us, having an extra $100 each was quite a bit.

During my first two years as a UIC doctoral student, mom's case seemed to have gotten lost in the criminal legal system. I didn't care, because I had managed to get my credit cleared with the police reports I filed. The banks stopped sending sheriffs to my door with foreclosure notices. Marx occasionally interacted with mom through Theo, who was still living with him, and he would tell me what she was up to if I asked. I learned from him that she got divorced from Andrew, got fired from the hospital for sleeping on the job, was still waitressing 10 hours a day but at a different restaurant, and that she was living in a dog grooming salon that she started running. She was officially homeless, but she managed to make herself a bedroom in the office of the grooming salon. She would shower in the grooming tub. I felt sad for her.

A few times, my dad brought me dog treats and outfits from mom's shop. He told me they were gifts from her for Cactus and Dingle, my rescued greyhounds, and that she missed me.

He always told me that she wanted to talk to me, but he supported my decision to keep away from her and the rest of her family. She once left me a voicemail crying like a child, begging me to call her saying that she was so depressed and had no one left in her life. I deleted the voicemail and made an emergency appointment to see my therapist the very next day. Marx later told me that the call had come after she and Andrew separated. Fuck her, I remember saying aloud even though I felt really sorry for her. I thought about changing my cell phone number or blocking her calls, but I didn't feel I could do that because the detective and banks had my number. Those calls I *had* to take.

While enrolled in a feminist theory doctoral seminar at UIC, I found myself in the middle of an academic discussion about the lived experiences of intersex people. I was so uncomfortable as my grad school friends, and our professor, sat around the conference table theorizing about intersex. No one was saying anything derogatory or problematic, but it made me uncomfortable. I had worked so hard to run away from a topic that they were openly and freely talking about. But suddenly in that space, a clearly feminist one, I felt that I could confront "intersex." I decided to focus on it for my seminar paper project. I first shared that I was intersex with the professor of the seminar, and then later to my friends who were also in the course. Everyone was very supportive, and they always listened to me as I shared what I was learning about intersex and my own medical history. Rather than fear or embarrassment, I felt liberated. I learned that my experiences were not unique. There was a global community of intersex people. Most of them had been lied to, forced to undergo (sometimes unknowingly) cosmetic surgeries, and generally shamed for being born in bodies that did not "make sense."[1]

That seminar changed the trajectory of my academic career.

I was drawn to study the lived experiences of intersex people. I wanted to learn more about my life and the struggles that so many intersex people face at the hands of deceptive medical providers who continue to rob us of our bodily autonomy. I wrote my dissertation on the topic and in the process confronted the pain that was wrapped up in the secrets that doctors didn't tell me about my body and that my family—somewhat deliberately, somewhat ignorantly—went along with. I was fortunate to piece together various funding sources to offset some of the cost of traveling around the U.S. to interview intersex people, parents of intersex individuals, and nearly every medical expert who treats intersex people. I also ended up taking out about $40,000 in student loans, which I used to pay for airfare, hotels, transcription of the interviews, and anything else I needed to finish my PhD.

With the research travel, studying, and teaching, I was very busy in grad school. I often dined at my local Pizza Hut, and scarfed down an entire large pizza while grading papers. I was getting fatter and fatter, and while I would go on a diet every now and then, I mostly just prayed (ironically) that the esophageal stricture would come back and I would once again not be able to eat anything. For nearly a year, I was taking multiple flights every week to collect data. Every time I stepped onto the plane, I would get anxious that the seatbelt wouldn't buckle or that I wouldn't fit into the seat. A few times it was a very close call, but I would push on my fat rolls and do whatever I could to squeeze into the seat, usually ending up with bruises all over my abdomen and thighs. My weight kept going up no matter what I did, which included joining gyms, hiring trainers, buying a bike that I rode around the neighborhood, and keeping track of what I was eating. You name it, and I tried it. I even took over-the-counter alli® pills and would get excited every time I had to take a shit because the medication minimizes the amount of fat the body absorbs while eating and expels it through greasy bowel movements. I tried so hard to lose weight, but any pounds that came off would eventually come right back on and bring more with them.

* * ✩ * *

During winter break in late 2008–early 2009, when I was studying for my PhD comprehensive exam, I made a promise to whatever higher power there might be that I would forgive mom and reach out to her if I passed the important academic milestone on my path to the PhD. Not long after I was notified that I had passed my comprehensive examination, I decided I would reconnect with her by taking my new puppy to the grooming salon she ran for a bath. I had foolishly bought Lucie, a pied French Bulldog, from a puppy mill for $3,000 using my student loan money after Cactus and Dingle both died of old age within a year of each other. When I walked in, I asked the groomer if they had an opening on their schedule to give Lucie a bath. She said sure, and while she was carrying Lucie into the back room, I asked if Ann was around. She said no but that she should be in soon. I figured she probably was still at the restaurant she waitressed at. I told the groomer that I was Ann's daughter, to which she replied with a smile, "Oh, you're Missy? Your mom is going to be so happy to see you. She should be here soon." She called out, "Scruffy, come here! Missy is here." Scruffy was the only dog still alive out of the four dogs that were evicted with us from our suburban Chicago home. Aside from limping and moving slowly, he looked the same, only with greyer fur. The groomer and I engaged in small talk while she tended to Lucie and the others that were also there for cuts or nail trims. I stood on the customer side of the counter waiting for mom to arrive. I hadn't talked to her in years, and I hadn't seen her since Papou's funeral. And then she walked in the door.

"Missy!" She had a huge smile on her face. "Did you bring Lucie for a haircut?" She knew my dog's name from Marx.

She hadn't changed much. She was wearing a white turtleneck and black pants. She had on black gym shoes, and her hair was up in a pony tail. She had on makeup, and was carrying a big purse and an apron that I assumed she wore at the restaurant.

"Lucie's getting a bath right now."

"Hold on a minute. I'm going to go put this stuff away. Did you see Scruffy?"

"Yeah, he looks good. I can't believe he is still alive."

She asked, "He must be 17 years old now, right?"

"I think so," I smiled.

I watched her walk to the office where I knew she slept every night. She immediately came back out and asked me if I was hungry and if I wanted to go get something to eat with her while Lucie was getting groomed. I said sure, as I was tired from standing around the store—it was loud from all the barking dogs and smelled nasty, too, from the dogs that were roaming around freely peeing and shitting everywhere.

As we drove to QDOBA, we made small talk about her side of the family, the grooming salon she ran, my pursuit of the PhD, and stuff like that. I told her that I hoped to land an assistant professorship in the next few years.

"Oh, that's good." She said before asking, "How much will you get paid?"

"It depends. But probably somewhere between $50,000 and $60,000."

"That's it?" She smirked. "You could make more than that as a waitress."

"It's a job for life," I said. "And I would get health insurance and retirement. And I wouldn't have to be on my feet all day running around to serve people. But whatever. You wouldn't understand."

The mundane conversation continued as we ate our food, which she insisted on paying for. On the way back, while I was driving and she was in the passenger seat, I looked at her and decided to say what I had been thinking for years.

"You know you really did me wrong." Her faced changed. "How could you do it? Why did you do all of that to me?"

"Please don't talk about that now. It's done with and over. Please leave it alone."

"I know, but it's really fucked up what you did to me. I forgive you, but I want you to know that you really hurt me."

She started picking her lips while saying, "Please don't start this again. It's over with now. Please just stop now."

I listened and let it go, in part because of the plea I made to the higher power to forgive her, but more so because of how nice it was to talk to her again. I missed her as much as it seemed she missed me.

Given how she responded to me, saying that it was over and to leave it alone, I had assumed that she reached some sort of agreement or settlement in the case. I didn't know, but didn't want to know either. What I did know, at the time, is that a year earlier, in April 2008, a U.S. Secret Service Agent had called me and asked me if the case was something I still wanted to proceed with. I was confused, because I didn't think I had a choice. But I also thought it was a trick question and that I might get in trouble if I said that I didn't want to pursue the criminal charges. My credit was cleared, and I thought if I said I wanted to drop the case, I might then again be responsible for all of the loans that mom had taken out in my name.

"Can I ask you something, sir?"

"Sure," the U.S. Secret Service Agent answered.

"Will she get a lot of jail time? I definitely don't want that but I also know what she did was wrong."

"She's cooperating," he said, "And because she is a first-time offender, she probably won't get any time. Maybe house arrest. But she might be ordered to serve time in federal prison. It would ultimately be up to the judge."

"Okay, well what she did was wrong. So, I guess you have to proceed."

The call lasted for only a few minutes, and I didn't hear anything about the case again until two years later. It was 2010, I had forgiven her, and we had been talking again for about a year when I received a victim notification letter in the mail. The letter was a formality to notify me, the victim, that mom had been indicted in federal court and that she would soon be formally charged and arrested. I immediately called mom at the restaurant she worked at and read the letter to her. She also had no idea about what was going on, but she asked me to look into it for her, which I did. I managed to find the indictment papers online in the federal court system. I downloaded them and emailed them to the criminal defense attorney who was representing her, along with information from the victim notification letter that I had received.

We were once again very close. Most weekends I would pick her up from the pet grooming salon and we would spend the evening in a casino. I would give Lucie a bath using the supplies in the store, and leave her there to dry while mom and I took off to Joliet, a suburb about an hour south of Chicago that had a cluster of casinos near one another. She loved the penny slot machines and would play them for hours. Her favorite was the Gold Fish Casino Slots. The game had a group of different fish that would roll in front of you and swim around the screen blowing bubbles and doing silly things like wishing one luck. While in theory you could play penny slots one penny at a time, if you wanted a chance at a jackpot or wanted to maximize the lines you were playing, you had to play far more than a penny with each spin. The way she played the penny slots, each spin cost her about 50 cents. When she was up, she was pleasant to be around. It was much easier for me to get her to leave when she was winning. But when she was down, she would get quiet and annoyed with me if I told her we needed to leave before she lost more money. She would tell me to shut up and that she was only playing pennies, but I would sit there and roll my eyes with each half dollar she wasted every three or four seconds.

"It's all rigged," I told her. "You aren't going to win. Let's go now before you lose more."

"It's gonna hit," she would angrily say with her hand continuously hitting the spin button and not taking her eyes off the screen. "It's going to hit any minute."

"Come on, let's go. I'm getting tired."

"Oh," she would say sarcastically, "you don't say that when we win."

Like Marx, she would split her winnings with me but never her losses. He would sometimes meet us at the casino, but I would usually spend time gambling and eating with them separately. Mom never played table games like Marx. I quickly realized that you had the potential to win far more at a slot machine with their rolling jackpots than you could at a table, but it also seemed liked you lost a lot more, too.[2] There is something about using your hands to move chips at a table game that makes it clear you are gambling with money compared to playing an expensive arcade game at a slot machine. You physically feel each loss as your stack of chips dwindles each time you make a new bet, but with the slot machine, you just keep hitting the spin button and don't physically feel each loss as much. On occasion, mom would win small jackpots of one or two thousand dollars, but it was far more likely we'd leave down a couple hundred dollars.

As she reached into her large purse for more money to feed the slot machine, I saw an unusual looking black device.

"What's that?"

"A stun gun," she answered me while repeatedly hitting spin on the machine.

"Why the fuck do you have that?"

"I open the restaurant early in the morning, and I have it for protection."

"How did you get it?"

"A friend gave it to me."

"Is it legal?"

"No, but I need it for protection. I'm the only one there in the morning opening the restaurant and I don't want to get killed or raped."

"You need to be careful."

"Why do you have all of that medicine?" I asked referring to the half a dozen prescription bottles I also saw in her bag.

"They are for my back and knees. You try being on your feet all day carrying trays of food."

Something seemed really fishy to me and it wasn't the fish machine she was playing.

"You're not selling them, are you?"

She stopped playing, zipped open her large purse, and pulled out a stack of large bills from deep down in her bag.

"Look at this," she said as she fanned the bills held together with a rubber band.

I'm sure my eyes almost popped out of my face.

"So, you sell them?"

"Mmhmm," she said while smirking, "Next question, hun."

When she was being sarcastic, she used "hun."

"My fucking God." I couldn't believe it. "You are going to get caught. What the fuck is wrong with you?"

"Mind your own business, hun, I just sell them to my friends."

"You are going to go to jail."

"Whatever. They are all prescribed to me. I'm not doing anything wrong."[3]

I understood, to some extent, her reasoning for carrying a stun gun. She was an older woman in her fifties whose job it was to open up a restaurant by herself. And she lived in a pet grooming salon. She could get robbed at the restaurant or grooming salon at any moment. But selling prescription drugs? My fucking God.

I asked Marx about it all the next day, and he already knew about the stun gun and her side drug business. He told me that there was a doctor in the south suburbs of Chicago who saw cash-only patients and would prescribe 180 hydrocodone pills, such as Norco, a month to anyone who presented with back pain and asked for them. She would then pay cash for the prescription at the pharmacy and sell each pill for substantially more than she paid. I got a feeling Marx was "seeing the doctor," too. But I was too scared to probe.

Around the same time that I learned she was selling prescription drugs and carried an illegal stun gun, I learned that the federal prosecutor was offering my mother a plea agreement for stealing my identity. She would plead guilty to certain federal charges outlined in the indictment that she was served in 2010, and she would get off easy with probation and not have to do any federal prison time. I was relieved that my credit was clear and no longer felt guilt for filing the police report because she wasn't going to have to be behind any bars.

* * ☆ * *

Amy and I were dating for about five years when we decided to separate. She had recently been admitted to a library sciences program. She planned on continuing to work her jewelry store job throughout the two-year community college library sciences program. We were constantly bickering with each other. I felt insecure, so I bombarded her with a lot of questions that she didn't like. Do you still love me? Are you unhappy with me? Maybe you're straight and want to be with a man? I couldn't figure out why she was so unhappy, and I pestered her about it all the time. I'm sure she would say that I was also really controlling, and to some extent she'd be right. On top of my insecurity, I didn't trust anyone after what mom did to me. I insisted on managing all of our household expenses, making sure everything got paid on time and usually weeks early.

Amy and I spent nearly a year in couples counseling. We talked about my control issues, our shared anxiety, our lack of sexual intimacy, and how our relationship morphed into an unhealthy situation that resembled a parent and child attachment rather than a romantic partnership. She wanted more excitement in her life, and I was comfortable sitting at home after school working on my dissertation, watching reality TV shows like *Big Brother* and *The Bachelor* or Showtime's *The L Word*, in between giving her advice about her education. In counseling, we came up with some ideas to reignite our relationship spark by going to community festivals and sports games, which we started doing. One hot early summer evening, we went to a Chicago Fire soccer match and had a blast. Things were looking up again in our relationship, until the next morning when I got out of bed and went to the living room and was confronted with something that ended up crumbling our efforts to build back a positive relationship. I sat in my recliner like I always did, while reaching for my laptop in order to get online and check my email. I then bent over and opened Lucie's plastic crate—she was only a year old and slept in the crate because she wasn't yet fully house-trained. She usually would stretch in the crate soon after I opened the door before running out of it and jumping on me. But when she didn't come out of the crate, I leaned over and saw that she was still on her back. I reached in to wake her up and immediately felt her stiff body. She was dead.

"AMY," I screamed, "Lucie's dead!!!"

She ran out from the bedroom and we immediately started crying. We opened up our door that led to a carpeted winding hallway and screamed to our downstairs neighbor, who was our landlord and friend, for help. Before I knew it, he was carrying out Lucie's crate with her dead body still in it. He told us that he would take her to a vet to be cremated.

I felt responsible for Lucie's death. Before Amy and I went to the soccer match, we had taken her on a long walk and she was heavily panting throughout it. When we got back from the match, I saw that she had thrown up around the house and I wondered if the walk we took her on caused her to overheat or have a heart attack or something like that. I knew from volunteering with the Chicago French Bulldog Rescue, something I did after learning about the horrors of puppy mills like the one Lucie came from, that the breed is prone to overheating owing to their short and flat faces. Why else would a dog barely over a year old die? It didn't make any sense to me, and I was devasted. Folks in the rescue told me to not be so hard on myself—that Lucie's death probably had more to do with how she was bred in the puppy mill than anything I did to her. Amy was devasted, too, but after a few days of grieving she told me I was being overly dramatic and needed to get over it. Our relationship was back on the downward swing.

After our year of couples counseling, many tears, nasty arguments, and me accusing her of cheating on me with a man, Amy moved out and rented a room in a house about a mile from where we had been living together. Our separation gutted me but also brought me relief. I imagine she felt the same way. I gave her some money to make sure she would be alright managing all of her expenses on her own. We had two cars, both of them were in my name. One was paid off, and the other I still owed a lot on. I gave her the paid-off one by transferring the title to her name. I wanted to make sure that she still had a reliable car to get to school and work, but I also didn't want my name on anything that I could no longer keep track of, like making sure the car insurance was paid on time.

We remained close friends for several months after we broke up. I would treat her to meals, and we would use the time together to gossip about who we were meeting through on-line dating websites. Because it would have been difficult for her to afford a pet-friendly rental that would allow our French Bulldog Penny (whom we adopted after Lucie died), and two cats Junie and Yoda, we agreed that all of our pets would stay with me and she would visit them whenever she wanted. Junie was a white tabby cat, and Yoda was a black cat with a few white spots on his toes. I assumed we would be close friends forever as we were with Claire, the woman we had both dated at earlier points in our lives.

For my thirtieth birthday in October of 2010, Claire and I left our partners at home and went to San Francisco together for a friends' trip. Claire was partnered with Elaine, a successful physician that I had encouraged her to date several years earlier. I was also in a relationship. After Amy and I broke up, I had started seeing Betty, a white 30-year-old social worker with shoulder-length dirty blonde hair. I had met Betty on OkCupid, an online dating site, and we were seeing each other off and on for several months as she jumped around from one temporary social work gig to the next, unable to secure a permanent full-time position. Amy agreed to look after Penny, Junie, and Yoda while I was on vacation with Claire, and I gave her some money for the inconvenience. When I got back from San Francisco, I found out from my downstairs neighbor that Amy had brought her new girlfriend to my place when I was gone, and that they were there together for the three nights I was on vacation. I was livid. I kept imagining them having sex on my bed. Or this random woman that Amy was dating snooping around my apartment, looking through my drawers and laughing at my granny panties. I had asked Amy to not bring her girlfriend to my place while I was gone, but she did so anyway. I freaked the fuck out and told Amy I never wanted to see her again, and that I hated her for disrespecting me the way that she did. It was an overreaction, for sure, but my therapist wondered if it had more to do with my unresolved trust issues from mom stealing my identity then it did with Amy bringing her girlfriend over to my place when I was out of town. My therapist at the time, a white lesbian, said she thought it was immature and selfish for Amy to have done that to me, but that my reaction, while understandable, was probably intensified because of my trust issues stemming from the identity theft case. Makes sense to me, I remember thinking. Amy and I didn't stay friends. The last time Amy and I talked was in the fall of 2011. She told me that she would always hope for the best for me and that she looked forward to googling me to watch me shine. I wished her well, too, and we haven't communicated since.

For the first time since the divorce in 2004 and learning all about mom stealing my identity shortly after that, my life felt stable. In the fall of 2010, I went on the academic job market and received two tenure track offers. I accepted a sociology professorship in a city that was just outside of St. Louis, Missouri. Despite that university offering me at the end of negotiations only $48,000, my other tenure track offer was from a university in Chicago for about $51,000. Given that the cost of living in Chicago was way more than living in southern Illinois, I accepted the professorship down south.

I spent the spring and summer semesters of 2011 finishing my dissertation and preparing for my move to Edwardsville, Illinois, which was about a four- to five-hour drive south of Chicago. For $1100 a month, I rented a home from an economics professor who left the Midwest for a professorship on the West Coast. He had been trying to sell the three-bedroom home that he lived in with his family for quite some time but wasn't getting any reasonable offers, so decided to rent it instead. It was a cute 1800-square-foot home built in 1925 and less than two miles from what would be my new campus. It didn't have a toilet on the main floor, but it had two bathrooms on the upper level, owing to an addition that had been put on at some point. There was also a toilet, by itself, in the unfinished basement next to the washer and dryer and your typical basement utility sink. The toilet was out in the open, leaving no privacy for the user, leaving me to laugh about it.

Betty, whom I had been dating for a little more than a year, was still in between temporary social work contract jobs when I was getting ready to move to Edwardsville. We wanted to move in together, so we saw my move to Edwardsville as the perfect reason to do so. It was better than trying to maintain a long-distance relationship, with her living in southeast Wisconsin and me soon to move to a small city near St. Louis, Missouri. I offered to pay for more than half of the rent because I had a permanent full-time job and she didn't yet. But six weeks after we got settled into our Edwardsville rental, she landed the perfect job, owing to her determination to find something other than dog walking, which she had been temporarily doing after we moved to southern Illinois. I'd like to think my editorial guidance on her cover letter and resume, and coaching on her interview, which I rounded off by paying for her to get her hair blow dried and styled the morning of an interview, all played a role, too. I explained to her that she is going to feel more confident in the interview with professionally styled hair. I convinced her to follow all of my advice, and a few days later she got an offer for full-time permanent employment.

When I told mom about the professor's home I was going to rent and how the owner had it on the market for around $167,000 but didn't get any reasonable offers, she told me to ask him if he would consider a rent-to-own agreement.

"Ask him if we would accept $139,500 for the home after a one-year rental lease at $1,100 a month. And, if so, if he would be willing to return 25% of the rent to you for the down payment."

"He would never go for that! That's almost $30,000 less than he is trying to sell the house for."

"What do you have to lose?" She told me to just ask him, and I did.

I was surprised when he agreed to my offer. We worked out the details between us, over email, without consulting any housing professionals. We treated our agreement as legally binding, not caring if it really was. The agreement began on July 1, 2011, and included a "Purchase Option" clause noting that I needed to make a decision about buying the home under our agreed-upon terms by April 15, 2012, with a target closing date of June 15, 2012. I did not have to buy the home, but he was obligated to sell it to me for the price we agreed on if I chose to proceed with the "Purchase Option."

* * * * *

On August 27th, 2011, I defended my sociology doctoral dissertation, which I titled "Gender Players and Gender Prisoners: When Intersex Activism, Medical Authority, and Terminology Collide," at the University of Illinois at Chicago. At UIC Sociology, dissertation defenses are open to the public but are often only attended by graduate students and faculty. At my defense, the sociology conference room was packed with my dissertation committee members, other faculty who were there to support me, fellow graduate student friends, my mom, my dad, Aunt Maria, and Aunt Athena and one of her daughters. Claire was also there, assuring me that she would keep an eye on my family to make sure they didn't say or do anything too problematic. I wanted my family there, but I also was afraid they'd embarrass me. Betty was working, so she wasn't able to make it. The conference room felt like a scene from *My Big Fat Greek Wedding*, leaving me to refer to the day as *My Big Fat Greek Dissertation Defense*. A few times during my presentation, I looked over at mom and saw her falling asleep, which still makes me laugh, given that she joked with me after my defense telling me that she had never in her life been so bored.

I couldn't find my mom. The cold winter days were getting shorter and darker, and as 5 o'clock drew closer I knew it would be getting dark. An employee at the grooming salon told me she didn't know where mom was. The manager at the restaurant mom waitressed at said he saw her leave around 3. Where the fuck could she be? My anxiety was at an all-time high, with terrible things racing through my mind. Did she get into a car accident? Without a cell phone, how would she call someone if she needed help? Aunt Maria and Aunt Athena weren't answering their cell phones. What was going on? Mom was always either at the restaurant she waitressed at, the grooming salon she lived at, or at a casino with one of her sisters. But it was a weekday, and they usually only went to a casino on the weekends. I was getting ready to make the drive from southern Illinois up to Chicago when Aunt Athena finally answered her cell after what must have been my fiftieth call.

"Do you know where my mom is? I can't find her anywhere."

"Oh, Missy, there are a lot of problems. Don't tell her I told you anything, but she got arrested."

"For what?" I asked, full panic-mode about to set in.

"I don't really know the details but she is in jail for selling drugs. She called me and asked me to get together the money to bond her out."

"Oh my fucking God. She's going to go to jail for a long time given the federal case. What the fuck is wrong with her? I told her to be careful."

I started crying.

"Oh, Missy, don't be upset. We will get through this."

"Are you going to get her now? How much is her bond?"

"Yeah, I've been trying to get together the money—she needs thousands—without letting Billy get wind of what happened."

Billy, a Greek-American, is Aunt Athena's husband. Aunt Athena often kept family things from him out of fear that he would tell his mother, who would announce everything to the entire Chicagoland Greek community.

"Should I drive up there now? I was about to before you answered."

"No, I wouldn't do that. If I need you, I will let you know."

"Well okay, but please tell my mom to call me right away when you see her."

"I will. Love you."

"Love you, too."

I didn't speak to mom until very late that night. Aunt Athena told me she bonded her out of jail and dropped her off at the grooming salon, but mom was avoiding me and not answering my calls.

When she finally answered, she was angry and short with me.

"Yeah, what do you want?"

"What the fuck? Why aren't you answering my calls? What's going on?"

"What do you want from me?"

"Well, what the fuck happened?"

"What do you want from me? Stop calling here. I'm sick to my stomach and can't talk."

"Did you call an attorney?"

"I said I don't want to talk right now."

"You need to call an attorney."

"Alright, you made your point. What else do you want from me?"

"Nothing. I'm just worried about you."

"Well, yeah, so am I. Now leave me alone."

She hung up on me. I called Aunt Athena in tears, scared about what was going to happen to mom. She calmed me down, telling me that my mom brought it on herself and would have to figure out what to do next. She told me to give her space, and I listened, but not before reminding Aunt Athena about the federal case.

"She needs to notify the pre-trial probation officer for the federal case because when she got arrested for that they released her on a signature bond. I think they said she was legally required to notify them if she had any interactions at all with the police while out on bond."

"Yeah, she knows."

"It's a fucking mess, Athena. She's going to end up doing a lot of jail time because on top of the federal case she now has a state case. I just don't see a way around it."

"I don't know, but I know it's not good."

"No, it isn't," I said through the tears, "It's not good at all."

"Take some Tylenol and try to sleep. There's nothing we can do at this point. She made her bed and has to sleep in it."

"Thanks, Athena. Thanks so much."

"It will be fine, honey. Just try to get some sleep."

"Okay, you too."

Mom never notified her pre-trial federal probation officer about the drug arrest. Nor did she tell the attorney she hired to represent her in the federal case that she was charged and arrested in state court with a new case. It took the federal court about a month to find out about the state charges, and I still don't know how they did. As soon as they learned of the new charges, they called for a status hearing, which I found out before mom did, on February 11, 2012, through the Department of Justice's automated Victim Notification System that alerted me mom was required to appear in federal court for a status hearing. Google taught me a status hearing was when the court needed to hear recent developments and make a plan for moving forward.

"Hey," I called mom at the restaurant, "there is a status hearing for your federal case next week. Do you know about it?"

"No, what's a status hearing?"

"I'm not really sure, but I googled it and it probably has to do with the state case. Did you tell them about it?"

"No."

"Well, that's fucked up because you were supposed to. I told you to tell them and it looks like they found out about it somehow."

"What do you think is going to happen?"

"I have no idea. Call an attorney."

"Do something, Missy, please. Do something. Please call the federal probation officer for me and tell them you don't want me to go to jail. She will listen to you because it's your case."

"They offered you a plea agreement, right? They can't take it away."

"They did but it wasn't finalized yet . . . not until the sentencing hearing. Do you think they are going to take it away?"

"I don't know."

"Please call the probation officer, Missy. Please."

"Call her and say what? What am I supposed to say?"

"Tell her you don't want me to go to jail. Please, Missy, do something."

"What the fuck. I told you to stop this shit."

"I have to go. It's busy here. Call me at the grooming salon later today."

"Okay."

Later that day, as I sat in my university office, I turned on Pandora and plugged in my earphones to listen to my Fleetwood Mac radio station that I had spent years cultivating by clicking thumbs-up to songs I liked and thumbs-down to songs I didn't. To this day, I always listen to music when I write. As Fleetwood Mac's hit song "Over My Head" traveled through the computer and into my ears, I opened up a blank MS Word document and used whatever writing skills I'd learned over the years to draft a letter to the judge overseeing mom's federal case. It was my Hail Mary attempt that I hoped would keep them from revoking mom's bond in the federal case and immediately take her into custody for violating the terms of her pretrial bond conditions.

After finding the judge's contact information through the Victim Notification System that updates me about mom's federal case, I started typing away, but not before first googling him to find out everything I could about him including his political leaning and educational background. In graduate school, we were always taught to consider our audience, and that is what I was determined to do as I crafted my letter. I learned he was a white, highly-respected federal judge with multiple Ivy League degrees and appointed to the federal bench by our country's 43rd President, George W. Bush. Because he was appointed by a Bush, I assumed he was on the right of the political spectrum, so I figured it would be best to play into the victim role and meritocracy myth that I taught my undergraduate sociology students was flawed.[1] I needed the judge to see me as a victim who was academically ambitious and always played by society's rules. I wouldn't dare share that I dropped out of school or that I, myself, sold drugs when I was a teenager. I needed him to feel like my savior. I deleted words. I added words. I changed words. It took me nearly two hours to settle on my written plea for his help.

> February 11, 2012
> Dear Judge,
> I would like to begin by thanking the courts for considering this Victim Impact Statement in the sentencing of my mother. I have felt the consequences of her action more than anyone else involved in this case. What she did was wrong. It was ethically, morally, and financially problematic. I will never forget her actions. However, I forgive them.
> She committed this crime when I was 23/24 years old and an undergraduate in college. Today, I am 31 years old,

I have a PhD, and am employed as an Assistant Professor at a state school where I am respectable citizen in our society living a happy, healthy, and honorable life. I have never been in trouble with the law, nor have I ever approached the courts in this manner.

In this statement, I am not only writing the courts but I am begging them to have leniency on my mother during sentencing.

In many ways she is already serving her sentence. She is homeless living in a dog kennel, has no health insurance, is in chronic pain due to breast tumors, and has untreated gynecological problems. She is poor. It pains me to see her live as she is, but it would hurt me even more to know that she was sentenced to jail for a crime that she has taken full ownership, is entirely remorseful, and has since followed the law which she's done her entire life up until this case.

I know that she is being accused in the state courts of criminal activity, but I beg the courts to let the facts of that case be heard and not let an accusation sway the sentencing of this separate case. The facts will prevail.

I am the sole victim in this identify theft case. The financial institutions, mortgage brokers, and the like are not victims. In my opinion, they are as guilty as she is for her actions. It is my strong belief that they had the obligation and duty to verify identity before issuing loans in my name. It has always been my assertion that the financial institutions, mortgage brokers, and the like are somehow escaping punishment. The financial institutions, mortgage brokers, and the like cared more about profiting from a loan than they ever did about my identity. I've stated this to detectives early on. I beg the courts to consider the entire situation—that is all of the parties truly involved—in their sentencing decision of the one and only person charged in this case.

My mother's actions caused me emotional pain and financial difficulty, but sentencing her to jail for this

crime will only exponentially create more emotional
pain and anxiety for me in my life as I continue with the
start of what I hope will be an honorable career that I've
worked hard to achieve for many, many years.

My mother takes full responsibility for her actions.
She is in poor health, has no medical insurance, and has
lived the last seven years in horrible conditions. Please
have mercy on her.

Please, from the bottom of my heart, take this
statement into account. I am the sole victim in this case,
and I beg the courts for leniency during their sentencing
decision.

Georgiann Davis

I went to the FedEx store and overnighted my hand-signed
letter directly to the judge's attention. I didn't know the best
and fastest way to get my letter in front of the judge, so I also
overnighted a copy to the judge's courtroom deputy, the victim
witness coordinator, and the pretrial federal probation officer
assigned to mom's case. One of the people, I hoped, would
make sure the judge saw my letter. I had no way to know if the
judge would read it before the status hearing, which was only a
few weeks away, but sending the letter to everyone I could think
of on the case was the only thing I came up with to help mom.

The evening before the status hearing, I drove to Aunt
Maria's house after I finished teaching three back-to-back sociology classes. I planned to spend the night at her house, not
wanting to get up super early the day of mom's hearing to make
the long drive from southern Illinois to Chicago. We had to be
at the federal courthouse by 9am. The mood at Aunt Maria's
house was somber. We were both worried that mom was going
to be taken into federal custody the next day, given she violated
her pretrial bond conditions with the state charges. Between
both cases, we assumed the worst and imagined her being
locked up for decades.

"What are we going to tell Yiayia?" I asked Aunt Maria. "She's
going to know something is up if my mom stops calling her."

Yiayia was in Greece and didn't know what was happening.

"We can't tell her anything," Aunt Maria warned in our typical dramatic family fashion, "If she finds out, she will have a heart attack and die."

"But she's going to want to talk to my mom and won't be able to because she will be in jail."

"Your mom can call me collect from jail, and I will put Yiayia in on a three-way call. She won't know anything that way."

"I think that's illegal, Maria. You can't three-way anyone from a jail call. I don't want you to get in trouble, too."

"Well then we will just tell her that your mom is being your mom and she's fine."

"But what if she gets sentenced years and years? I mean you can't keep it from her forever."

"I don't know, I guess we will play it by ear."

I couldn't sleep that night. I kept thinking about mom in a cell behind bars.

Early the next morning Aunt Maria and I drove to the grooming salon to pick up mom. She didn't say anything to me as I got out of my aunt's SUV and moved to the backseat to give her the front passenger seat. Aunt Athena was going to meet us at the federal courthouse. Sitting in the backseat, I could see mom scratching her scalp and biting her lips. She handed me an envelope of about two thousand dollars. On the envelope was contact information for her federal attorney as well as contact information for an attorney she somehow found that she wanted for the state case.

"Promise me you both will take care of my dogs if they lock me up."

"We will," Aunt Maria answered.

"Don't worry." I told mom, "I will take them with me to Edwardsville."

"All of them. Please," She continued, "They are old and I don't want them to be put to sleep at a shelter. You know a shelter will kill them because they are old."

She had five dogs, but Scruffy, the very old schnauzer that we got when I was about 12 years old, had recently died so she was down to four. There was Precious, a medium-sized brown dog rescue, that was very old and blind and deaf—like her dog Sophie, a brown cocker spaniel who was just as old. And then there were Timbies and Jake, dogs she adopted when we weren't talking. Timbies was a medium-sized 7- or 8-year-old white dog with black spots. And Jake was a similarly middle-aged dog that looked like a mix of German Shepherd and Alaskan Husky.

Back at home, I had Penny, a young French Bulldog that I rescued two years earlier after Lucie died, as well as my two middle-aged cats, Junie and Yoda. Although Betty and I together took care of the animals we shared our house with, I had no idea how we were also going to take care of mom's four untrained dogs. I was a neat freak and couldn't imagine what I was going to do with them pissing and shitting all over the home we were renting.

"I will take care of them. Don't worry," I told her. "It will all be okay."

"Easy for you to say. You aren't the one going to jail. They are going to beat me up and rape me."

"That's not true," I said. "It's not like that."

"Whatever," she said. "Just promise me you will take care of my dogs."

"I will."

As we drove to the courthouse, I texted back and forth with some of my closest friends. In different ways, I told them that I was devastated and scared for mom. They supported me the best they could with every reply and by sharing my pain.

We met Aunt Athena outside the main entrance of the federal courthouse. As we emptied our pockets at the security checkpoint before proceeding through the body scanners, I felt numb. My body was there doing the necessary motions, but everything around and inside me felt blurry. I was only brought back to clarity when I saw a group of news crews with bright video lights and flashing cameras charge a huddle of people leaving an elevator. I didn't know what was going on or who was in the center of the huddle, nor did I care. But I recall one of my aunts making a joke that it was probably former Illinois Governor Rod

Blagojevich, who was arrested back in 2008 for trying to sell off the United States Senate seat that Barack Obama vacated when he was elected America's 44th President.[2] Blagojevich's federal case went on for years. He was found guilty of 18 federal charges, and reported to federal prison in March of 2012, where he was sentenced to serve 14 years. However, President Donald Trump commuted his sentence, during his first term, and he was released in February 2020 after only serving about eight years. Given that Blagojevich was once a contestant on Trump's reality TV show *The Celebrity Apprentice*, I'm going to assume they were friends.

The courtroom we needed to report to was a large windowless room with high ceilings and dark wood everywhere, from the benches where we sat, to the jury box, to the two oversized desks that faced the judge's elevated platform. I learned from watching the O. J. Simpson trial in 1995 as a middle school dropout that the defendant usually faced the judge by sitting on the left side of the room, so I took a seat in the last row of the left side. Mom, and her sisters, followed me. We were early and the only ones in the room, which was eerily quiet and odorless. I don't know what kind of smell I expected, but because the space felt like a mix of stately and intimidating, I guess the courtroom reminded me a bit of a Greek Church. We were only missing the traditional livani incense that hits your nose as soon as you enter the building. Mom and her sisters were speaking Greek to one another, mostly telling mom that everything would be fine. I stayed silent, with my stomach turning. As time passed, people started entering the room, including a white man in his forties wearing a traditional men's suit and tie, and two white women dressed in pantsuits. The man and the women congregated near what I correctly assumed was the prosecutor's area. They were chatting with one another, but were speaking so softly that I couldn't make out what they were saying. Mom told my aunts to stop talking, explaining that the prosecutor was Greek and might understand everything they were saying. They immediately stopped. Then two white men, who looked like they were in their thirties, entered the room and stood in the back. They had on black polo shirts, khaki cargo pants, and black shoes that might have been boots. They each had what I assumed was a gun on their waist alongside handcuffs. They stood in silence like soldiers reporting for war. Their polos had yellow letters on them that read "POLICE" followed by "U. S. Marshal." Mom saw them and started whispering in Greek to my aunts.

"Do you think they are here to arrest me?"

"I don't know," they both calmly answered her, with words that didn't match their faces.

Mom looked at me and asked me in Greek: "Do you think they are going to take me?"

"I'm not sure but whatever happens it will be okay."

One of the white women approached us and started speaking to mom.

"Hi, Ann. How are you doing?"

"I'm okay."

"Are they going to arrest me?"

"That's up to the Judge, but I know he got your daughter's letter."

The woman looked at me.

"You must be Ann's daughter?"

"Yes, I am Georgiann Davis."

She extended her hand and introduced herself.

"Nice to meet you. My name is Jessica and I am your mother's pretrial probation officer and I received your letter. We all did."

"Okay, thank you."

"I gave a copy to the prosecutor, too."

"Thank you. I appreciate it. I just want the court to have mercy on my mom."

"We know that. We all just met with the judge."

"ALL RISE." Someone said something of that nature as the judge I'd googled a few weeks earlier made his way to his desk. Jessica simultaneously walked over to the prosecutor as mom's attorney, who I must have missed quietly entering the room, touched mom's shoulder and directed her to the defendant's table.

The Judge started speaking.

"Hello, Ms. Markozis."

"Hello, your honor," Mom quietly responded.

"We all know why we are here. Ms. Markozis, very serious charges were brought to my attention, and it's my understanding your family is here with you today?"

"Yes, your honor. My sisters and my daughter are here with me."

The judge looked at me.

"You must be Georgiann Davis?"

"Yes, that's me, your honor," I said from the back of the courtroom, wondering if he had googled me like I googled him.

"Thank you for sending me your letter," he told me before turning his eyes back on my mother.

"Ms. Markozis, you have an incredible daughter here who has accomplished so much in her life. You should be very proud of her."

"I am. Thank you your honor."

"We are going to go off record here." The judge stood up and walked to where I was. He personally introduced himself to me as I stood up and we shook hands.

"I was really moved by your letter, Professor Davis, and it's clear you have been through a lot and still manage to do great things."

He called the prosecutor, pretrial probation officer, my mother, and her attorney over to where he and I were standing and facing one another.

"I'm going to go to my chambers while you all discuss an arrangement that works for everyone. When you reach an agreement, come and get me."

I had no idea what he was suggesting, but it was all happening so fast. Before I knew it, the judge was gone and I was sitting at the prosecutor's desk with mom, her attorney, the prosecutor, and pretrial probation officer. My aunts moved from the back left row of the courtroom to the front right row so they could hear everything that we were discussing.

Everything was very blurry, but the pretrial probation officer, prosecutor, and mom's attorney were throwing words around including "third-party custodian."[3] It became a little clearer that the prosecution was offering that to mom instead of taking her into custody for violation of her pretrial release conditions. They then asked me if I was willing to be her third-party custodian.

"What is that?" I asked.

The pretrial probation officer answered.

"You will be responsible for your mother. You will be legally required to notify us if she violates any conditions of her release. If you fail to do so, you could be held legally accountable."

"Okay," I said.

"Are you willing to be your mother's third-party custodian? She will have to live with you."

"Yes, I can, but I don't live in Chicago. I live in southern Illinois. Does she have to live with me?"

"Yes, she has to live with you. If you aren't willing to be her third-party custodian, then we will have to take your mom into custody for violating her pretrial release conditions."

"For how long will she be in custody?"

"Until sentencing."

"But I live in southern Illinois. Will she not be able to stay here in Chicago?"

"No, she will need to live with you. We can ask the Southern District of Illinois to oversee her pretrial probation until sentencing. Does this work for you?"

"Yes, it's fine."

What the fuck was going on and so quickly? What was I agreeing to? I mean I understood what was being said, but I wasn't at all prepared to respond. Before I knew it, I was sitting next to my aunts in the front row and the judge was back at his desk addressing me:

"Ms. Davis, would you please come up to the stand."

"Okay."

He asked me to spell my name for the court reporter before continuing on with his questions.

"Ms. Davis, do you understand what it means to be a third-party custodian?"

"Yes, I think so."

"Do you understand that you are legally responsible for your mother and are legally required to notify the courts if she violates her pretrial probation conditions?"

"Yes, I do. But am I responsible if she does something wrong? Could I be charged instead of her?"

"No, but you are legally required to notify us if she violates her pretrial probation conditions. If you fail to notify us, you could be charged."

"Okay."

"Do you understand?"

"Yes, I do."

"And you agree to be her third-party custodian?"

"Yes, I do."

The U. S. Marshals quietly left the courtroom and mom evaded arrest. The pretrial probation officer asked me for my home address and phone number and gave me her card. She instructed me to keep her posted about what was happening in the state case. She told me that she was going to reach out to the Southern District of Illinois to inform their pretrial office of the circumstances of mom's case and give them my contact information. A federal pretrial probation officer who works out of the Southern District of Illinois, she said, would be in touch with me in the next couple of days. As we walked out of the courtroom, I felt relieved that mom wasn't taken into custody, but I suddenly felt like I was the one on pretrial probation.

As mom, her sisters, and I stepped into an empty elevator that would take us to the ground floor, they were speaking in Greek with smiles on their faces, acting like the federal case was over—while I was realizing that the court left me with a false choice. It was either mom moves in with me or they take her into custody.

"This is serious," I reminded all of them before directly looking at mom. "You can't fuck up or I'm going to be the one going to jail."

Mom jokingly smirked and winked at me.

While I often parented mom more than she parented me, my responsibility was now legally reinforced with my new status as her third-party custodian. On the way back from the federal courthouse as my mom's third-party custodian, I texted Betty to let her know that mom was going to be moving in with us. She was always supportive, and this time was no different, but I could sense her disappointment with what the court did.

Mom insisted that I allow her to bring her four dogs with her.

"Missy, they are all I have. They have to come with me. Please."

"I can't have your four dogs and my dog in the house. If my landlord finds out, I will get kicked out."

"How will he know? He doesn't even live in the state."

"But your dogs aren't trained and you know I'm a neat freak. They can't fuck up the house. I don't have any money to pay for dog damage."

"I will take care of them. Please. I've lost everything and they are the only good things in my life. They will be put down if I don't take them with me. I just can't leave them to die."

Our back and forth continued as Aunt Maria drove us from the federal courthouse to her home, where I had left my car. I finally caved and agreed to let her bring her four untrained dogs with her. Betty, who was an animal lover like me, was fine with it but I probably wouldn't have changed my decision even if she wasn't. An hour or so later, mom was following me to Edwardsville with four dogs crammed in the back of her old and beat-up SUV alongside a few garbage bags full of her clothes.

* ★ ☆ ★ *

Out of fear that I would be in violation of my agreement with the federal court, I kept in regular email communication with her federal pretrial probation officers in both northern and southern Illinois. I used email because I wanted a paper trail of everything in order to protect myself in the event the court falsely accused me of not adhering to my now legally binding obligations. I don't know how much of my fear was driven by anxiety, but I was deathly afraid of being in violation of the agreement and somehow ending up, myself, in federal prison. I notified the federal probation officers about my efforts to get mom into therapy, and I let them know when I found a local resource center in southern Illinois that not only provided her with mental health counseling but also managed to get her on public assistance.

Mom's federal case was in pre-sentencing limbo. Although the federal prosecutor offered her a plea agreement that would keep her under probation but out of prison, that offer was not yet finalized when she was charged and arrested at the state level with narcotic distribution. With the new charges, the federal prosecutor withdrew his offer, and he did so saying that he would wait to see how the state's case evolved before revisiting any plea agreement discussions.

* ★ ☆ ★ *

Mom had been with me, her third-party custodian, for only a few weeks when I dropped her off at an Amtrak Station in southern Illinois. She had a state court hearing up in northern Illinois, and I couldn't take her myself because I had to teach. It was only my second semester in my first professorship, and I thought it would reflect poorly on me if I canceled class. Aunt Maria promised me that she would pick mom up at a Chicagoland Amtrak station and bring her to the state court hearing, which we figured would just be a continuance because mom was going to ask for time to secure legal representation. We were right. The judge granted mom a continuance but only for one week, and thankfully on a day of the week that I was not teaching so I was able to make the four hour or so each way drive with her.

* ★ ☆ ★ *

The state court building felt very different from the federal court building that I was in only a month or so earlier. There were a lot more people of color, presumably defendants and their supporters, making their way through the security check-points. The officers overseeing the scanners were incredibly rude to those of us in line.[1] One white man officer shouted to the crowd of people in the queue:

"For the umpteenth time, I said take everything out of your pockets! Why don't you people listen?"

I felt scared. I had visited state courtrooms a few times before with Theo to support him during his court cases, but somehow it felt different now. Maybe because I was older and knew more about the criminal legal system then I did when I was a child. Or more likely it was because I was there this time to support my mother, and everything society tells us about our parents, especially our mothers, is that outside of their senior health care needs, they will always be there to support their children and not the other way around.

"If you don't want another case," the officer continued, "leave your cell phones and weapons in your car!"

I was glad mom warned me to leave my cell phone in the car, or I would have felt more afraid than I already was.

Aside from fear, I felt anger—and not just towards the officers who were treating all of us like shit in the security line. I also felt anger towards mom for putting me in this position, and

I remember thinking that I—a new professor—didn't belong there, as if I was somehow superior to those around me.

The courtroom that mom had to report to was packed. We could barely find a place to sit, and we even arrived early, as I always tend to do for everything in my life from social gatherings to work meetings. The cases were quickly called one after another. There appeared to be public defenders, mostly younger white people of all genders, using the defendant's table as their work station, occasionally joining some of the defendants who were called up to the judge. Some other folks in suits, presumably private attorneys, who looked a lot like the public defenders (only, on average, older), would enter the courtroom and join the defense table only moments before their respective clients' cases were called. They either had psychic powers and knew the exact time to arrive or they had a more detailed schedule that listed the order in which cases would be heard. The defendants and their supporters, on the other hand, all had a general time to report to the courtroom, not knowing when their case would be called. The court's time was clearly more valuable than the defendant's time.

Occasionally folks in prison scrubs would be brought in from a side room adjacent to the courtroom. An officer who stood outside the side room would escort the incarcerated defendants, already handcuffed, into the courtroom. The incarcerated defendants were almost always men of color, with the occasional woman or white man thrown in, too. The officer would quickly escort each defendant up to the judge, only to return them to the side room minutes later—but not before, in many cases, the defendant tried to quickly do a modified handcuffed wave by wiggling their fingers and smiling at a loved one who returned the gesture. I remember being in awe that the loved ones of those in custody would deal with a busy parking garage, the offensive security line officers, and crowded courtroom for these few seconds of reciprocal love. The currently free defendants, and their supporters, sitting around me were far more racially diverse than those in the side room, albeit people of color were still in the majority.[2]

The courtroom got emptier and emptier as case after case was heard. What's taking so long, I thought to myself. Finally, after nearly two hours, mom's case was called. She was going to ask for another continuance, noting that she still hadn't secured legal representation. I figured we only had a few more minutes of waiting as I stared at her back as she stood in front of the judge. I couldn't hear anything that was being said, but the next thing I knew the side room officer walked up behind mom and placed her in handcuffs.

What the fuck is happening? My heart started beating faster. What the fuck is going on? As the officer turned my handcuffed mother around, she had tears streaming down her face. She didn't wave at me like the other defendants in custody. Instead, in shock by what just happened, she mouthed to me, "Help me, please. Please, help me. Help me. Help me."

I didn't know what to do. I couldn't call anyone because I didn't have my phone. I went up to the defendant's table and explained, holding back my tears, that the woman just taken into custody was my mother and that I was her federal court appointed third-party custodian.

"Why did they take her into custody?" I asked a butch-looking white woman who I assumed was a public defender. "She was out on bond."

"I'm not sure. Let me see what I can find out for you."

She approached the prosecutor's table and whispered back and forth with someone sitting there as the few remaining cases were being called up one after another.

"It seems there was a warrant out for her arrest. If she has an attorney, I would reach out to them as soon as possible."

"Okay, thank you."

I left the court room set on running to my car in order to get my cell phone and immediately call my aunts for help. As I was making my way to an escalator, I coincidentally saw the attorney who was representing mom in the federal case. I ran up to him.

"Mr. Jackson, they just took my mom into custody. I don't know what is going on but apparently there was a warrant out for her arrest."

"Which judge did she see?"

"I don't know," I said as I fumbled through mom's paperwork that she had me hold onto when her case was called. "We were in Room 1201."

"Let me see what I can find out about the warrant."

We walked together to the courtroom and mom's federal attorney walked up to the prosecutor's table. I was near him but still in the now mostly empty audience section of the courtroom.

"Excuse me," I interrupted the prosecutor as he spoke with Mr. Jackson. "I am my mother's federally appointed third-party custodian. Please tell me what is going on."

The prosecutor ignored me, but mom's federal attorney responded.

"Missy, I will meet you in the hall. Please go wait there and give me a few minutes."

"Okay," I said before making my way out of the courtroom.

Without my phone to reach out to someone, anyone, for support, I felt lost waiting. Mom's federal attorney eventually met me in the hall like he promised.

"So, it seems, as you know, they initially charged your mom with the distribution of drugs, and she bonded out on those charges. But they have since added a new charge related to a weapon of some kind that she had on her."

"Can I bond her out?"

"After a bond hearing on the new charge, sure. If the judge offers bond."

"You don't think he will?"

"I don't know the details of the case, so I can't answer that for you."

"Can I hire you for this case?"

"I mostly work in the federal court these days, but yes, you could retain me for this case if you wish. Here's my card."

"Okay, thank you for your help. I will talk to my aunts and call your office. When will I be able to see my mom?"

"Not for a while. She has to get processed and that takes a while. And then the county jail has set visiting hours. You should be able to find what they are on their website. Are you heading back to southern Illinois?"

"Yes, I have to because I teach tomorrow."

"Drive safely and call my office after you speak to your aunts."

"Okay. Thanks again."

I ran back to my car to phone my aunts. After updating them while still parked in the courthouse parking garage, I decided to drive back to Edwardsville. I had to teach the next morning, and I didn't want to miss class. I was left with a lot of unknowns, too. Would she get bond? How much would it be? I also wanted to hire a private attorney to represent her in the state case, but before I even thought about doing that I needed to know if she would get bond on the weapons charge. I didn't have any savings, so any money I needed to retain an attorney for her and/or bond her out was limited to the cash advance available on my credit card. My aunts said they would help me come up with any money I needed by pawning off their jewelry, but I didn't know if they meant what they said.

As I was driving back to Edwardsville, my cell phone rang and "Unknown" popped up on the screen. Mom. It must be mom.

"Hello?"

"You have a collect call from, 'Ann,' an inmate at the county jail. To accept the charges, press 1."

The message was spoken by an automated women's voice, but interjected in the automated message was my mother's voice who said 'Ann.' Her voice was shaky and she was clearly in tears.

I pressed '1' as quickly as I could.

"Hello? Ma? Are you there?"

"Missy! Get me out of here! Please! Please! I don't have long! Please get me out of here!"

"I'm trying. I saw Mr. Jackson and he said they added on a weapons charge and that's why they arrested you. He doesn't know if they will give you a new bond. I'm going to hire him."

"Don't do that! He's a fucking idiot! What does he mean I'm not going to get a bond?"

"I don't know."

"I have a bond hearing tomorrow morning. You need to get the bond money. Whatever it is. Tell Maria and Athena to get the money you don't have and bond me out. I can't stay here." She started crying and screaming. "They will rape and kill me, Missy!"

"I'm going to take a credit card cash advance and drive back to Chicago after I teach."

"Where are you now?"

"I'm driving to Edwardsville. I have to teach tomorrow morning."

"Please come back tomorrow. Please! And bring whatever money you have and can get. I promise you I will give it back to you."

"Don't worry about the money. I will figure it out. But, you don't want me to hire Mr. Jackson?"

"NO! Don't do that! He's a fucking idiot."

"Do you want me to hire the other guy—the card you gave me? I can't remember his name."

"I don't know. I will hire an attorney when I get out. Just get me out of here."

An automated message interrupted us. "You have 1 minute remaining"

"Missy, it's going to disconnect! Please get me out of here! Please! They will kill me!"

"I'm doing what I can," I said, too anxious to call out her racism this time but familiar with it enough to know she was using "they" as a stand in for "people of color."

"You have to get me out of here. I can't stay here. Get as much cash as you can from the credit card."

"How much do you think it will be?"

"I don't know. Get as much as you can. And tell Maria and Athena, too. They owe me a lot of money. Tell them they have to. I can't stay here!"

"What time is your bond hearing tomorrow?" The line cut. "Hello? Hello?"

I immediately phoned Aunt Athena. And then added Aunt Maria into the call via a three-way connection, all while doing

75 mph on I-55 South. I recounted mom's collect call with them and asked them to meet me at the county jail at 6pm the next day with whatever money they could come up with. By 6pm, I figured she would have seen a judge and have been given a bond amount. I told them that I thought I would be able to get a $5,000 credit card cash advance but that I thought I would need more. I never took a credit card cash advance before, although I recalled seeing from marketing letters that I did have access to a cash line, albeit with an outrageous interest rate. As we hung up, I drove the rest of the way home feeling drained. I had no more tears to cry. I didn't flip through the radio stations as I always did. I just stared ahead driving on autopilot. I didn't eat or drink anything that day. After cleaning up after mom's dogs by mopping the basement floor with hot bleach water, I just crawled into bed, miserably replaying the day's events in my head. Betty tried to comfort me when she got home quite late from work, but I told her that I wanted to be left alone.

The next morning, I went to campus and taught like my life wasn't crumbling around me. After teaching three back-to-back classes, I walked to my car and made the long drive back up to Chicago. Aunt Maria and Aunt Athena met me in the jail parking lot as they promised they would. They were only able to collectively come up with about $1,000. I had on me $5,000 in cash that I managed to get by cashing a credit card cash advance check that I paid to myself. I think the interest rate was nearly 30%, but nothing was going to deter me from bonding mom out of jail.

The three of us, with our $6,000 cash, walked up to the bond window and asked an officer about mom's bond hearing. We quickly learned we didn't have enough. There was a little confusion because mom was facing multiple felony charges, but the officer told us that we needed more than $20,000 cash given the charges, but that the bond amount would likely be reduced the next day in a follow-up bond hearing. I still don't understand the process, but I knew then that we'd never be able to come up with $20,000. As the three of us walked back to our cars, we discussed what we should do and I said that I think it's best to use our money to retain a defense attorney. They agreed. Given that mom didn't like Mr. Jackson, I made the decision to contact the defense attorney—whose card she had, which was with the paperwork she told me to hold onto before she got called up to the judge and subsequently arrested. I think she met him once about the state case—why else would she have his card?—but I wasn't sure and obviously couldn't call mom and ask her. The attorney answered my call and, after a brief conversation, said he could handle mom's case for a $5,000 retainer. He told me he could get her probation since she didn't technically have a record, given that the federal case was still pending. He happened to be at the courthouse, which was adjacent to the jail, so he met us in the parking lot and I gave him the $5,000 cash I had on me, officially retaining him to represent mom in her state case. My aunts kept their money. He was an unremarkable white man who looked like he was of Italian descent, but those few minutes would be all that I would ever see of him—although he would be there with mom at each of her subsequent state court dates. A few hours later, I got another collect call from mom.

"Where are you?"

"I'm driving back to Edwardsville. Your bond was too much and we didn't have it."

"They are going to lower it tomorrow. You have to bond me out of here. I can't stay here, Missy. They are going to kill me. Please!"

"I hired that attorney. The one whose card you had."

"What? Why the fuck did you do that?"

"Because I wanted you to have an attorney and you didn't want me to hire Mr. Jackson."

"Oh no! No! Why did you do that? How much did you give him?"

"$5,000."

"Now how the fuck are you going to bond me out?"

"I don't know but your bond was like $20,000. I had no choice."

"Didn't Maria and Athena give you any money?"

"They had about $1,000."

"Figures. I wish you wouldn't have hired that attorney. I told you to get me out of here and then I would hire an attorney."

"But there was no choice. And you need an attorney."

An automated message interrupted us. "You have 1 minute remaining."

"Now what? Why the fuck did you do that, Missy?" She started screaming and crying, "Get me out of here!!"

"Please stop. Please. There's nothing I can do. I will see what else I can come up with. Please don't be mad at me. And please call me tomorrow. I'm really worried about you."

"How am I going to stay in here. It's horrible in here. They are going to kill me."

"Just keep to yourself."

"Yeah, you try that."

The call disconnected.

I was really worried about mom. Yeah, she fucked me over so many times, and logically you'd think I wouldn't care about her. But that's not actually easy to do when we are bombarded with messages from just about everyone about the unconditional and uncontested reciprocal love biological families should share. "Blood is thicker than water." "Your mother is your mother." "Family first." This bullshit is what makes it difficult to create healthy boundaries around hurtful people.

My mind was wandering to dark places. I was picturing her sitting in a jail cell alone, crying, and scared. It was too much for me to handle on my own, so I called Marx, who reminded me that she created this mess for herself.

I then did something I never did. I asked my dad to put Theo on the phone. Unless he was locked up, he was always around either our dad or our mom, usually strung out on drugs or passed out on alcohol. But this time he sounded different. He was there for me when I opened up to him about our mother being in jail. He told me she'd be fine and that jail wasn't like what they show on TV. "It ain't that bad, Missy. Don't worry. No one will fuck with her. She's too old."

I needed to believe him.

* ★ ☆ ★ *

A few weeks had passed by the time the judge in mom's weapon and drugs case lowered her bond. And soon thereafter the prosecutor offered mom a plea agreement that would total to, accounting for good behavior and credit for time already served, about 90 days of total jail time. She was taken into custody in mid-March, and was set to be released on June 16, 2012.

Although the private attorney I hired for her in the state case did essentially nothing, I was glad that I'd used the credit card cash advance to hire him rather than bond her out. If I'd bonded mom out instead, I'm sure she would have refused the prosecutor's plea agreement, given how much she feared incarceration. The case would have continued on and on, resulting in more and more legal fees, long drives from southern Illinois to the court in northern Illinois, and more demeaning interactions, for both of us, with the court's security officers.

Mom got used to jail and even made a few friends while in custody. I imagined it helped that I put one, sometimes two, hundred dollars on her commissary account on a weekly basis so that she could buy, and share with other inmates even if it wasn't allowed, snacks, toiletries, and anything else she wanted that the commissary sold. I also asked her to call me—collect—at least once a day to ease my anxiety about her well-being. Our calls were costly and short and limited to minutes, but enough time for a check in. She would mostly ask about her aging dogs. And I would update her about their health. And when her dog Precious was unable to walk anymore and stopped eating and drinking, she gave me the go-ahead to put her to sleep. She asked me to stay with Precious after the final injection until she passed on, and I did. As I drove away from the vet's office, I was in tears not because I was attached to Precious (I wasn't), but because mom wasn't able to be there with her dog.

When we weren't talking about her dogs, she would tell me about the friends that she made, what they were charged with, and how when cases were settled, folks were moved out of the county jail and into a state prison or were released. She would use their names when we spoke about them, and after our call, I would occasionally go to the Illinois Department of Corrections website and look them up. Maybe it's voyeuristically fucked up, but I found it comforting to put faces with names, to know who mom was sharing space with. Many times, when we spoke, she would tell me to write down phone numbers to call and pass along messages from her jail mates. The messages usually went something like this, "Hello! Jazmine wants you to know that she misses you and thinks about you all the time!" Or "Hi, I'm calling for Holly. She is wondering if you could please put some money on her commissary account and find out what is happening with her attorney." Many of the women mom was incarcerated with were far younger than she, although in for similar drug charges. There were also people in for retail theft, sex work, and DUIs.

The only person she spoke of that was in for a violent crime was a middle-aged white woman who was charged with murdering her daughter. I read about the case in the Chicago media, and I learned that the woman slit her daughter's throat. She claimed she was having delusions and had pled not guilty by reason of insanity. The court eventually agreed with her plea and she was committed to a mental health institution. Mom told me that a handful of other jail mates felt the woman was getting off easy, so they allegedly taunted and tormented her when the local news reported the decision. While the woman was curled up on her bed alone in her cell after lights out, they would yell: "Mommy, mommy, don't kill me! Please mommy don't kill me!" Mom said the woman had pictures of all of her kids, not only the one she murdered, in her cell, and that others mocked her for that, too. The harassment supposedly continued for days until the woman was transferred out of the county jail and into the mental health institution that she was sentenced to. Mom is a liar, so I don't know if the woman was actually treated this way by other jail mates or if mom made some, or all, of it up.

I only visited mom once when she was in jail, and I went with my Aunt Maria, who with Aunt Athena visited mom more frequently because they both lived less than an hour from the jail. As Aunt Maria and I sat facing mom, separated by glass, we talked through jail phones and did so mostly in Greek to afford us some level of privacy. We weren't allowed to meet for long, I think around 30 minutes, which to me wasn't worth the drive from southern Illinois. Our collect call check-ins, while expensive, were fine by me and enough for both of us. When the guard said time was up, we followed what you see in the movies. She placed her hand on the glass and I placed my hand over hers. She continuously waved at me walking towards the guards, as did several of her friends to their loved ones whom they had just finished meeting with. I recognized some of mom's friends from their mugshots.

There were only a handful of days that mom was in jail that we didn't speak. The first time she didn't call me to check in, I thought the worst and couldn't sleep all night. I feared there was a riot and kept checking local Chicago news to ease my concerns. It turned out there was a lockdown because a few women got in a physical altercation, so everyone had to stay in their cells. The next time she wasn't able to call, I was still afraid, wondering if this time she was the one involved in a fight, but not as worried as I was the first time—given that mom was viewed as an elder in jail and mostly left alone.

Then there was a three-day period that she didn't call me, in order to punish me for refusing to pay her, Marx's, and Theo's life insurance premiums. She'd taken out the life insurance policies a few years earlier, admitting to me that she was banking on getting rich from either Marx's or Theo's death. She knew Marx wasn't taking care of his health and believed he wouldn't live long, and we all knew Theo was a drug addict who probably would die young from an overdose. Now, she claimed that all three policies, including hers, were to help me when any of them died. I told her I didn't want that money and to not involve me in any way, but she didn't listen. The total quarterly premium for all of the policies was nearly $1,000, totaling to about $4,000 a year. The policies only ranged from $10,000 to $25,000 each. And looking into them, I learned they came with all sorts of exclusions—including drug overdose and suicide—yet mom didn't believe me when I told her. I explained to her how illogical it was to have these types of what I felt were predatory life insurance policies, but she refused to listen to me. In my mind, they were a rip-off.

When she first went to jail, she begged me on a collect call to pay the then-overdue premiums in order to not lose the policies. Like a fool, I used another credit card cash advance and did. When the premiums were due again, I refused to pay them a second time. I think the saying is, "Fool me once, shame on you. Fool me twice, shame on me. . . ." My refusal pissed her off, so she hung up on me, knowing damn well she would leave me with a tremendous amount of anxiety. What's worse, she didn't call me for three days. And since those incarcerated can't receive calls while in jail, I was left feeling anxious and worrying about her without any way of reaching her. When she eventually called me on the fourth day, I asked her why she didn't call to check in with me as she promised she always would, and she said she was very upset with me for being an asshole and not paying her life insurance premiums. I again reminded her that I only made $48,000 a year, had a car payment, student loans, and a rent payment for the house I shared with Betty. And that I also paid for our collect calls and sent her commissary money. She said, "I don't want to talk about it anymore. How are my dogs?" And that was the death of her life insurance policies.

* * * * *

Although I had defended my dissertation in August of 2011 and was already working as an assistant professor down in southern Illinois, I didn't officially graduate with my PhD until December of that year. I'm not sure why UIC didn't have a winter commencement for graduate students, but because they didn't, I wasn't eligible to walk in the UIC commencement until their spring 2012 ceremony, which fell on May 6. My dissertation advisor emailed me when the commencement date was announced.

"Am I going to have the honor of hooding you?"

Faculty, administrators, and graduating students all wear regalia to commencement. The gowns that the graduates wear typically reflect the school colors—UIC's are flame red and indigo blue, whereas those worn by faculty and administrators are reflective of their alma mater colors. Those who have earned graduate degrees wear hoods over the graduation gowns. Sometimes the hoods are in complementary school colors and other times they represent the discipline in which one has earned an advanced degree. While colors vary across institutions, the one thing that doesn't is that one's graduate advisor is the one that ceremonially hoods their graduating advisee at the graduation ceremony. The advisee typically kneels in front of their advisor, a gesture intended to reflect respect and the formal mentorship that took place, while they place the hood over their student's head and straighten it so it neatly drapes down their back.

I wanted to participate in the ritual but felt guilty about celebrating while mom was in jail. Other than my family and close friends, no one knew what I was dealing with at home. And I was too embarrassed to share. I vaguely responded to her email.

"Hi, I am on the fence about whether or not to go to the graduation since I have to be at my university's graduation the day before, but it would be nice to experience my own official graduation. Will you be in town? I believe the ceremony is on Sunday, 5/6."

The hooding ceremony is as much a celebration of the advisee as it is the advisor.

"Yes and I think you SHOULD. Your family will love it, and we can all go out to celebrate after. Actually, how about this, we can come back to my house and toast with champagne and cake?"

With mom in jail, I couldn't imagine celebrating anything. But I was too ashamed to share what I was going through, so I agreed and figured I would back out later.

"Sounds great! :)" I replied.

A few weeks before the commencement, I emailed my advisor and asked her if she had some time to talk. On the call I told her that I wasn't going to be able to make it to the commencement ceremony after all. She was sad but understood once I explained to her that mom was in jail and that I couldn't find it in me to celebrate anything when she was locked up. Out of embarrassment, I withheld many of the details of what she was locked up for and what I had been going through, and instead downplayed the seriousness of it all. She was very empathetic, and the following year—without me knowing—even unsuccessfully petitioned UIC administrators to allow me to walk at the commencement. They didn't, but I was there anyway in the audience. cheering on one of my closest graduate school friends as our advisor hooded her while I sat next to her partner in the stands.

* * ☆ ★ *

Betty was a huge help to me when mom was in jail. She was busy in her new job, but always helped me care for mom's dogs when she could. And caring for four untrained older dogs, three after Precious died, wasn't easy. Mopping up shit and piss after a long day's work wasn't an ideal activity, but we each did it many times.

* * ☆ ★ *

On June 16, 2012, mom was released from jail after being locked up for three months. I was there hours before her release time, waiting for her to walk out of the inmate release doors. She left the jail with a garbage bag of belongings, mostly junk she bought from the commissary. Several other inmates were released at the same time. A man being released asked me if he could use my phone. I said sure, and while handing him my phone I offered him a ride, for which he thanked me but refused, saying that his girlfriend should be there soon. It turns out she was stuck in traffic.

Mom was starving and craving White Castle fast food. So, as we drove away from the jail, my GPS brought us to the closest one and we soon found ourselves sitting in a hard plastic booth eating sliders, fries, and onion rings. Not wanting to burden either of my aunts by staying at either of their homes, I booked a cheap motel for us to stay in that night. I would have driven back to Edwardsville after she was released, but her sisters wanted to see her and I was tired from driving. As soon as we got to the hotel, I logged into Skype and phoned Yiayia's landline so she and mom could speak—the first time in more than three months. We used Skype's phone feature, not the video chat. Yiayia doesn't have, nor does she know how to use, a computer. Yiayia never knew mom was in jail. My aunts just told her she was busy working and dealing with health issues. They talked, in Greek, like nothing had happened.

Mom took a long hot shower, and then put on the new light blue summer shorts and a matching t-shirt that I'd bought for her at Walmart a week earlier in anticipation of her release. When she was arrested, it was the tail end of Chicago's winter and she was wearing sweatpants and a hooded sweatshirt. She walked out of the jail in the middle of June wearing those same clothes, which were now way too big for her given that she lost a lot of weight while in custody. We were both very tired—me from making the drive to Chicago, and her from not getting a good night's sleep in months. I closed the motel drapes and we both fell asleep on the king bed, but only after we made plans with Maria and Athena to meet for dinner later that night at a casino restaurant. My aunts, who like to gamble, have always been able to get their steak and lobster dinners comped because they'd spend a few hours playing high roller slots or table games after dinner. Once again, everything seemed back to normal.

On June 19th, 2012, three days after mom's release, I bought the house I was renting from that professor for about $140,000. With the money he returned to me given our rent-to-own agreement that mom had helped me craft a year earlier, I had enough money to put down the $4,670 that was required for the FHA loan I took out. I was in no position to buy a house, but with mom's dogs living in the basement, and my rent-to-own lease only good for one year, I didn't know what else to do. He had asked me a few months before my rent-to-own lease expired if I wanted to move forward with the purchase, and if not, he had said he was going to put his property on the market. How in the hell could I allow him to put his house on the market with mom's three surviving dogs living in the basement? My lease allowed pets, but only one dog, Penny, and my two cats, Yoda and Junie. If he put his house on the market, he'd know I was violating our lease agreement, and I didn't want that to happen. I also knew that mom was required to live with me, given that I'd agreed in federal court to be her third-party custodian. And I knew I'd never be able to find a rental that would allow my pets along with mom's three untrained dogs, so I reluctantly decided to buy the house I was renting.

I was able to book a hair appointment for mom that same week with Shelly, a hair stylist I'd been seeing at a mall salon since I moved to southern Illinois. Mom's grey roots were long and her hair was frizzy with split ends everywhere. Shelly was a friendly white woman raising two kids on her own, and although Shelly and I only had a surface relationship where we talked about our respective jobs, new restaurants, and her kids' antics, I knew she would treat mom with respect despite how her hair looked. Mom asked Shelly to make her look glamourous, explaining to her that she had been really sick—she wasn't—rather than telling her that she'd just gotten out of jail. Shelly recommended that mom go with a chin-length dark brown bob with dark auburn highlights. Mom was hesitant because she didn't want shorter hair. She was afraid she'd look, in her words, "like an old hag." Shelly laughed but eased mom's fears by showing her some pictures of what she had in mind. I sat next to mom as Shelly worked her magic over the course of three hours. And magic it was. Mom looked amazing, and she felt it, too. As we were driving home from the salon, mom had the visor down and mirror open putting on eyeliner and lipstick that she had in her purse.

She smacked her lips, and said aloud, "Welcome back, Ann, welcome back."

"Oh my fucking God," I laughed, "you are so ridiculous."

Still looking in the mirror, she half-sincerely asked me: "Why don't you find me a rich professor I can date? I mean, who could turn this down?"

"I can't with you!" I laughed. "I just can't. Shelly did a nice job though, didn't she?"

"Yeah, she did."

"I told you she was great."

* * ✮ ★ *

On October 12, 2012, I was back in a federal courtroom for mom's sentencing hearing in the identity theft case. I was again pleading with the judge, the same one who appointed me as mom's third-party custodian, to have leniency on her. How fitting, I thought: mom was being sentenced in a federal courtroom in Chicago for stealing my identity less than 10 miles away from the suburban hospital where she gave birth to me 32 years, to the day, earlier. I went from celebrating my birthday with extravagant cakes that mom used to get me when I was kid, to spending my 32nd birthday in a federal courtroom where my mom was facing multiple counts of federal felonies.

As I stood next to mom as we both faced the judge, I listened to him discuss the severity of the charges, the financial consequences she left numerous banks, and the pain and suffering she caused me. He then looked directly at mom and said something similar to what he said many months earlier when I first met him.

"You have an incredible daughter, Ms. Markozis. I hope you know that. You should be very proud of her."

"I am very proud," mom quietly responded.

The judge sentenced mom to six months in federal prison along with restitution related to the financial costs of the crime. She would also be subjected to federal probation for two additional years. I was so hoping that she'd only get house arrest and federal probation that I stopped listening after he sentenced her to six months. I thought about mom going back to prison. I didn't catch the restitution amount, nor to be honest, did I care about that part of the sentencing decision. The judge said he would allow mom to choose when to begin her sentence, and to make it easier on me, would request that she serve her sentence in a minimum-security satellite camp for females in southern

Illinois. He mentioned FCI Greenville, a federal correctional institution located in Greenville, Illinois, about 35 minutes from my home. While FCI Greenville is a medium-security prison, he explained it has a minimum-security camp for females attached to it. Given she would be imprisoned not far from my home, he said I could more easily visit her when permitted.

"Do you want to go now?" I looked at mom and asked her. "To get it over with?"

"Are you crazy? No."

"But when will you go?" I looked to my Aunts Maria and Athena, who were standing near us to lend support, but they stayed silent and apparently didn't want to get involved.

"I don't know, but not now."

"But it's only six months and it will be done with before you know it."

"Easy for you to say. You're not the one going."

The judge interrupted our conversation and told us we could work out the details with federal probation officers.

Mom didn't say much on our long drive back to southern Illinois. When I reassured her that it wouldn't be that bad, she snapped back telling me to leave her alone. She eventually opened up and said she couldn't do six more months in jail behind bars, and being dramatic, she said she'd rather die.

After we got home from mom's federal sentencing, she went directly to the basement to be with her dogs, and I jumped onto my computer to read about FCI Greenville. I read everything about the female camp that I could, including the classes offered, the number of inmates, and the visitation rules. I even found myself reading prison reviews and blogs written by those who were once incarcerated at FCI Greenville or who had family members who were. I then took to google maps to take a virtual tour around the facility. The prison was surrounded by green trees and grass. It looked peaceful, or at least that is what I was trying to convince myself.

The next morning, in an effort to ease her fears and anxieties, I told mom everything I learned about FCI Greenville.

"It's way nicer than the county jail you were at," I said with confidence. "They have classes on all sorts of things. And the camp prisoners are all women and can even walk around outside not behind bars or anything. It looks more like a school than a prison to me."

She listened to me but wasn't convinced.

"Do you want to go for a drive with me to see it?"

"You can't do that," she said.

"I don't see why not. We will just drive by it so we know where it is."

She reluctantly agreed, and stayed silent for most of the 35-minute drive to the facility. The entire drive there, I kept re-iterating everything I learned about the facility. She stayed quiet but was listening.

As I pulled into the camp's parking lot, we saw women in prison scrubs walking around outside.

"Look," I said to mom, "they are just walking around outside on the sidewalk. And they have earrings and makeup on. It doesn't look so bad."

She didn't say anything.

"I mean they are just out in the open and could run if they wanted to but they don't. This doesn't look bad at all."

She didn't say anything.

"Maybe we can talk to one of the women?"

"Are you fucking crazy?" she asked. "You can't do that. You will get arrested."

"For what? Saying hello?" My questions were genuine.

"Hey," I instructed her, "Let's go inside and talk to the guards."

"Missy, I know you can't be that fucking stupid."

"What are you taking about. I'm your third-party custodian and I will just say that and tell them that you will soon be re-porting here."

As I opened my door, she said, "I can't believe you. You are going to get arrested."

"Come with me," I instructed her. And she reluctantly fol-lowed my directions, mumbling shit about me as she got out of the car.

We walked into the visitor's entrance and were greeted by two prison guards who appeared to be white men.

"Hello, my name is Georgiann Davis, and I am a professor of sociology." I pointed to mom. "I'm also my mother's third-party custodian. She was sentenced to six months federal prison by the Northern District of Illinois because of a white-collar crime she committed, and she is very scared about being in prison. I know this is a weird question, but can you tell us a little bit about the facility?"

The prison guards looked at me like I was an entitled alien.

"Do you mean visiting hours?" One of the guards asked.

"No, like . . . would it at all be possible to get a tour?"

They chuckled.

"I know it's a ridiculous request. But I thought I'd ask."

"Sorry, we can't do that."

"Okay, but can you tell us anything about the facility?"

"Sorry, we can't and you shouldn't be here."

"Okay, we will leave now. Thank you for your time."

"No problem."

As we walked back to my car and crossed paths with several women prisoners, I whispered to mom in Greek, "See, it doesn't seem that bad." She stayed silent but I feel like she agreed with me.

* * * * *

By May of 2013, about seven months had passed since mom was sentenced to six months in federal prison. Mom had been permitted to delay serving her sentence, as the court allowed it, given she stayed in regular contact with her federal probation officers. I finally convinced her to begin her sentence early in June 2013. She would celebrate her birthday, in May, and then a few days later report to federal prison. I would visit her as much as they allowed, and I assured her that the six-month sentence would fly by. She'd even be out before Christmas.

In preparation for her six-month sentence, I told her to finally get the lumps protruding through her left breast checked out. Because she had them for a few years, I just assumed they were benign fatty deposits. But a diagnostic mammogram, and follow up imaging including biopsies, revealed otherwise.

In 2013, mom was diagnosed with advanced, but slow growing, breast cancer. The oncologist wanted to immediately begin chemotherapy, which mom agreed to only because it would delay her federal prison sentence. With the support of her federal probation officers, the judge agreed to allow her to postpone her prison sentence until her breast cancer was stabilized, despite knowing that treatment could be ongoing for several years.

More than 11 years have passed, and mom has yet to serve any time in federal prison.

* * ☆ * *

In September 2013, with mom bald from her ongoing chemotherapy treatments, I heard her talking on her cell phone, one that I got her in my name, to someone about pain pills—the same ones she was arrested for selling in northern Illinois a year and half earlier. She was in the basement with her dogs, but was speaking loudly probably not realizing I could make out a lot of what she was saying.

I was scared and in shock. What the fuck is going on? I was still her third-party custodian and afraid that if she was selling drugs again that I'd also be charged with a crime.

I laid on the hardwood floor, one level up from where her bed was in the basement. I placed my right ear as tightly as I could against the floor, hoping to more clearly hear what she was saying. She was still talking loudly about pain pills, but I didn't find out who she was talking to or know for a fact that she was trying to sell them.

But I snapped.

I ran down the basement stairs screaming on the top of my lungs.

"Get the fuck out of my house! You fucking bitch! I'm going to end up going to jail because of you! You fucking lying bitch!"

I phoned Aunt Athena.

"I think she's selling drugs again!" I screamed and cried. "I'm going to end up in jail!"

"What's going on?" Aunt Athena asked.

I started throwing mom's shit into bags, ignoring Athena who was still on the phone.

Looking at mom, I screamed, "How could you do this to me? You fucking bitch! I hate you!"

Aunt Athena tried to calm me down.

"Missy, she is really sick. She could have a heart attack. You have to calm down, honey."

"Fuck this shit! I don't care! How could you all do this to me? How could you allow this to happen to me? What the fuck did I do to any of you?"

I looked back at mom.

"I'm not fucking around! Get the fuck out of my house! Now!"

"Okay, you'll get your way," she quietly said. "But where am I going to go with my dogs?"

"I don't give a fuck about you or your dogs! I want you and your dogs gone now or I'm calling the police on you!"

Aunt Athena interrupted me.

"Missy, her car won't make it to Chicago. What do you want her to do?"

"I don't know and I don't care! I want her gone! Now!"

"But what about the court thing? She has to stay with you."

"I'm going to email them right now and tell them she can't live with me anymore."

"But they might make her go to jail if she can't stay with you and she needs her treatment."

"I don't fucking care!"

"Put your mom on the phone."

I handed my phone to mom and heard her denying everything and complaining about me saying that I was a miserable person who didn't care about her.

I wouldn't let up and even brought her three dogs to her car. She followed with two plastic garbage bags of her things and sat in her car running on my driveway for more than five hours until Marx eventually made his way from Chicago to southern Illinois. She was afraid to drive to Chicago on her own, worried that she'd be stranded on the side of the road if her old car broke down, so she asked Marx to drive down to southern Illinois and then follow behind her in his car as they drove to Chicago.

As Marx made multiple trips from the basement to his car moving out more of her belongings, I yelled at him.

"How could you do this to me? What the fuck is wrong with all of you? All of you knew I could go to jail if she did anything wrong! And you didn't fucking care! I hate all of you!"

He didn't say anything to me, but I saw tears in his eyes. I took mom's phone from her because it was in my name, and I didn't want anything to do with her. I told her that I was going to tell her federal probation officer first thing in the morning that she no longer lives with me, and I told her that it was in her best interest to follow up with them. I watched out the window as Marx drove away from my home with his car packed with her stuff following mom, bald from chemo, with her three dogs hanging out the rear windows of her SUV.

The next morning, from my university office, I emailed mom's federal probation officer:

> Hello,
> By now you should have heard directly from her, but I wanted to also let you know that my mother is going to be living in the Chicagoland area again.
>   You should be able to reach her at XXX-XXX-XXXX (my father's cell number) or XXX-XXX-XXXX (my aunt's cell number/her sister's phone number).
> Thank you for all of your support.
> Georgiann Davis

During my first professorship, I would spend about 50 hours per week in my university office. The college had bought new furniture for the entire building the summer before I joined the faculty and my office felt, at least to me, sophisticated and inviting. It was a nice change from the chaos of my home. I put a few house plants I bought at The Home Depot up against the large windows. And I placed a handful of family and pet photos around the space, which I lit with two desk lamps to avoid the need to use the hideous fluorescent ceiling lights that made my office look like a drab and dirty industrial basement. I kept all of my books neatly organized by topic and reserved a shelf for my teaching materials, which included papers that I needed to grade. I often worked on my laptop while sitting in my ridiculously comfortable oversized brown fake leather armchair that I bought from a discount furniture store and nestled in the corner of my small office. I always kept my door open when I was in the office and loved it when colleagues or students stopped by to chat. The building custodian, an older thin white woman named Susie, was a regular visitor. She would sit in my armchair as we shared university gossip. Occasionally she would tell me about her adult children and we'd often discuss how she missed her husband, who had died from a heart attack. I told her to stop by any time she needed a break, and she regularly did but sometimes she'd stop by when I was on a writing roll—and I didn't want to break my flow—so I'd tell her to come on in and relax but that I needed to keep working and couldn't talk. We closed my office door so she wouldn't get caught resting on an unapproved break.

My other regular office visitor was Dr. Lilly Rantz, a colleague whose office was next to mine. But unlike Susie, I didn't just enjoy her visits, I needed them. My time with Lilly was more useful than any therapy I've ever had, and we talked on an almost daily basis. She was the only one at my first professorship that knew what I was going through with mom, how I felt about my weight (which was continuing to climb), and my lack of emotional intimacy with Betty, which had me doubting the future of our relationship. I don't remember when or why I first opened up to Lilly, but I remember it involved lots of tears that I couldn't keep to myself anymore. We, of course, also talked about work things, and she was just as supportive of my research and teaching as I tried to be of hers.

I was professionally really productive during my time in my first professorship, in part because work was my way of escaping my family drama. I published numerous peer-reviewed research papers, worked on a book proposal for *Contesting Intersex*, and landed a contract for it with New York University Press.[1] I also volunteered for numerous university committees and was active in various organizations inside my discipline, but also in the intersex community, serving as board president for one of the largest intersex support groups in the world.

I was making $48,000 and teaching three classes in the fall and three in the spring, so I often took on two summer courses, the maximum I could, to bump up my annual salary another $10,000 or so. I needed the money to get by. I had student loans to repay, having accumulated about $40,000 worth during the course of my dissertation data collection. And I was paying $400 a month on them to try to pay them down as fast as I could. I had a monthly car payment of around $350, housing costs that came to about $1,000, and vet expenses for my animals and mom's dogs that came to another $400 or $500 (depending on what medications I needed for any of them that month). I'd also put money on mom's jail commissary and supported her when she was released and living with me, including buying her food and paying her car insurance and cell phone bill. She didn't go back to waitressing because her body no longer allowed her to do the physical labor. Instead, she lived off of my faculty salary, finally understanding that working as a professor was a much better job than waitressing even if, in my case, it paid less. I didn't have any money in savings.

I did feel that the university where I had my first professorship was underpaying their faculty. I would ask my sociology friends at comparable state universities in similar cities what they were making and learned they were all making at least $10,000 a year more than me. I had an informal coffee meeting with a high-up administrator about my salary disparity and even brought data from the American Sociological Association with me.[2] She was supportive, but her only advice was to go on the job market. The only way to get a salary adjustment, she said, was to have a job offer in hand that my current university could make a counteroffer against to retain me. I never wanted to leave my first professorship, but it seemed the only way that I could get a raise was to go on the job market and pretend that I wanted a new opportunity. So, in the fall of 2013, with Lilly's support, I did. I applied to about 24 university positions around the country that I felt were a good fit for me in terms of research and teaching expertise. And I landed three interviews, all at research-intensive universities with lower teaching loads, unlike my current university, which had fewer research requirements but more teaching obligations. I knew that research universities paid more, but when University of Nevada, Las Vegas made me a tenure track offer and agreed to a $66,000 annual salary, I couldn't refuse it and didn't even visit the other two universities that invited me to on-campus interviews. I didn't know if the others would even offer me a position or what they paid, so I ended up removing myself from their hiring pools and accepting UNLV's offer after my current university said that there was no way they could match it.

I was only in my first professorship for three years, but it was really hard for me to leave it, in part because I knew I would no longer have Lilly close by to lean on emotionally. Several colleagues organized a goodbye gathering at a local Italian restaurant the day before I left for Vegas. As I walked out of the restaurant with Lilly, and her partner who was also a colleague, I cried and hugged her and did my best to find the words to convey how much I appreciated her for unconditionally being there for me. I cried the entire way home. Although I have no doubt that she would be there for me today if I needed her, physical distance changed our friendship and we rarely talk these days.

* ★ ✮ ★ *

A few weeks before I moved to Las Vegas for my new job, I called mom. The last time I'd spoken to her was when I kicked her out of my house for fear that she was selling prescription pain pills and putting me, her (at the time) third-party custodian, at risk of criminal charges. I still remember shouting at her bald-from-the-chemo head as she left my house: "Stay the fuck out of my life, you fucking bitch! I never want to see you again!" She stayed silent as I screamed my last words, "I don't give a fuck about you or what happens to you! I fucking hate you!"

Although I was still angry with her for everything she had put me through, I was still worried about her health and genuinely feared I might never see her again once I moved across the country. She answered my call and spoke to me as if nothing ever happened. I guess that's how abusive relationships work. The abuser minimizes, denies, or outright ignores the harm they've caused.

She gave me her address—an apartment in a small city in southern Illinois that a social worker she met when she was living with me in Edwardsville helped her rent. It was a run-down, but affordable, two-bedroom apartment. She told me to come by before I moved to Vegas, so that I could see her dogs, and say hello to Theo and Yiayia, too. Theo was just released from prison, having completed one of his many sentences with more to follow. I'm not sure why he chose to stay with mom rather than Marx after getting out, but he might have done so to spend time with our Yiayia, who was in the United States from Greece visiting her daughters and grandkids. I don't know how long Yiayia had been in the U.S. by that time—no one told me she was in town until I learned from mom that she was staying with her.

When I pulled up to mom's apartment, I was greeted by mom and Yiayia waiting at the building's main entrance. We were sitting in her living room on hand-me-down couches that I recognized from Aunt Maria's house, mostly making small talk about my new job in Vegas when Theo came out of one of the bedrooms to say hello, shifting our conversation to his release from prison. He seemed to be doing so much better now that he was off of drugs and alcohol—at least for the time being, given that he didn't have access to drugs and alcohol while he was locked up. He wasn't skinny as fuck, and he didn't seem so angry at everything and everyone, like he usually was when he was strung out. He complimented my shoes—dark brown cloth loafers. I'd gotten them at DSW a few weeks earlier, and they still looked new. "Do you want them? They are men's size 10." He smiled, "Yeah, but I don't want to take your shoes." "It's okay, man, I have more shoes at home. Here," I kicked them off my feet and flung them towards him, "See if they fit you." As he put them on, he said, "Oh these are nice. Thanks, Missy. Are you sure you don't need them? I don't want to take them if you need them." "No, for real, it's fine. I don't need them." "Thanks, Missy," I could tell he meant it, "I really like them and will pay you back for them when I get a job." "Seriously, man," I told him, "Don't worry about it." It was the least I could do, as I felt my survivor's guilt rushing through my body.[3] We grew up in the same home, facing a lot of the same shit, but I ended up as a professor when I easily could have ended up like him. We all made small talk for another hour or so, with mom's dogs jumping around, before I said goodbye and walked barefoot back to my car.

Betty moved to Las Vegas with me, although we ended up breaking up not long after. I was glad that I didn't have to move out West alone, but I was also, at least I think, open with her about our relationship issues: I told her that we needed to go to couples counseling. Before we left, as we sat in a large office next to each other on an oversized sofa, we discussed our issues with both of our individual therapists present. I expressed my need for more emotional intimacy along with my frustration about her financial secrecy. If we were going to continue living together, and I was going to continue to pay for more than half of our living expenses, I thought it was reasonable to want to know how much she made, how much she had in savings, how much debt she had, and stuff like that. She had some sort of blockage and never wanted to share any of that information with me. She had nothing to add to the session, aside from saying she felt everything was fine. Our couples counseling wasn't exactly helpful, but given that Betty landed a job in Las Vegas comparable to the one she had in southern Illinois, I didn't see the harm in her moving with me—especially since she said she was moving to Vegas whether or not we lived together. She didn't want a long-distance relationship. And neither of us was willing to break up, until a few months after we'd been living in Vegas, in individual therapy, I got the courage to end it and pursue a relationship with Ranita, a colleague and fellow sociologist, with whom I was developing the deep emotional intimacy that I always craved.

* * ☆ * *

"You make me want to throw up!" Ranita blurted out. I kicked her under the conference room table. I was worried that what she said was going to bite her in her untenured ass. We were in a university meeting and someone said something that could be construed as racist. Ranita doesn't talk shit behind people's back. She speaks what comes to her mind, to whomever and whenever.

In academia, mentors often advise new professors to keep quiet in their new departments until they earn tenure, which is a job guaranteed for life. Faculty of color, like Nikole Hannah-Jones,[4] Steven Salaita,[5] Sara Ahmed,[6] and others who speak out against white supremacy, support Palestine rights, and/or are critical of their institution's Title IX office and the like, have found themselves under fire—or even fired—before, or even after, tenure. Make no mistake that academia continues to be a white privileged space, even as more minorities—students and faculty alike, although not in equal numbers to each other—push their way through its closed doors.[7] Kiese Laymon, a Black writer and faculty member originally from Mississippi, was even told by multiple white colleagues during his first week teaching at Vassar that he was "lucky" to be there.[8] It was him, though, who was, years later, named a 2022 MacArthur Fellow.

Assistant professors on the tenure track, like Ranita and I were at the time when she publicly said that a university colleague made her want to throw up, typically serve a probation period often lasting around six years. At the end of the probationary period, an assistant professor can apply for tenure and promotion to associate professor. The promotion to associate professor and the granting of tenure are two career milestones that usually happen at the same time. Tenured departmental colleagues are the first of many in the university to assess their junior colleague's tenure case, which is supposed to be based on one's performance, vaguely defined, during the probationary period. The performance metrics for tenure vary significantly by institution, discipline, and department, and there is a lot of ambiguity in this arbitrary assessment, which disadvantages marginalized faculty. White cis straight faculty often use this ambiguity to overlook their own professional mediocrity as well as that of their white colleagues (whom they consider to be collegial friends), while simultaneously drawing on the same ambiguity to hold marginalized faculty to a higher standard. But far too many of my fellow white academics pretend this doesn't happen, and instead claim to be outside these patterns and not responsible for the lack of people of color, LGBTQI folks, and disabled individuals across tenure track faculty ranks.[9] Marginalized mentors know this, but there isn't much they can do about it other than warn their new PhDs who are fortunate enough to land tenure track positions to lay low, focus on their teaching and research, and avoid departmental politics, at least until they are tenured. Taking this advice won't protect marginalized faculty from discriminatory practices. However, it will hopefully prevent an even brighter spotlight from following them around campus. Most folks heed this advice, but not my partner Ranita, an immigrant from India, who feels that if people don't speak up before tenure, they probably never will. It's what I love the most about her, and it is also what my family prepared me for.

She doesn't hold back for anyone. Even me. At one faculty meeting, after we were dating on the down low for about a year, she called me out in front of everyone: "Your syllabus is so white, Georgiann." Damn her. But she was right. It took me a moment before saying, "Yup, I agree. I need to change it." Our colleagues were surprised that I welcomed Ranita's feedback during a faculty discussion, which she had initiated, about "decolonizing" syllabi. The syllabus I created, and was using to teach doctoral students about gender, tokenized scholars of color. I incorporated work by one scholar of color here or there, unlike work by white scholars who were included up and down my syllabus, thereby contributing to the perpetuation of scholarly racism.[10] This was especially shameful because the university's student body was, and still is, one of the most diverse in the country.

I've learned a lot from Ranita. She introduced me to what she was reading about the prison abolition movement from scholars and activists like Angela Davis, Gina Dent, Erica Meiners, Beth Richie, and Derecka Purnell. I found their arguments convincing—prisons need to be replaced with community social services that do not enact racist and classist systems of punishment for social problems.[11] I used to think I was a hypocrite for embracing the prison abolition movement yet still wanting my brother behind bars. How could I see prison as the best place for Theo and still be against it?

When Theo is in prison, he's the state's problem, not ours. Mom, in particular, has a better relationship with him when he is locked up then when he is free.[12] And because he is a white cis straight man, we aren't worried that racist prison guards will murder him. When he is on the streets, we fear that he will be killed or will not come back from overdosing. He has gotten into numerous street fights over the years that have left him with scars and chipped teeth. And he has been revived many times by Chicagoland paramedics and ER personnel after someone finds him unconscious in an alley or on a sidewalk. My family is accustomed to calling hospitals searching for him, worrying that one day we will learn he is gone. Mom often describes him as "100 pounds soaking wet" when he isn't in prison. But when he gets out after a long stay, he has nearly doubled his weight, looking like a handsome six-foot middle-aged white man with a receding hair line. His healthier appearance doesn't last for long, though, as he goes right back to drugs and alcohol. The cycle continues because prisons are a key cause of the societal problems they purport to address. In 2017, more than 300 billion dollars was spent across our criminal legal system on police, courts, and corrections.[13] What if, instead of fueling the prison industrial complex, we do as the prison abolitionists call for and allocate those funds to drug and alcohol rehab facilities, universal health care, and food security programs?[14] What if Theo could get into a rehab as easily as prison? Maybe then I wouldn't see prison as his only answer.

* ★ ☆ ★ *

A little more than a year after I moved to Vegas, the American Sociological Association held its Annual Meeting in Chicago. It was August 2015. Although my book *Contesting Intersex* had an official publication date of September 2015, it was already out and was going to be on display at the New York University Press booth during the ASA meeting. I wanted to celebrate its publication, so I decided to throw a dinner party at Greek Islands restaurant in downtown Chicago, which was just down the road from the conference location. When my dissertation advisor heard of my plans, she arranged for me to do a book reading at a local bookstore immediately before the dinner. I invited anyone and everyone to join me at the book reading and dinner that followed, as I celebrated alongside my family, many colleagues, students, and friends, including intersex people I've met along the way. Kelly, one of my best friends from childhood who was also my maid of honor when I married Charlie 14 years earlier, was even there. It was a celebration that I will never forget.

But a few hours earlier, after Ranita and I had landed in Chicago, we took an Uber to the conference hotel. As our Uber made its way down Lake Shore Drive, I couldn't help but openly reflect on my journey.

G: It's so fucking surreal. I can't believe that my book is out. I never thought I could do it—you know, from dropping out of school to publishing a book. It's unbelievable and being back in Chicago is bringing back so many memories.

R: Yeah, but you should think sociologically about it all, too.

G: What do you mean? I don't understand.

R: Just think about why you were able to do it and so many others, especially POC, can't, you know, drop out of school and then go on to get a PhD and publish a book.

I was annoyed but tried to laugh it off.

G: Hey, do you have a safety pin?

R: What? Why?

G: Because you just popped my bubble.

Versions of that conversation continued for years. While I often drew on humor to defend the mobility story that I had constructed and truly believed in, and even wrote about, I also shed many tears questioning Ranita's support.[15] Couldn't she just be happy for me?

I had to come to terms with the fact that despite the many obstacles—from my body being deemed abnormal in many ways to my family's financial failures—my whiteness was always there for me, helping me at every turn, like a security blanket that I never need shed. I had to confront my belief in my race neutral mobility story. I had to own the fact that I benefitted from racism. Ranita was patient with me, sharing tweets, blogs, and formal writings from working class Black, Brown, and Third World activists that she came across that cemented her points and encouraged me to rethink my mobility narrative.

I eventually grew to a place that I can question the role whiteness played throughout my life, including how it granted me access to incredible mentorship throughout my education—from my days at the community college to now as a tenured professor—unlike people of color in my life who were just as ambitious and even more hardworking than I was.

I want to be very clear here. By acknowledging the role whiteness has played in my life, I am not diminishing all of my hard work. I am, though, showing how my efforts were amplified.

I did a lot of self-promotion when my book came out, and I was well positioned to do so, given that I was on the board of two major intersex organizations—one that offers support to intersex people and the other that advocates for the human rights of intersex children. I was invited to appear in 2015 on the *Dr. Phil* show, on an episode entitled "Mama's Little Boy or Daddy's Little Girl: Identity Confusion or Brainwashing?"[16] I shared a little bit of my experience on the show and reassured the parents of an intersex child who were featured that toy preferences don't determine one's gender. And, in 2017, I appeared in the *National Geographic* documentary "Gender Revolution: A Journey with Katie Couric."[17] While Katie interviewed me about my personal intersex experience, intersex activism, and research for more than an hour, in a multimillion-dollar home the production company rented for the day, I only appeared for a few moments in the two-hour documentary, which primarily focused on trans lives. But I didn't care. Meeting Katie felt surreal. I wanted to ask her for her autograph when we first met, but instead, I played it cool, walking onto the makeshift set pretending she wasn't even there. I think my nonchalant attitude took her by surprise, given that she approached me and introduced herself rather than the other way around. She was wearing a white zipped-up blazer and black pants, but then, after complimenting me on my outfit—a black blazer over a black t-shirt that read in white letters "too cute to be binary," dark jeans, classic black slip-on Vans, and white eyeglass frames, she called her assistant over and said she needed something hipper and trendier to match my style. She changed into a black short dress with seams held together with silver hoops. She laughed when I said she looked much better in her new outfit. Before the cameras started rolling, she asked me if there was anything I wanted her to discuss or avoid, and I said, "No, but could you please begin the interview commenting on my gorgeous home and then pan the living area?" The big home was quite a contrast with the small place that I had just told her I lived in back in Las Vegas. We laughed again, as did most of the production team standing around us holding cameras and positioning stage lights.

* * ☆ * *

In 2018, I earned tenure and was promoted to associate professor. I now had a job for life, as well as a 10% pay bump that came with my new associate professor title. To celebrate my achievement, I decided to throw myself a party at an outdoor tiki lounge not far from campus. I invited the entire sociology faculty and staff, including a dozen or so colleagues from around campus, as well as community friends I'd met through my university contacts, to my open-bar-and-finger-foods celebration.

I also invited some family. The party was as much for mom as it was for me. I wanted her to leave her worries behind in the Midwest for a few days and fly out to Vegas to celebrate alongside me. We had been through a lot together, from the medical lies, to losing the Italian ice businesses and our home, to her criminal court cases. I thought the party would be a momentary escape from it all, and allow us to feel like the right kind of white that we were always chasing. I used airline points to book mom, Aunt Maria, and Aunt Athena on the same flight from Chicago to Vegas, and my aunts used their elite privileges at the Chicagoland casinos they always gambled at to get comped hotel rooms at a casino on the strip.

They never made it.

Mom got really sick from a round of chemo she just completed and was admitted to the hospital severely dehydrated, without the ability to keep anything down. It happened a lot like this since her breast cancer diagnosis. She would start chemo. Have a treatment. Get really sick from it. Refuse further treatments. And then, after many months went by, she would give chemo another try. This time she insisted that the doctors release her, against medical advice, but my aunts and I all convinced her that leaving the hospital was the dumbest thing she could do. I canceled their flights and got my airline points back.

The party went on, but the nearly $2,000 bill I paid felt far more wasteful than it would have if mom were able to make it.

My body was also growing, alongside my career.

When I moved to Vegas in 2014, I was over 350 pounds. I started embracing my fatness, and did so by calling out anti-fat discourse after reading fat activist Marilyn Wann's 1998 book *Fat!So?: Because You Don't Have to Apologize for your Size!*[1] I even placed a weight diversity flyer—a key piece of fat activism that Wann created—on my office door at the university that read, *"Welcome! Weight diversity is celebrated here. Kindly refrain from diet talk, body disparagement, and other unpleasantries. Thank you!"* I was ready, as a now seasoned intersex activist, to take up fat activism and fight the fat oppression, discrimination, and stigma[2] that are rampant throughout the western world.[3]

But I failed at fat activism, not being able to overcome my internalized anti-fatness. In 2017, a year before I was tenured and promoted, I turned my back on my dream of fat positivity, as I was approaching 390 pounds in a society that hates fat people and sees us as lazy and unattractive slobs.

At an annual physical, my primary care physician, a thin Asian-American woman in her mid-thirties, shared with me that my blood work was all in normal ranges before shifting her focus entirely onto my weight gain. She asked me if I ever considered a revision of the bariatric surgery that I'd had more than 20 years earlier. I wasn't having any physical health issues, but I was struggling with my growing body. The staples they had placed into my stomach to minimize how much it could hold either had dissolved or the piece of the stomach they had portioned off had stretched. Regardless of what was happening to my stomach, the one thing that was clear was that the surgery was no longer working. I was having trouble finding clothes I liked that fit me, it was getting increasingly uncomfortable squeezing into armed chairs around campus, at restaurants, movie theaters, and more, and I was regularly getting heat rashes on my thighs caused by them rubbing together when I walked.

Of course, none of my individual struggles with my fatness compared to how I was repeatedly treated by strangers. I've had strangers puff out their cheeks and mock me because I was eating a donut. One man walked up to me when I was eating in a shopping mall food court and loudly told me I needed to go on a diet because I was killing myself with food. Another person demanded a flight attendant re-seat her on a plane because she wasn't comfortable sitting next to me. And then there was the time I was traveling to an academic conference and an older Greek couple sitting a row behind and over from me started making disgusting remarks about the size of my queer body in Greek, not realizing I understood everything they were saying. As I'm so used to doing, I covered up my shame with humor in these instances by, for example, looking directly at the Greek couple and telling them in Greek that they are an embarrassment to our culture and nothing but dirty wet dogs for gossiping about people. Although I mask my pain with humor, the fat harm I've experienced at the hands of strangers has always been more painful than any heat rash my kissing thighs left for me or any bruises I got from squeezing my fat legs into a far-too-small chair.

My doctor's question about considering revising my weight loss surgery tapped into all of my fat pain. I was given a referral to a bariatric surgeon and decided to make an appointment to discuss the possibility of a revision.

So much for fat activism.

When I called the bariatric surgeon's office to schedule a consultation, I was told I would need to attend one of their "Weight-Loss Seminars" before an appointment with one of the two office bariatric surgeons could be scheduled. I registered for the next open seminar that fit my schedule, and just like that, it was August 27, 2016, and I was sitting in a full conference room next to the bariatric surgeon's office with more than 50 other people, mostly middle-aged, white women of different body sizes ranging from what my internalized anti-fat self-classified as "OMG, *you* aren't even big! Why are you here?" to, I'm ashamed to admit, "OMG, thankfully I'm not *that* fat." As I took a seat in an oversized armchair in the back of the conference room, I could feel my internalized anti-fatness flow through my entire body.

The surgeon who led the seminar was a 40- or 50-something-year-old white man with light brown hair that was slicked back, but not in a sleazy way. Let's call him Dr. Vegas. He was lean but muscular, or at least he seemed to be, based on what I gathered while observing him as he moved about the conference room in professional, but casual, attire. He had a noticeable tan, as if he spent his personal time in the pool or at the golf course. However, what stood out to me most about Dr. Vegas was his ability to express fat empathy with his fat audience.

As he flipped through his PowerPoint slide presentation, it was clear that Dr. Vegas had his bariatric surgery pitch memorized as he introduced us to the three bariatric surgeries his office offered: lap band, gastric bypass, and vertical sleeve gastrectomy. His memorization wasn't surprising given that his office hosts these weight-loss seminars twice a month. Dr. Vegas told his captive audience that "morbid obesity is genetic" and clinically defined it as having a body mass index (BMI) equal to or greater than 35—ignoring the criticism about the measure. As I knew, the BMI scale, first introduced by the Belgian scientist Lambert Adolphe Jacques Quetelet in the early 19th century, has been described as a flawed[4] scale that the inventor never intended to be used as a measure of one's fatness.[5] BMI standardizes one's size by taking into account one's height together with one's weight, but it has always been a crude and arbitrary measure. "No matter what you do, it will be virtually impossible to lose a substantial amount of weight and keep it off," Dr. Vegas continued: "I'm sure you've all tried diet after diet and failed"—the audience giggled and expressed agreement—"But it's not your fault." I had mixed feelings throughout Dr. Vegas's presentation, ranging from disgust about the way he presented fatness to love for the kindness he seemed to extend to the audience as he moved about the room and later as he answered our questions during the Q&A. Fat people know all too well how poorly medical providers treat us, so this was—at least for me—a very welcome change. Of course, it depresses me to know that medical kindness is a rare commodity for fat patients.[6]

After the weight-loss seminar concluded, I got the go-ahead to sign up for the three-month medically supervised diet offered through a medical group affiliated with my primary care physician's office. In order for my HMO to cover most of the costs associated with bariatric surgery (revision or otherwise), I needed to prove to my health insurer that I had unsuccessfully tried to lose weight under a medical professional's care. So, I signed up for three dietician visits over three months or so, which I came to call "fat classes." I was curious about what the classes would entail. I told myself, my family, and close friends that I wasn't seriously considering bariatric surgery (only very close friends in my inner circle knew I'd had stomach stapling when I was a child), but rather, that I was intellectually curious about the content of the fat classes, who attended them, and so forth. First, however, I would fly to deliver a keynote address on intersex at the University of Surrey's "After the Recognition of Intersex Human Rights" conference in late September 2016.[7]

During a social outing in Surrey after the conference with other intersex activists from around the world, we casually started discussing flying while fat, and I shared my thoughts about anti-fatness within the intersex community. Because of that conversation, in early October 2016, an intersex activist and curator from the Intersex Day Project invited me to write a blog post for their project on the intersection of intersex and fatness in honor of Intersex Awareness Day. The Intersex Day Project is a virtual installation that "promotes human rights actions for Intersex Awareness Day (October 26) and the Intersex Day of Solidarity (November 8), and documents and shares the histories and works of the intersex movement."[8] I was honored to participate in the project and gladly accepted the invitation. And the timing was perfect, as I was just about to begin my three-month medically supervised diet, which would force me to reflect on my fatness.

I nervously (or maybe it was with a bad attitude?) walked into the site of my first fat class on a mid-October evening in 2016. It was in a medical center in downtown Las Vegas, with far more working-class people of color than in the outskirts of the Vegas Valley. Signs at the main entrance directed attendees to a classroom-type auditorium space that could easily hold 50 or more people. After I signed in with the instructor—a thin white woman I will call "Erin," who was seated at the front of the classroom facing the mostly empty chairs—I was given a workbook. I proceeded to take a seat in the second row next to a Black woman who looked like she was in her forties. There were five or six other people in the room, all fat women of color, except for a white woman who sat in the front row directly in front of the instructor. I remember rolling my eyes and thinking, "That woman isn't even fat! What is she doing here?" She was quietly, and exclusively, talking with Erin about calorie-counting programs, ignoring everyone else in the room. "Racist, queerphobic, kiss ass," I thought. As Erin stood up and was about to begin class, a fat balding white man in his late thirties or early forties, wearing flip-flops, shorts, and a solid color t-shirt and holding a very large water bottle, walked in and apologized for being late. He explained that he was coming from work, as if others in the room weren't also coming from some sort of commitment.

Erin introduced the class and instructed all of us to open our workbooks to page 5 to complete the "Readiness Questionnaire." It read:

> There is no "magic pill" for weight loss. This workbook is based on sound principles of nutrition and physical activity combined with a behavioral approach for successful weight loss. *Behavioral* refers to actions, and *behavior modification* is a science that involves the use of specific strategies to replace undesirable behaviors. Behavior modification will involve identifying current behaviors, factors that trigger those behaviors and establishing ways to reinforce desirable behaviors.[9]

Erin asked us to fill out all 12 prompts, and clarified that we needed to go through these necessary steps to ensure insurance coverage. At this point, I was confused. I thought fat class was supposed to teach fat people about nutrition (as if we don't already know and/or don't eat nutritiously!), not prepare us for bariatric surgery. I filled in each prompt; these ranged from concerns about my weight to how I would overcome barriers that would prevent a lifestyle change. Unable to set aside my sociological imagination for the activity, I responded to each prompt with a snarky attitude that brought me back to larger institutions and structures of domination that control our lives. For example, in answer to the question, "Name an individual who may not support you (sic) efforts." I wrote, "Flight attendants who assume fat people are lazy while ignoring the fact that airlines seats are getting smaller for profit." To the question, "What do you think reaching a healthy weight will do for you? In the next year or two and beyond," I wrote, "What is healthy? I am healthy now without any abnormal lab results or other medical problems. I do believe I will have less anxiety if I lost weight because I will be subjected to less discrimination."

After Erin gave everyone some time to complete the prompts, she asked us, "Who would like to share what they wrote?" Immediately, the white woman in the front row raised her hand and spewed off some rhetoric to the effect that she was looking forward to having more energy to play with her kids and to exercise. The only man in the room shared that he hoped he would be more productive at work—a physically demanding job. I couldn't keep my snarkiness to myself anymore. I raised my hand, and when called upon I said, "I'm a sociologist who studies bodies and inequalities. Being fat doesn't prevent us from playing with our kids, exercising, or working." I then shared what I wrote about fat discrimination. The Black woman next to me loudly replied, "Umm, yes!" and then she snapped her fingers. A Latina a few rows back from where I was sitting added, "Yeah, I'm sick and tired of being treated like I'm lazy."

Erin nodded, and then swiftly moved us to the next section of the class—pre-operative dieting. She explained it would help all of us if we lost weight before our bariatric surgeries. Our livers would get smaller, and it would be easier for the surgeon to see our stomach and modify it according to the bariatric surgery we've chosen. The white woman raised her hand and said, "What if we are on the BMI borderline without any co-morbidities?" Most insurance companies will only approve bariatric surgery for those who have a BMI equal to or greater than 40, although they will allow a slightly lower BMI if the person also has at least one co-morbidity such as type II diabetes, high blood pressure, or sleep apnea. I just about fell off my chair when Erin said, "I would be careful and not lose any weight before you have the surgery. Your weight on the day of surgery is what most insurance companies go by." I doubt that there could be stronger evidence that bariatric surgery isn't about health—not that there is a relationship between size and health in the first place.

After the lecture portion of the class was over, Erin instructed us to line up in the hall around the corner. One by one, she weighed us and recorded our weight as proof for our insurance companies that we were participating in a medically supervised nutrition program. I was the last one to be weighed, and as I walked out of the medical center to my car, I cringed as I replayed everything I had just experienced over and over again in my head. I was angry that I had gone to the fat class.

My second fat class was at the end of November 2016, in the medical center's much more affluent suburban location. I entered the class with my workbook in hand, as Erin had requested. Although Erin wasn't instructing this fat class, she could have been. My new instructor looked and acted a lot like Erin. She was white, thin, plain, and forgettable. The classroom at the suburban location was much smaller, and the eight attendees, myself included, were all white. There was more gender diversity in this class, though, with half of the attendees presenting as men. This class was a continuation of the first fat class, with more fat shaming and victim blaming. Only this time I was smart enough to ask the instructor, a licensed nutritionist, in front of the entire class why it was that the surgeon at the "Weight-Loss Seminar" we had all attended had framed fatness (I consciously said "fat" and not "obesity") as genetic and out of our control, and yet she and the other nutritionists were framing fatness as something we were capable of controlling. No one snapped their fingers or supported my resistance during this fat class. Instead, my fellow fat classmates stared at me in a way that made me think they were all annoyed with me. The nutritionist quickly shut me down: "It's both, really." And then she went on to tell us all about the dangers of high-caloric sodas, as if we weren't aware of these.

My third and final fat class was a one-on-one appointment in mid-January 2017 with one of the medical center's nutritionists. I'd be lying if I didn't admit how relieved I was to be scheduled to meet with a nutritionist I hadn't yet met. I was afraid the two nutritionists I'd previously interacted with at the fat classes wouldn't be so kind to me, given how I had intentionally, and admittedly disruptively, asked questions or raised concerns I knew weren't in line with the medical framing of fatness I'd experienced in the world of bariatric surgery. Also telling to me, as a feminist who studies gender inequality, is that I didn't similarly challenge the surgeon, a white man, at any point during the weight-loss seminar. Instead, I kept my snarkiness to myself, only to later let it out on white women nutritionists. I was admittedly more vulnerable in my one-on-one fat class, and I don't know why—but I felt this third nutritionist was more empathetic than the others. She really listened when I expressed my concerns that I hated being fat but felt that societal discrimination and fat shaming fueled such feelings. She also listened to me as I discussed research that problematizes the assumption that there is a strict correlation between body size and health. She nodded as I spoke, and her eyes never left mine. I felt comfortable enough with her that I shared that I'd had bariatric surgery more than 20 years earlier and that I didn't really want a revision, but I was considering it. She listened, allowing me to be the expert regarding my body. As our hour-long fat class that morphed into a therapy session came to an end, she hugged me and said I could meet with her any time, regardless of whether I chose to go forward with a bariatric revision surgery.

On September 20, 2017, I stood outside of the same conference room where I had attended Dr. Vegas's "Weight-Loss Seminar" 13 months earlier. There were at least 15 other people waiting outside with me. We were all waiting for someone from Dr. Vegas's staff to unlock the conference room so we could receive our final pre- and post-operative bariatric surgery instructions in a lecture format and then pay our insurance co-pays to the surgeon and hospital. We had all been individually instructed that if we came late to the presentation or missed it, our surgery date would be canceled and we would have to wait to be rescheduled. We were also told that Dr. Vegas's practice was scheduling surgeries four to five months out, and thus, if we missed our opportunity in the queue, we would have to wait another four to five months for a surgery date and—depending on our insurance—might also have to go through another three-month medically supervised diet. No one, it seemed, wanted to do any of that. So, there we were, a group of fat people congregated outside a locked conference room waiting to get in so we could get part of our stomachs sealed off or cut out.

A 40-something-year-old average sized white woman walked up and we all gathered closer to the door, thinking she worked for Dr. Vegas and would be letting us in to escape the September Vegas heat. By my assessment, she looked upper middle class. Her blondish-brown hair was perfectly styled to her shoulders, her makeup was light but on point, and she was wearing a fashionable shawl, bangles, and dress pants and high-heeled shoes. She looked like she just walked out of a Nordstrom. Much to our surprise, she joined us in line. A Black fat woman who looked like she was in her fifties asked, "You aren't here to let us in?" The white woman replied, "No, I'm a patient." "WHAT?!?," the Black woman loudly exclaimed. Others similarly chimed in. The white woman responded, "Oh, I'm a lot bigger than I look." Confused, we all went back to waiting, most of us scrolling through our smartphones until a representative from Dr. Vegas's practice eventually showed up and let us all in.

Following presentations by one of the practice's physician assistants and a nutritionist, the office manager informed us that we would be called up one by one to pay our hospital co-pay (to the hospital biller who was in attendance) and physician co-pay. My co-pays were $500 and $3,000, respectively. We would also be told when our surgery was scheduled and would additionally be called up by a medical assistant who would take our picture for our health records. I was called up for my photo before the billing folks called me up, and as I stood in front of a background imprinted with the bariatric surgeon's logo, I smiled widely and chuckled. The medical assistant joked, "Don't look so happy in the pre-op photo! Save it for the post-op photo!" I erased the smile from my face and thought, "Here I go again." Only this time, it was my choice—or was it really my choice? Roxane Gay, *The New York Times* bestselling author of, among other books, the 2017 memoir *Hunger: A Memoir of (My) Body*, shared in a blog in April 2018 that she, too, after considerable deliberation, had bariatric surgery in January 2017.[10] She explained something that I wish I'd articulated first: "I had to face the extent of my unhappiness and how much of that unhappiness was connected to my body. I had to accept that I could change my fat body faster than this culture will change how it views, treats, and accommodates fat bodies."[11]

* ★ ✬ ★ *

As the sun was rising in Las Vegas on September 25, 2017, I was on my way to a local hospital to convert the vertical banded gastroplasty that I had in 1995 when I was 14 years old, which involved stapling my stomach into two parts to reduce its capacity, to a vertical sleeve gastrectomy where the surgeon was set to remove 80 percent of my stomach. Ranita was by my side. I was nervous, but I was also ready to get it done and over with. I didn't take medical leave from work. I was teaching undergraduate statistics face to face on Mondays and Wednesdays and an online masculinities course. My graduate assistant covered for me on Monday, the day of my surgery, and I planned ahead for Wednesday by giving the students an out-of-class group assignment meant to prepare them for an exam I would administer one week after my surgery. I didn't tell my students I was going to have surgery. In fact, I didn't tell many people aside from my closest friends about what I had signed up for. I was embarrassed. I truly felt like a sell-out who caved to the diet industrial complex. But what does selling out even mean, and who has the burden for challenging fat oppression?

In the preoperative surgical waiting room, a very thin and older white woman in her late fifties called my name, weighed me, and got me ready for surgery. She was the nurse who would walk me through all the consent forms I needed to sign. As she took my blood pressure and got me ready for my hospital bed, she shared, "You will be fine. I had the same surgery a few years ago." Dr. Vegas's practice partner had performed her surgery, and she explained that she had lost all of her "excess body weight" and that while she "had a rough recovery due to an intolerance to the protein shakes" that bariatric surgery patients are instructed to consume after surgery, both to help the stomach heal and because solid food intake is strictly prohibited for weeks if not months (every surgeon's office has a different post-op protocol) after the surgery, she managed and ended up "stronger and healthier than ever."

The nurse walked me to a large room with four hospital beds that were separated by thin curtains to offer each patient some privacy. I could hear that the person next to me was also scheduled for bariatric surgery with Dr. Vegas. Trying to be respectful of his privacy, I did my best to tune out his conversations with medical personnel. A different nurse, an average-sized middle-aged Asian woman, came to my bed to start my IV and give me the necessary preoperative medications. I was resting in my bed completely naked except for my thick white eyeglass frames and a thin hospital gown, which fortunately was large enough to fit me comfortably (this is problematic, as many medical providers don't carry hospital gowns that comfortably fit all body sizes). She told me I would need to provide a urine specimen so they could run a pregnancy test. I explained to her that for more reasons than one—I didn't have a uterus, I was intersex, and I was queer and partnered with a woman—there was no way I could be pregnant. She respectfully accepted my explanation and even asked thoughtful questions about my intersex trait and medical history. It was a surprisingly pleasant interaction. After the IV drip began working and I was patiently, but nervously, waiting for my time to be rolled into the operating room—I was told I was next—the nurse who began my IV returned. Apologizing, she said, "Because of your age and sex, the computer won't let us move you to the next stage of preoperative care until you take the pregnancy test. Will you please take it?" Reluctantly, I did. Although I wasn't angry at her, for I thought she was genuinely empathetic, I thought to myself, "What bureaucratic bullshit."

Before I knew it, I was in recovery. The postoperative nurses told me the surgery was "successful" and I would soon be transferred to my inpatient room. I remember being asked whether I was in pain, and I said, "No, I'm fine." I slept a lot that day, but I did get up to walk and use the bathroom. I was uncomfortable, but much to my surprise, I didn't need any pain medicine. The laparoscopic bariatric surgery was so very different from the incredibly painful open-incision bariatric surgery and the just-as-painful open-incision removal of my testes that I had when I was a teenager. I was beyond relieved for the lack of unbearable physical pain that came with having 80 percent of my stomach removed.

I spent only one night in the hospital. Because my stomach was really swollen, it was difficult to drink more than an ounce of fluid at a time (my choices were limited to water, ice chips, and/or chilled protein shake). However, I managed, and I was discharged less than 24 hours after my surgery, when Dr. Vegas's practice partner said I was recovering exceptionally well and could continue to heal outside of the hospital. Ranita drove me home, where I would rest and do my best to recover as smoothly and quickly as possible. I never did need pain medication, but I was really struggling with exhaustion, something I wrestled with for a few months. I had no energy, and I could barely keep my eyes open long enough to try to consume the necessary fluids. I was back to work a few days after the surgery to attend a college meeting. One week after my surgery, I was administering an exam in my undergraduate statistics class. My students had no idea I just underwent major surgery. No one who saw me on a regular basis seemed to notice my body was getting smaller until I had lost more than 50 pounds. It was then that people started commenting on my weight loss.

I regularly saw the bariatric surgeon's team for a year following the surgery. While the primary focus of the follow-up visits was always my weight loss, they did monitor my overall health through blood draws and inquiries about both my physical and emotional well-being. I was in their bariatric program for a year before I was discharged from it and asked to only follow up if I had any concerns or changes in my overall health. In total, I lost about 100 pounds and most of it, eight years later, has stayed off without any complications aside from heartburn, which I continue to treat with an over-the-counter antacid. I'd say it was a success, but I'd be lying if I didn't say I was disappointed that I hadn't lost more weight.

Mom couldn't believe I was discharged the day after my second stomach surgery, given that I was in the hospital for nearly a week the first time my stomach was operated on. She also didn't believe me when I told her it was far less painful for me than my 1995 stomach stapling. But it was. Soon after I was discharged, she asked me what pain meds the doctors prescribed, and I said I didn't know and didn't care because I wasn't going to take them, because I didn't need them and, even if I did, I was too scared of getting addicted. I explained to her that the hospital filled my prescriptions and gave them to me when I was discharged but I didn't bother with them. She didn't believe me when I told her the pain was tolerable. She thought I was allowing my fear of drug addiction to keep me in pain. "Missy, don't be stupid! Take the pills. You won't get addicted." "I don't need them, for real," I told her, "I'm not even taking Tylenol."

In jest, she said, "Well, let me know, hun, if you want me to take them off your hands because I can get you a lot of money for them."

"Oh my fucking God," I said, partially skeptical that she was only joking, "Will you ever learn?"

Marx was in multi-organ failure. It was 2017 and not long after my revised bariatric surgery. I took the earliest flight out from Vegas to Chicago to see dad and assess in person just how bad he was. The hospital staff told us he was a 61-year-old guy in a 90-year-old's body. Marx smirked but was confident he would get better. He tried to sit up but was too weak and couldn't.

Ten years had passed since his quadruple bypass heart surgery. The hospitalist, by my account a young South Asian man, playfully scolded him in front of mom, Theo, and me, who were all there to see him: "George! You never followed up with the cardiologist after your surgery. You didn't stop smoking. And you're diabetic. You're in deep water, man!" It was always weird to hear people refer to dad as "George," his real name. Marx smirked at the doctor. It was the first I learned how serious his health situation had become. I don't know why I thought Marx treated his insides any differently than his outsides.

After losing his paid-cash-under-the-table mechanic job several years earlier because he couldn't keep up as a self-taught mechanic with the technological advancements of the auto industry, he let himself go and lived off social security disability insurance, which he qualified for because of a lifelong mental illness.

The last time I had seen Marx, he hadn't shaved in days. His hair was unkempt and looked dirty. I was in town for one night to attend a Human Rights Watch press conference, which I did before stopping by my Aunt Maria's house. I didn't have much time before my return flight home, but I wanted to see as many family members as I could. I asked Marx to pick me up from Aunt Maria's and give me a ride to the airport. We stopped at a gas station so I could fill up his tank. My flight was scheduled to depart in a little more than an hour but a Walmart was in sight.

While I was standing outside his car pumping gas, my survivor's guilt surfaced again, and I asked him: "What size clothes and underwear do you wear? What about Theo?"

He answered, guessing what prompted my questions.

I ran as fast as I could into that Walmart, picking up as many shirts, jeans, socks, and underwear I could quickly find for them. I threw the bags in Marx's car, noticing small tears forming in his eyes.

"Thank you, Missy," he said before taking another drag from his cigarette.

"Dude, don't worry about it. It's nothing. Just hurry because I can't miss this flight. I teach tomorrow."

I was silent for a few seconds and then added, "And keep the windows open. Your cigarette smoke makes me sick."

I was half joking about getting sick from the smoke. I always gave Marx shit for being a chain smoker ever since he was a teenager. After his heart bypass surgery, he stayed with me to recover in the attic apartment I was renting. I prohibited him from smoking. And I fed him carrot sticks and veggie dogs from Trader Joe's, telling him they were gourmet Italian sausages. He only lasted with me for a few days before wanting to be on his own out in the world, eating off the McDonald's dollar menu between cigarettes. Those were some of our best times together.

It would have been less stressful to just give him money instead of running around Walmart like a fool on the game show *Supermarket Sweep*, but I was afraid he'd gamble it away or give it to Theo for drugs and alcohol. Later, mom, who was still living on her own down in southern Illinois, told me Theo would probably return everything for a gift card and sell it on the street for less than what it's worth for drug money. I don't know if that's what happened, but I wouldn't be surprised, given the countless media stories I've come across that claim gift card crime is fueling drug addiction—albeit in most of those stories the drug users are stealing stuff from one store and returning the stolen goods to another for a gift card that they exchange on the streets at a discount for drug money.[1] I didn't care, I just wanted to do something nice for them to appease my survivor's guilt.[2]

I wasn't as naïve as Marx about his prognosis. But I have to admit I was fooled because he looked cleaner and healthier on his deathbed than he had in recent years. I knew his best chance of coming out of this alive was to get into continuous care. He needed to go to a nursing home until he could get better. But there was a big problem. Theo would have nowhere to live. He used Marx for everything from the roof over his head to the heroin he smoked.

Over Marx's hospital bed, I told him there wasn't a choice to make. He was going to the publicly-funded nursing home that the hospital social worker recommended and I agreed to. Theo was against my plan.

"What about me? Where the fuck am I going to go?" Theo asked the room, but I knew the questions were directed at me.

I looked at him and yelled: "I don't give a fuck about you! Take care of yourself you piece of shit! He is dying and all you care about is yourself!"

He looked at me with his piercing brown eyes and his jaw so clenched that he looked like he was about to jump me. "You fat fucking selfish bitch! Why don't you worry about yourself?!? What are you 400 pounds?"

I wanted to hurt him. "Whatever, crackhead. Or is it heroin? I can't keep track."

Mom quietly sat in the corner of the hospital room picking at her lips. She knew better than to get involved.

He wasn't going to concede. "Are you a man or a woman? You fucking freak!"

But neither was I. "Fuck you, you piece of shit!"

Marx interjected by mustering the strength to whisper, "Stop it. Please." I didn't get my way. Marx went back to his illegal basement apartment that he shared with Theo. They kept it warm with a space heater.

Marx kept needing frequent trips to the emergency room and admissions to the hospital. Like the one time when he was immobile on the floor and phoned Aunt Maria for help. He couldn't get up. Aunt Maria arrived as quickly as she could and somehow managed to drag her brother-in-law by herself to her car. On the way to the hospital, Aunt Maria called me and told me what was going on and how disappointed she was in Theo, who was too strung out to get off the couch to help her, or to care.

Marx eventually agreed to go to a nursing home, but only after Theo got locked up pending yet another criminal trial. He had been locked up so many times since he was 15 years old, I've lost count. I could say he never learned from his mistakes, but to do so I would have to reject everything I know about the criminal legal system and how, as a for-profit system with prisons popping up all over rural America, it thrives on repeat customers, who are disproportionately from urban areas.[3] I also can't help but question the role whiteness has played in giving him chance after chance to escape the cycle through shorter sentences, multiple chances, and a belief that he, a white guy, is worthy of rehabilitation. The criminal legal system continues to approach him with a mental health lens, while its players rarely extend the same empathy to the overwhelming percentage of Black and Brown folks they incarcerate because of the ongoing "War on Drugs."[4] A 2017 United States Sentencing Commission report revealed, for example, that Black men receive federal sentences that are, on average, about 19 percent longer than their "similarly situated" white peers.[5]

* ★ ☆ ★ *

Marx died on January 9, 2018. I was at a Korean restaurant with Ranita and our friend, Cassaundra, when I glanced at my phone and saw two back-to-back missed calls and voicemails from the nursing home. My heart sank. I knew my dad was gone. I stepped away from the table and walked to my car to return the nurse's calls.

The nursed informed me: "I'm so sorry, but your dad passed away this evening. When I went to give him his evening medicine, he was no longer with us."

I was surprisingly calm. "Thank you for telling me. What are the next steps? I live in Vegas, and I'm not sure what to do."

I could tell this wasn't the nurse's first rodeo. He asked, "Do you have a funeral home picked out? If you call them, they will come and pick up his body and you can go from there."

"Okay, thank you. I appreciate it. If they have any questions I can't answer, can I give them your name and number?"

"Of course," he said, ending my last phone call to the nursing home.

I immediately texted Aunt Maria, and Aunt Athena, with the news. Unlike mom, they both know how to text. I then called mom.

"Hey, Marx is dead."

"Oh no," mom quietly responded.

"Yup. He's dead," I said. "Marx is gone."

There was a lot of silence as tears rained from my eyes. Aunt Maria and Aunt Athena were calling me, but I let their calls go to voicemail. I'm sure mom shed some tears of her own. They were legally divorced and hadn't lived together for years, but they still loved each other. Mom visited Marx in the nursing home whenever she could, with Arby's roast beef sandwiches, Popeyes fried chicken, or whatever else he wanted.

I asked mom to mother me: "What am I going to do? I'm so sad."

"Call Maria," she said.

"Okay."

Even in this moment, she directed me to her sister for the mothering that I needed. I wasn't really surprised. Everything around me felt blurry except for the phone.

"Hey, Maria."

"Oh, Missy, I'm so sorry," Aunt Maria said, comforting me with her soft words while holding back tears.

"I don't know what I'm going to do. They told me to call a funeral home."

Aunt Maria always had helpful advice: "Missy, call the Drapo Funeral Home. It's across the street from Holy Sky."

Holy Sky is a Greek Church just outside of Chicago that my family was loosely connected to over the years, for weddings, baptisms, and even funeral services when Papou Theo died more than a decade earlier. Growing up, my maternal grandparents—Papou Theo and Yiayia Gia—took us to the Holy Sky Summer Festival every year for souvlaki, which is Greek seasoned meat on a stick, and loukoumades, a Greek donut-like pastry smothered in honey and cinnamon and sometimes nuts. It was symbolically comforting to me to have a funeral home near Holy Sky take care of Marx's body.

"Do I call now?" I asked her. It was after 11pm in Chicago, and I wasn't sure if funeral homes close.

"Yes, call them, Missy. Do you want me to call them for you?" She has always been so helpful.

"No, it's okay."

And she somehow always knew what to say: "Missy, I'm so sorry. I love you. Marx loved you, too."

"Thanks, Maria. I love you, too. I will call you later."

I remembered that Ranita and Cassaundra were still inside the restaurant. I called Ranita and told her what was going on. They rushed out moments later.

Aunt Athena phoned me.

"Hey, Athena," is all I needed to say.

"Oh my God, Missy. I'm so sorry."

"Thanks," is all I could come up with, followed by telling her the obvious: "I'm so sad."

"I know honey. I know." Aunt Athena comforted me as she had done most of my life. She and Aunt Maria were like mothers to me and better at delivering traditional mothering than my mother.

Aunt Athena sincerely asked: "Do you need money? I can help you with anything." I knew she would gather up any money I needed. But I also know that she didn't have it sitting comfortably in a bank.

"That's okay. I will figure it out."

I believed her when she said, "Let me know what you need. I'm here for you."

"Thank you so much, Athena. I love you."

"Love you, too."

I didn't have prior experience, but working with a funeral home director was a lot easier than I anticipated it would be.

After a few rings, a man answered the phone ready to help. I said, "Hi, my father just passed away. He is in a nursing home. Can you help me?"

The man's voice was deep, soothing, and matter-of-fact.

"Of course. I'm sorry for your loss."

After giving him Marx's demographic information, the topic turned to arrangements.

"I think I want him cremated. I'm not sure yet."

I didn't feel pressured or rushed: "Take your time," he said. "We will pick up your father tonight and we can talk tomorrow."

"Okay, I'm going to fly out to Chicago either tonight or first thing in the morning."

He invited me to meet him at the funeral home after I arrived, to discuss options and to get the necessary information to file the death certificate.

Ranita was in the passenger seat gently rubbing my shoulder. Cassaundra was in the back seat. I caught some tears rolling down Cassaundra's cheeks. I don't even remember them entering the car. Several iPhones later and the nurse's voicemails are still on my phone. I can't muster the strength to delete them from the cloud.

* ★ ☆ ★ *

I never came out to my family. While the popular narrative may be that all queer people have a big coming-out-of-the-closet moment with their family, that wasn't my experience, nor is it for so many others.[6] After I amicably (and predictably, given that I got married in my early twenties while attending a community college in the north suburbs of Chicago) divorced from my ex-husband Charlie in 2004 after two and half years of marriage, I just started showing up to birthdays and holiday gatherings with a "best friend" who was always a woman.[7] My "best friend" changed a number of times over the years until I settled down with Ranita. I'm sure mom knew "best friend" was my queer cover.

I'm not sure if Marx knew I was queer. The last time I saw him alive I was visiting him at the nursing home. I had my laptop with me and was able to show him pictures of the home Ranita and I were about to buy. He raised his eyebrows in awe and said he was proud of me, all while scarfing down the gyros I brought him.

"Where did you get this from?" he asked.

"The airport. Why?"

He confidently responded: "Because it fucking sucks."

He was right, but I was left to ask: "It has to be better than the food here, no?"

As tzatziki sauce was running down his chin, he smiled and answered, "Well, yeah, the food here is nasty."

"Then stop complaining!" I jokingly shouted.

We both laughed. He was fucking with me because he knew my options were limited. When he entered the nursing home, I made sure to call him at least twice a day. If he didn't answer, which he often didn't because his phone would be out of reach and he was immobile towards the end, I would call a nurse asking if they could check on him and make sure his phone was within his reach. I have a lot of anxiety about everything, which, in the case of his wellbeing, I dealt with by calling him throughout the day. I also tried to visit my dad as much as I could, but that was much more difficult given that I worked on the other side of the country. However, I made cross-country day trips affordably happen several times, owing to the fact that Las Vegas and Chicago are major hubs for several airlines. My trips were hectic but worth it:

Set the alarm for 4:30am.

Depart Vegas on the first flight to Chicago.

Land at Midway.

Take an Uber to the nursing home.

Spend a couple of hours laughing with Marx.

Uber back to Midway.

Depart Chicago on the last flight to Vegas.

Land at Vegas.

Go to bed around 2:00am.

Teach in the morning.

On one of my first day trips, I asked Marx what his thoughts were on cremation. We were sitting on a bench outside the nursing home.

"Greeks aren't supposed to do that," he reminded me.

"I know. If you want, I will have you buried. But it's such bullshit and so expensive."

I didn't tell him that I already did my googling and found out that funeral and cemetery expenses would put me under thousands and thousands of dollars.

"I don't want you to waste your money, Missy."

"Marx, I have it."

It was my third year living in a university dorm. I was UNLV's first professor-in-residence, and in exchange for hosting social events with students who lived on campus, I got free housing, utilities, and a generous meal plan. It wasn't just university service. It was a full-blown part-time job and the only legal way I could supplement my $66,000 faculty salary without violating my university contract, which greatly restricts outside employment. Aside from guest talks at universities that paid honorariums of rarely more than a couple hundred dollars, and summer teaching, $66,000 is what I earned. Faculty appointments are structured with the privileged academic in mind and ignore those like me, from a working-class family, who experienced mobility but who have loans to pay and parents and siblings to help support. I was one of two finalists for the housing position, which I was so glad to get because I knew it would help me pay off my student loans and save up for a home. I managed to save about $30,000—which I knew would be enough to buy my dad a casket, a cemetery plot and marker, and cover the funeral home fees for embalming and a small service. Whatever was left, I would be able to put towards my student loans. But I knew that wouldn't be much.

I proudly shared with Marx: "I have about $30,000."

"Wow. That's a lot." He raised his eyebrows and smirked.

"I will do whatever you want, Marx."

"Listen, girl, I'm gonna be dead. Don't waste your money on me. You worked too damn hard all on your own for it."

He was always so understanding, and he was always so apologetic for not being able to help me pay for college or graduate school.

"Okay. I will cremate you and keep you with me wherever I am. When I die, I will be cremated, too. And I will make sure my ashes are spread with your ashes wherever I decide I want to be."

"That sounds good," he said, but I didn't believe him.

"Are you sure?"

He didn't hesitate. "Yeah."

"Marx, I love you so much and you are going to be alive a lot longer. I just want you to be okay with whatever."

He put his hands together as if he were praying but I knew he wasn't. He fidgeted a lot, and that is what he was doing. He held back a laugh with a half-smile.

I asked him, "Do you love me or Theo more?"

"You. Of course," he answered my ridiculous question.

We laughed. We both knew I was being silly. I pulled out my phone and started a video recording.

"Say it again. I want proof to show him when he gets out of jail. Who do you love more? Me or Theo?"

He went along with it and said, "You." He then laughed with the sense of humor we shared.

"Are you sure?" I asked through a smile.

"Yes," he quickly reassured me.

Uber Eats drove up with the large sausage pizza that I ordered. I pushed his wheelchair over to the picnic tables and we dug in.

* ★ ☆ ★ *

I was so thankful that Ranita was by my side when I flew to Chicago to see Marx's body for the last time. I was in and out of tears the entire flight. The funeral director was expecting me when Uber dropped us off at the funeral home.

"Hello. I'm George Markozis's daughter."

He directed us to a conference room.

"I'm so sorry for your loss," the funeral director, dressed in a suit and tie, said.

"Thank you. Is his body here?"

"Yes, it is."

"Can I see him?"

"Yes, just give me a couple of minutes."

He handed me a folder with what looked like a menu of afterlife services. My eyes went to the cost of cremation.

"I will go prepare your father for a viewing. Take a look at these materials and we can go over the details after the viewing."

As I flipped through the paperwork, I looked to Ranita for approval.

"Boo, do you think it's okay I go with cremation? He said he was okay with it."

"Yeah, of course. He will be with us."

The funeral director walked back in and peacefully told me, "Your father is ready now." The funeral director held the conference room door open as Ranita and I walked out into the hall. He directed us to a room that only I entered. I remember it as beige, boring, and sterile. Marx looked peaceful laying on the metal table with a white sheet draped over his body up to his chest. He wasn't fidgeting like I was used to seeing him. I did the Greek cross, knowing damn well I wasn't religious, while standing over him as tears rushed down my cheeks. Ranita and the funeral director were standing in the hall.

"Marx, I love you so much," I told his body, knowing that he wasn't there.

I only stood over him for a handful of seconds but it seemed like forever. I walked towards the door as I wiped away my tears.

I looked at the funeral director as I left his body behind: "Thank you."

"Of course."

As we walked back to the conference room, I asked Marx to give me a sign that he was there with me. I was on the verge of more tears so, in an attempt to compose myself, I started asking the funeral director questions about his job.

"It must be so difficult to be in your profession. To see people sad all of the time?"

"It can be," he said. "But it is a time to support people when they really need it."

I let drop the fact that Ranita and I were professors. I often do this when I feel like I am being judged for any of a number of reasons, ranging from my gender performance to being in a queer relationship. I know that professors are afforded a lot of prestige, so I use it to my advantage, hoping that it will mitigate problematic judgments about me or my family.

"As a sociologist, I find this whole process so interesting. Like the cause of death on the death certificate. Or what the person did for a living. Or their age at death. These are things that some sociologists draw on to study all sorts of things. It's not what I study, but others do."

"What do you study?" he asked.

"I mostly study gender." I looked over at Ranita. "And she studies poverty and inequalities."

The funeral director came out to me. I don't recall how he did, I just remember having a conversation about him being gay and how he navigates his personal life alongside his business. We talked a bit about queerphobia, but it is all a blur. I was in an auto-pilot conversation, not paying attention to any details. Instead, I was fixated on the fact that Marx delivered a sign that he was with me. And not just any sign, but one that made it clear he approved of my queer relationship—the funeral director was queer like me.

As I proceeded with the plans for cremation, I told the funeral director that I was going to be returning to Vegas the next evening because I had to teach and didn't want to cancel class. I asked him if I could take Marx's ashes with me so that I wouldn't have to worry about collecting his remains. He said he would do his best to have everything ready before I needed to leave for the airport. He also advised me to not pick out an urn, because I likely wouldn't be able to fly with it on the plane. Marx's remains would be packaged in a cardboard box the size of a shoebox. I was told that I could purchase an urn on the internet or from a funeral home out in Vegas and transfer Marx's ashes myself or have someone else do it for me.

"Will you cremate him tonight or tomorrow?" I had a reason to ask.

"Early tomorrow morning," he answered.

"Can I call you later today to confirm that cremation is what I want?"

I lied and went on to say that I had to check with other family members. But in reality, I just needed to sit a bit longer with my decision. I knew the cremation was going against Greek Orthodox tradition and, because of that, the Greek church wouldn't conduct a memorial or funeral service for him. To save my family's face in the Chicago Greek community, mom and her sisters lied and told people who found about Marx's death from my social media that I flew his body to Las Vegas and had traditional services out there where I lived.

"That's fine," the funeral director said. "Just call me on my cell as soon as you can. If anything, we can arrange to have his remains shipped to you if we aren't able to finalize the cremation before your return flight home."

I paid the $1,416 bill with my credit card. It included the cost of a couple of death certificates in case I needed them down the road. I ordered an Uber, and Ranita and I were on our way to our hotel.

* ⭐ ⭐ ⭐ *

It wasn't the first time I saw a dead family member. But it was the first time I was the one responsible for all of the afterlife decisions.

Theo was at the beginning of a two-year prison sentence for driving under the influence of drugs and alcohol. He had been driving Marx's car without a license and slammed into another car on the highway. Marx told me it was a hit and run, and that Theo fucked up his car. No one was seriously injured. But because he left the scene, was driving on a revoked driver's license, and had a long rap sheet including a separate pending drug and alcohol related offense, we all knew Theo was going to have to do time again when he eventually got caught. Although I still would've been the one to make Marx's afterlife decisions if Theo wasn't in prison, it would have been nice to have him by my side.

Mom, on the other hand, had no excuse. She should have met me at the funeral home. Yes, she was divorced from Marx, but they were still family. And, regardless, she should have showed up for me. Instead, she did what she does best—avoidance. She told me she was really sick with a tooth infection, so she conveniently went to an emergency room the morning after Marx died, while I was on a flight to Chicago. They admitted her— she knew they would—because the infection was out of control. I don't doubt it. She had been complaining to me about her tooth for weeks, but now, all of a sudden, she wanted to get it looked at despite my telling her every day to go see a dentist or doctor? Please. I'm familiar with her games. I know she didn't want to see Marx's dead body, so she had herself admitted to a hospital to get out of it. She always told me she wasn't afraid of anything except dead bodies, snakes, and jail. I didn't give a damn though. She should have mothered me that day.

When I booked my flight to Chicago, I also decided to reserve a room at a Greektown hotel. I chose the same hotel I stayed in the night before I defended my doctoral dissertation at the University of Illinois at Chicago. The hotel was filled with happy memories for me. And it was across the street from Greek Islands restaurant—a place where my family went to celebrate things when we were growing up. It was also the same place I took my grad school friends, some faculty, and my family for lunch after my doctoral dissertation defense. I just knew Marx would want me to celebrate his life there. After I said my goodbyes to his body, I invited Aunt Maria and Aunt Athena, and their families, out to Greek Islands for dinner as a way to honor Marx's memory. Mom was in the hospital, so I knew she couldn't come. I thought it would be nice to have my aunts there instead. But they weren't able to make it, or so they said.

Thank God for Ranita.

We sat at a table for two, enjoying a Greek feast. Holding back my tears in the crowded restaurant, we toasted Marx (red wine for Ranita, iced tea for me) as we shared Greek salad, avgolemono, saganaki, pastitsio, dolmades, fasolakia, and crusty Greek bread that we ate with the best imported feta cheese and Kalamata olives.

When we left the restaurant, I saw someone walking two French Bulldogs. "Look!" I told Ranita, "Another sign from Marx." Marx knew how much I loved French Bulldogs. So when I saw the two Frenchies walking outside of the Greek Islands restaurant after doing my best to celebrate his life, I felt it was his supernatural way of telling me that he was with me, and that everything would be okay. I don't usually believe in signs from superpowers or whatever like these, but I do when I emotionally need them.

I phoned the funeral director and told him to proceed with the cremation. It wasn't easy rejecting the Greek custom, but I did it. There was no lavish funeral nor a final resting place in an overpriced burial plot surrounded by trees. And there was no decorated marble headstone that would have read "loving father" followed by "chain smoker" to make sure he was also remembered for his sense of humor. The $30,000 I had accumulated by living for close to three years in a university dorm room as UNLV's first professor-in-residence stayed in my savings account, along with the guilt I felt for choosing cremation.

The next morning, I picked up Marx—who was now a pile of ashes stuffed in a plastic bag inside of a cheesy shoebox made to resemble the blue and white sky. I apologized to his remains before turning to our shared humor to make both of us feel better. "Now get your ass in my bag," I said aloud as I stuffed the box into my laptop bag and flew him home with me to Las Vegas where he would rest next to the TV in my university dorm room. But his remains didn't rest in my dorm for long.

Less than a month after Marx died, Ranita and I bought our first home together, a $400,000 four-bedroom newly built home in Henderson, Nevada. I used much of the $30,000 I had saved for my portion of the downpayment. As I drove Marx's box of ashes to our new home, I blasted Fleetwood Mac and told him about our new house. I assuaged my guilt about cremating him by taking comfort in the fact that his resting place was with me as I had promised him, and not in some cold wet hole in the ground.

Our new home was fresh but without character. The builder had chosen a neutral and ever-so-popular grey and white color palette for everything from the quartz countertops to the two-toned cabinets. A boring house, but perfect for the family we wished to grow.

* ★ ✬ ★ *

Mom waited several months before telling Theo about Marx's death. She was afraid he wouldn't be able to handle the news in prison and might end up "hanging himself with a sheet." We are all dramatic in our family, but hands down, mom wins this award. It was an easy lie for mom to keep because Theo was in prison without a way to phone the nursing home. And Theo and I avoid any contact. We prefer to find out about one another through mom. When mom did get the courage to tell Theo at one of her many visits with him in prison, he had questions.

He stared at her and asked, "Oh. That sucks. How'd he die?"

Mom had prepared months for this moment: "In his sleep at the nursing home."

"When?" Theo asked, leaving mom and I to later wonder if he somehow knew we were keeping the truth from him.

"A few months ago. I didn't want you to be upset so I didn't tell you."

"Where is he?"

"Missy had him cremated. She has his ashes at home with her in Vegas."

I imagine him sitting there in prison scrubs, sad about Marx and angry at me when he calmly said: "That's fucked up. Greeks don't cremate. She shouldn't have done that."

Mom wanted the conversation to end when she said, "I don't know what to say."

He continued eating his vending machine meal, which mom always purchased for him when they met in the prisoners' visiting room. On the way out of the prison that day, mom told a guard that she gave Theo some sad news and that she was worried about him. She asked the guard if he could notify the chaplain or have someone else check on him. The guard said he would. Mom didn't see Theo again until he was released nearly a year later. The Illinois Department of Corrections prohibited her from visiting him again because she withheld the fact that she was a convicted felon on the Prospective Visitor's Information Form, which asked about her criminal background.

* * ☆ * *

In August of 2019, I sat in our guest room, which doubled as a home office, with a vial of frozen sperm in my hand. The warmth of my hand was slowly defrosting the sperm that I was praying would make our baby. I was staring at Marx's remains, pleading with him to use whatever superpowers the dead have to help us make this insemination work. It was our third time trying to get pregnant, and although the first two times failed, I was reassured by online queer conception groups that it was too soon to be concerned about infertility. They'd remind me that straight folks have to be actively trying to conceive for a year before most medical providers will recommend running tests to assess fertility. But I was worried. I wanted to be a mother so badly. I tracked Ranita's ovulation like it was my day job, ordering the frozen sperm in preparation for her peak fertility. Our midwife was on call for us, and would show up when I thought the timing was just right.

I would hand the vial of thawed cryobank-prepared sperm to her and assist her as she inserted the sperm through the vaginal canal and directly into Ranita's uterus. The third time worked. In May of 2020, during the height of the COVID-19 pandemic, our son was born. I know it's cliché, but I never felt love like I did for him when he entered the world.

With COVID-19 shutting down the world as we knew it, including the Las Vegas Strip for nearly 80 days,[8] Ranita and I, with our jobs as university professors, were able to do all of our work from home during our son's first year of life. It was a special time, alone with just the three of us. I will always be grateful for that time, and look back on it fondly even though in the moment I was longing for pre-COVID life.

Ranita's parents and sister would video chat with us from India every day to connect with our son. And I would talk with mom on her landline—she still didn't have a smart phone—nearly every day, too. She would send her grandson boxes full of toys and designer baby clothes that she picked out from a one-of-a-kind children's boutique in Chicago. When she received our 2021 New Year's card with Ranita, our son, and I all wearing matching rainbow pajamas standing in front of our decorated Christmas tree, she jokingly called us the "Griswolds."

With nowhere else to go now that Marx was dead, Theo moved in with mom after he got out of prison. They lived together in her run-down two-bedroom apartment in southern Illinois. They were constantly fighting and screaming at each other. Sometimes, when I'd call her landline, he'd answer, asking me, "What that fuck do you want?" He never asked about my son, but if I happened to call when they were in the middle of an argument, I'd hear him in the background screaming, "Tell that stupid fat bitch that kid isn't hers!" or "He ain't our blood!" or "Stop raising someone else's kid you dumb bitch!" He had been saying such horrible things ever since he found out, when he was in prison, that Ranita and I spent "a shitload of money" on sperm to make a baby. He was pissed that we wouldn't wait until he got out so he could sell us some of his. He wanted our money. But I wanted sperm from a highly educated athlete, in case everything I teach my students about nature versus nurture is wrong. "Why are you letting him say that shit?" I'd be upset and ask mom. "What do you want me to do? You think I can control him?" she'd helplessly respond.

Every once in a while, I'd tell her to put him on the phone, which she would do only reluctantly, given that our conversation would go something like this:

"Yeah, did you want something from me, you fat bitch?"

"Fuck you, crackhead! Now listen to me. You keep my son's name out of your mouth or you will be fucking sorry!"

"What are you going to do? Call the police on me? I don't give a fuuuuuuuck!"

"Why don't you leave us alone! Aren't you too old to be living off your mommy?"

"This bitch, listen to me, this bitch has done nothing for me. She's a horrible piece-of-shit of a mother."

"Keep me out of it!" I would hear mom yelling in the background.

"She's done nothing for me," he'd continue. "She ruined my life."

"Ruin your life? What life? You mean your drug addicted self? Take care of your fucking self, man. She's done nothing for me either but you don't see me acting like you. Move out on your own and get a job like everyone else."

"I can't Missy! This bitch mother of ours ruined my life! I'm a felon. No one will hire me!"

"That's not fucking true. Every job you've had, you've lost because you were too strung out to work. That's no one's fault but your own."

"Alright are you done? Why don't you help me out? I'm your brother. I'm your blood, man. That kid isn't yours. You're being used, you stupid fatass!"

"You crackhead motherfucker! Shut the fuck up or you'll be fucking sorry!"

"She's using you, Missy! She wants you to raise her kid!"

"He is my kid you piece of shit! I can't stand you, motherfucker. Why don't you OD already?"

"Fuck you, you fucking fat bitch! I will kill you and her and that kid, too!"

"Go ahead motherfucker! Try it! I will get your ass locked up so fast that you won't ever get out!"

"I don't give a fuck!"

"I'm fucking recording this call you piece of shit! I'm going to call the police right now!"

"Do it you fat fucking bitch!" he'd scream one final time before hanging up.

He knew I wasn't recording the call. I did call the police on him a number of times, but it mostly was because mom would call me and tell me that he'd tried to strangle her, that he had attacked her, or was threating to "slit her throat." When the police would come, they'd separate them, sometimes taking him to the police station for the night like some sort of de-escalation white boy staycation. The next morning he'd leave the jail and walk right back to mom's apartment. They would just let him go because mom would never press charges.

I'd beg her: "You have to press charges or at least don't let him come back. The same shit just keeps happening again and again and again."

"Yeah, easy for you to say. Where is he going to go?"

"That's not on you," I'd remind her. "He's a grown-ass man."

"I can't leave him under the bridge to die."

"Stop being dramatic and stop enabling him. He can't keep staying with you like this."

"He makes my life a living hell. I wish he'd just kill me already."

"That's real fucked up you'd say that. Just kick him out."

"Do you know how much money I've given him?"

"Just kick him out," I'd keep saying it even though she wasn't listening to me.

"He is such an angry person. Why do you think he got like that?"

"I don't know, but you have to kick him out."

This back-and-forth would go on as long as I'd stay on the phone, which wouldn't be long, as I'd get tired of hearing her complain. Empathy only lasts so long.

When my son was born, my heart exploded. I knew at that moment what unconditional love felt like. I'd do anything for him. For the first time, I understood why mom, and Marx before he passed, always enabled Theo even at the expense of their own mental and financial well-being. Tough love isn't easy.

But being a parent also deepened the disappointment I had in my own mother. She knowingly harmed me when she stole my identity even though she didn't do it for the purpose of harming me. I know my bar is low, but Marx would never do such a thing, much like I couldn't fathom harming my own child. When Marx first heard that mom stole my identity, he told me that he once opened a piece of mail that was addressed to "G Markozis." He thought it was for him but quickly realized that the approval letter inside along with a new credit card was meant for me. Even though he "was broke," he told me he never thought about using my card as his own.

The similarities of our names, which made it easier for mom to steal my identity, is one reason why I never went back to the last name I was given at birth and instead continue to use my ex-husband's last name. It's also why I rejected the Greek tradition of recycling first names in the family when it came time to choose a name for our son and, two years later, our daughter.

Ranita and I love parenting so much that we knew quite quickly that we'd try for another child. Soon after our son was born, I bought more of the same donor's sperm, which we ended up using in September of 2021. As I did previously, I used my hand to thaw a vial of frozen sperm while waiting for our midwife to come over and do the intrauterine insemination. As the sperm was thawing, I prayed to Marx's ashes, begging him to use the dead's superpowers to once again help us get pregnant. We were working with a new midwife this time, given that we had moved from faculty positions at UNLV to similar posts at the University of New Mexico. And we were in a new house in the foothills of the Sandia Mountains. It was newly built like our first home, and unsurprisingly—given it's a cookie-cutter house—it has a similar grey and white color palette. Much to our surprise, the insemination took, and we were pregnant with our daughter after only one cycle of trying.

In late December 2021, Ranita and I made last-minute plans to celebrate the new year with friends who live in Wisconsin. Ranita was several months pregnant with our second child, and we wanted a vacation after quarantining in Albuquerque, our new city, without many friends for most of the still ongoing COVID-19 pandemic. Fearing we'd get COVID, we didn't want to fly, especially since we were traveling with our 18-month-old son who couldn't be vaccinated against it yet. So, to play it safe, we ended up taking a 20-hour road trip from Albuquerque to Milwaukee. We planned two overnight stops. The first was an uneventful night in Oklahoma City. Our second stay was in southern Illinois, not far from where mom lives.

Mom was looking forward to finally getting to meet our son in person. Since our son was born, I bought, and she had me cancel airline tickets for her to visit us multiple times. She was going through an eviction at her two-bedroom apartment for violating her lease by allowing Theo and Yiayia to stay with her. Her lease agreement said anyone who lived in their unit needed to go through a background check and be approved to live on their premises. Mom never did that. I'm sure the apartment management didn't care about my nearly 90-year-old Yiayia riding out the pandemic with mom in one of their run-down units. But they definitely didn't want Theo around, given the screaming fights he'd get in with mom, her neighbors, and sometimes even Yiayia. In the six months after the apartment management found out that Theo was staying with mom, he had at least 16 interactions with the local police department for assault, resisting arrest, public intoxication, and more, resulting in numerous and still ongoing criminal court cases. The apartment management declined to renew mom's lease, citing that she violated the terms of her rental agreement. But she refused to move out. She had been living in her apartment for nearly eight years, never late paying the rent. She didn't want to uproot herself. So, she went to court and tried to fight the eviction case, claiming that Theo and Yiayia were just her guests.

Mom was going to put her eviction case aside for a night and stay with us in our southern Illinois hotel room so we could maximize our time with one another. She was going to bring Yiayia with her. But the plan never materialized. I didn't even allow them to meet my son. When they got to the hotel, I walked out into the parking lot to greet them, only to find that Theo had tagged along. On our way up to southern Illinois, I repeatedly asked mom to not bring him. I didn't want to see Theo, and I definitely didn't want him around my son. He had been threatening me for months on the phone telling me that he was going to kill me, Ranita, and our son, who he refused to acknowledge was mine. I wasn't genuinely scared of him. I just didn't want to be around him. Being a new parent myself helped to crystallize this decision. I was unwavering. Mom thought I was overreacting when I yelled at her for disrespecting my boundaries by bringing him. She told me he was going to wait in the car and that she and Yiayia were only going to stay for a little bit. But I feared Theo would eventually get restless waiting for them and would eventually make his way into the hotel lobby, drunk or drugged out, and make a scene trying to find out which room we were in.

"Why in the fuck did you bring him?" I asked mom in the hotel parking lot. "I told you many times to leave him at home."

"He wanted to come for the ride!" she yelled. "He's going to wait in the car!"

"I don't care!" I interrupted.

"We are only going to stay for a few minutes. He's not even bothering you."

"I don't care. I told you not to bring him."

"We just want to meet the baby!"

"I don't care. He's in the room and I'm not bringing him down. You can try again on our way back down to Albuquerque in a few days."

"Whatever." She yelled at the top of her lungs as she got back into her car while my nearly 90-year-old Yiayia held on to her for walking support. "I hope you're fucking happy, Missy."

"Yiayia," I loudly asked her while pointing to Theo, "Why did you bring him with?"

"Shame on you, Missy," Yiayia voiced with disgust, "he's your brother."

Afterwards I had a panic attack, a rare occurrence these days, brought on by feeling terrible for not allowing mom and Yiayia to meet my son. But more than that, I regretted telling them that we were going to be in the area, and I even regretted planning the trip.

Within a few hours, however, my feelings calmed. On our drive back home a few nights later, mom and Yiayia finally got to meet the baby. They left Theo at home this time, respecting my wishes, and hung out with us in our room for about an hour. Mom and Yiayia gave my son a few Christmas presents—a stuffed doll and some small cars, which they watched him play with as they made small talk in Greek to each other about the baby. They both tried to pick him up multiple times, but he would whine, forcing them to just let him stay on the floor where he could play with his presents.

Mom asked Ranita and I about our work. And I told her about the new book that I was writing.

"What's it about?"

"My life, but from a sociological lens."

"You mean like your illness?"

"Intersex isn't an illness."

"Well, yeah, but you know what I mean."

"Yeah, I'm writing about being intersex but also everything else, too."

"Like what?"

"Just everything. Like how I dropped out of seventh grade and am now a professor. Theo, stuff like that."

"Oh, me? Great."

"I'm just writing about my life, from my perspective."

"At my expense though."

"I'm just using sociology to make sense of it all."

"How?"

"It's complicated. I can't really explain it right now."

"Well, try."

"I'm just writing about how I dropped out of the seventh grade and was still able to get a PhD and become a professor."

"Because you're smart? You know I took these brain pills when I was pregnant with you."

"No," I rolled my eyes and laughed. "Because my efforts to get ahead are doubled, tripled, and quadrupled because I'm white. And how Theo gets chance after chance, when people of color don't."

"What's going to be on the cover?"

"I have no idea. It won't be out for a while."

"Are you going to have another book party?"

"I want to. But I have to finish it first."

"Do you think they will make a movie out of it? Because if they do, I want someone good to play me. Don't get anyone homely."

We laughed.

As they were leaving, mom asked me to follow her out to her car because she had more presents for my son. I told her she should have saved her money instead of wasting it on toys he didn't need, but she said she wanted to give him things to remember her by. Her car was filled with all sorts of new, but unwrapped, toddler toys—from a school bus that you ride on to a kitchen set to a walking-and-talking dinosaur. She also got him a bag full of new clothes. I was barely able to fit all of the gifts into our SUV. She hugged us goodbye, placed her hand on Ranita's belly saying "bye, baby" to our fetus that was growing, and then told us to call her when we got home.

* * 🟊 * *

In May of 2022, almost exactly two years after our son was born, our daughter joined our family. The life I dreamt of—loving family, stable career, nice home—was coming to fruition. My anxiety was also under control with the help of a therapist and daily medication.

Mom has also been in therapy, and has been for the last decade or so, ever since I got her connected with social services when the federal court appointed me her third-party custodian. Although my custodian status didn't last for long, she continues to see a therapist and as far as I know is no longer doing anything illegal.

It has taken nearly 20 years since mom started stealing my identity in 2004 for her to accept at least some accountability for her actions. She acknowledges her mistakes, and while she stops short of directly apologizing for them, I'm okay with that for now. My bar is low but she's meeting it.

She also regularly tells me how fortunate our kids are to have two amazing parents, and she regularly compliments us on how much we do for our kids—saving for their college education or spending so much quality time with them. I quickly dismiss her praise, noting that we are just doing what we can with what we have. I put it bluntly: "That's what parents are supposed to do." "Whatever," she'd say and then continue, "I was just being nice." I don't retract my hurtful words. She's better at grandmothering than she's ever been at mothering. But she still doesn't show up in meaningful ways. She skips everything from our kids' birthday parties to holidays with us even when she knows I will pay for her airfare. She overcompensates for her absenteeism with boxes upon boxes of gifts that she sends to our kids on a quarterly basis. She wants to show her love with presents, but she doesn't always know that presents aren't the same as love. I try to protect my kids from this all-too-familiar pattern from my childhood.

Although I wish my mother was more actively involved in the lives of my children, I soften the blow by reminding myself that kids only need their grandparents when their parents aren't as involved as they ought to be. Ranita and I will always be there for our kids—welcoming, of course, any other guides into their lives but in supplemental rather than primary roles.

My parents were not my primary guides. And they weren't for Theo either. When I was a kid, I looked to Yiayia and Papou to fill those roles, and when they were in Greece (where they lived), I filled the parental gaps in my life with other meaningful adults. Theo had people fill the parental gaps in his life, too, like the time my Aunt Athena allowed him to live with her for close to a year after Marx died and mom and he weren't getting along. She tried to guide him but wasn't successful. "He's not the same Theo you and I used to know," she shared with me after she told him he had to leave her house. "He's very angry, Missy. He looks at me like he can snap at any moment," and she continued, "I have my own kids to worry about and can't have him around anymore." I understood, and couldn't believe she allowed him to live with her as long as she did.

With nowhere else to go, he moved back in with mom. But she got evicted from the two-bedroom apartment she was renting because, according to the property manager, "Theo was a huge problem in the complex." She ended up moving into a trailer park not far from the apartment in southern Illinois she rented for nearly eight years. She didn't listen to me when I told her not to let him live with her again. She even acknowledged that it was just a matter of time before she was evicted again because of Theo's actions. She begged him to stay in the trailer and not go outside. He promised her that he'd stay inside and no one would know that he was living with her. His promise didn't last for long.

Within a week, he was getting in screaming matches with her again and even, according to her, attempted to strangle her on more than one occasion. He even got in a fight with some neighbor in a common area of the trailer park. I'm not sure for what, but mom said a steel pipe was involved and he was "badly fucked up," as were the others involved in the altercation. When the trailer park management got word of the incident, they told mom that they were going to start eviction proceedings because she was housing someone who wasn't on the lease. This made mom furious at Theo but also at the management. To the management, she'd accuse them of harassing her and would lie and say that Theo was just visiting. This was the same unsuccessful lie that she'd told her previous management company, that did end up evicting her. I guess she always has to blame someone. She'd then, and rightfully so, scream at Theo because he was causing yet another eviction. During one of their screaming matches, Theo went to the trailer park's management office and started threatening them. The police got involved, and the eviction process continued to progress through the court.

After one physical altercation with mom, Theo eventually moved out for good. She somehow got away from him and ran to the trailer of a neighbor, who called the police for her. When the police arrived, she assumed they would take her side, but instead, they, according to her, were taking his side because he told them that she was a convicted state and federal felon. The police told her that they couldn't legally make him leave the trailer because he had mail addressed to him at the trailer, which served as proof that he'd been living there. It didn't matter that he wasn't on the lease.

Theo volunteered to leave the trailer after a county social worker got involved. Mom didn't know what happened to him for weeks. But after contacting the police department, she learned that the social worker got him into a Salvation Army residential rehab facility in central Illinois. When our mom asked for a phone number to get a hold of him, the social worker informed her that it was best that they not have any contact with each other. She promised mom that she would keep in touch with her about Theo's progress. But she rarely did.

Theo reached out to mom a few months later. He asked her to send him money, which she did. She didn't know why he needed the money, only that he had been kicked out of the residential rehab facility for getting into an altercation with a fellow resident. When mom pressed him for details, he said he didn't want to talk about it. He was still unhoused but now in a different Salvation Army residential rehab facility.

These days, when he calls her, she panics, hoping he's not going to ask her to pick him up and let him live with her again. The trailer park stopped the eviction when the social worker informed them that Theo was no longer living with mom. They did tell the social worker that they'd proceed with the eviction if he ever returned to their community.

But as of now, Theo doesn't want to live with mom. He only calls her for money, which she sends him whenever he asks for it even if she doesn't have it. I'm not sure how she can afford to send him money or how much she sends him. All I know is that she sends whatever he asks for to keep him from living with her again.

I haven't talked to Theo in years. I do think about him though, especially when I see unhoused people on the streets of Albuquerque. I read their signs, and give cash when I have it on me, often wondering what would be on Theo's sign. When we speak, even if it's just a few words of thanks or have a good day or something like that, I feel like I'm connecting with Theo. I also regularly google Theo's name to check in on him, hoping that something tragic doesn't appear in my internet search. I worry about him and regularly ask Marx to use the dead's superpowers to watch over him.

It's a weird feeling, having a silent conversation with Marx's ashes. I find comfort doing it, though, and am grateful his remains have always stayed with me, making wherever I'm living feel like a home. And upstairs, beside a photo of him that I framed, is a cigarette that I've left out to make him feel at home, too. I imagine my Marx smiling: "What the fuck, Missy! I need a lighter!" He'd be so proud of me today, and not just because of the college savings account I've been growing for my kids, or that I'm debt free aside from a home mortgage. He'd take a cigarette drag and say something like, "You did good, girl. You did damn good." And I'd lie, and tell him, "It's all because of you, man, you know I got your brains." He'd laugh and say through a smirk, "You know that's bullshit." Lying is something I hardly do these days because I don't need to. I'm living the life I dreamed of as a kid. I'm in a career with good pay, and I'm doing my best to build a stable, loving, and supportive home so my kids never feel compelled to lie. And we don't keep secrets in our home, which my four-year-old son reminds me of whenever we share a chocolate bar before dinner and I ask him not to let his sister know. "You're right," I'd laugh as we stuff the chocolate into our mouths. "We don't keep secrets, but we have to eat it quickly before she sees us." "Mama, that's a great idea," he'd say right as she runs to us asking, "Can I have some? Please? Of course?" We'd share our not-so-secret chocolate with her and laugh as she thanks us with chocolate all over her two-year-old face. But these are things Marx already knows, as he witnesses my life while tucked away in my hall closet.

ACKNOWLEDGMENTS

I rewrote this book so many times with the help of far too many people to name everyone here. But I must thank the following folks for their unconditional support in seeing to it that I follow through with my goal of bringing it to fruition: Ranita Ray, Jennifer Kontny, Rebecca Southworth, Koyel Khan, Maggie Hagerman, Michelle Manno, Cassaundra Rodriguez, Cati Connell, Jennifer Hauptman, Rachel Allison, Amy Brainer, Pallavi Banerjee, Kimberly Zieselman, Sharon Preves, Lizzie Reis, Susila Gurusami, Chandra Waring, Shweta Adur, Nicole Jenkins, Korey Tillman, Celine Ayala, and Linda Markowitz.

I also wish to thank those I've met through the UNM community for their encouragement, especially Aaron Cayer, Nancy López, Owen Whooley, Jessica Goodkind, Shannon McKigney, Lisa Broidy, Michelle Gurule, and Daisy Atterbury.

For her patience, encouragement, and editorial expertise, I owe Ilene Kalish and her team at NYU Press, including Valerie Zaborski and James Michael Reilly. I've now had the privilege of publishing two books with Ilene, and I seriously couldn't ask for a better editor. This book wouldn't exist without her believing in me and my unconventional ways of writing academic ideas. A special thank you to Priyanka Ray for her editorial assistance during the production process. I also wish to thank the anonymous reviewers who read earlier drafts of this book and offered helpful ways to strengthen it. And I would be remiss if I didn't thank Heather Kreidler of Fact or Fiction, LLC for offering her meticulous skills that have strengthened this book.

Albuquerque is more than just my workplace because of the people who offer community and a much-needed writing break. They know who they are, and I thank them, and all of their children, for the laughter and good food!

My family shaped who I am and how I see the world, and for that, I will forever be thankful to them for standing beside me even when my words make them uncomfortable.

Most of all I thank my partner, Ranita. I'm fortunate to share a home with her unmatched intellectual and creative energy that provides me with so much including her suggestion of titling this book *Five Star White Trash*—which I like to think of as payback from when I came up with "Identity of Distance" for her award-winning *Social Problems* article. I thank her, and our children, for bringing so much happiness into my life. The three of them will always be my everything.

NOTES

1. MIDDLE SCHOOL DROPOUT

1 For a discussion of white flight in Chicago, see Erick Howenstine, "Ethnic Change and Segregation in Chicago," in *EthniCity: Geographic Perspectives on Ethnic Change in Modern Cities*, ed. C. C. Roseman, H. D. Laux, and G. Thieme, 31–50 (Lanham, MD: Rowman and Littlefield, 1996). For more on white flight, albeit in Atlanta, see Kevin M. Kruse, *White Flight: Atlanta and the Making of Modern Conservatism* (Princeton, NJ: Princeton University Press, 2005). And for a scholarly overview of racial residential segregation, see Camille Zubrinsky Charles, "The Dynamics of Racial Residential Segregation," *Annual Review of Sociology* 29, no. 1 (2003): 167–207.

2 In the State of Illinois, it was, and still is today, compulsory to be enrolled in a public school, or equivalent educational program, until 17 years of age or graduation. For a report on compulsory school age requirements in the United States, see Marga Mikulecky, "Compulsory School Age Require-ments," Education Commission of the States, April 2013, www.ecs.org/clear-inghouse/01/07/03/10703.pdf. Because of age restrictions, few youth drop out before entering high school, which may be why the National Center for Education Statistics does not have reliable data on the few who never make it to the ninth grade. Around the time I dropped out of the seventh grade, the high school dropout rate was around 4.5 percent, as noted in Marilyn M. McMillen, Phillip Kaufman, and Summer D. Whitener, "Dropout Rates in the United States: 1993," National Center for Education Statistics, U.S. Department

of Education, Office of Educational Research and Improvement, 1994, NCED 94–669.

3 For a discussion of whiteness, see Ruth Frankenberg, *White Women, Race Matters: The Social Construction of Whiteness* (Minneapolis: University of Minnesota Press, 1993). For a discussion of the white working class, see Monica McDermott, *Working Class White: The Making and Unmaking of Race Relations* (Berkeley: University of California Press, 2006). See also Monica McDermott, *Whiteness in America* (Cambridge, UK: Polity Press, 2020).

4 For a discussion of "white trash," including the origins of the term, see the introduction in Annalee Newitz and Matt Wray, *White Trash: Race and Class in America* (New York: Routledge, 1997). See also Matt Wray, *Not Quite White: White Trash and the Boundaries of Whiteness* (Durham, NC: Duke University Press, 2006).

5 Five star white trash is a different kind of "white trash." I conceptualize it as having access to money at any cost, be it borrowed or stolen, and mobilizing it to appear wealthy. Five star white trash overlaps with what sociologist and economist Thorstein Veblen referred to as "conspicuous consumption" in his book *The Theory of the Leisure Class: An Economic Study in the Evolution of Institutions* (New York: The Macmillan Company, 1899). But five star white trash is different in that money is obtained by any means possible and the mobilization of the money tends to exist alongside the devaluation of other markers of a privileged social class position, including education, concern for physical and mental well-being, financial planning for retirement, and more.

6 For a historical review of beauty standards, see Dimitre Dimitrov and George Kroumpouzos, "Beauty Perception: A Historical and Contemporary Review," Clinics in Dermatology 41, no. 1 (2023): 33–40.

7 See Candace West and Don H. Zimmerman, "Doing Gender," *Gender & Society* 1, no. 2 (1987): 125–51. See also Judith Butler, *Gender Trouble: Feminism and the Subversion of Identity* (New York: Routledge, 1990).

8 For more information about Greek immigration to the United States, see "Greeks," *The Encyclopedia of Chicago*, accessed September 13, 2024, www.encyclopedia.chicagohistory.org/pages/548.html.

9 Salvador Minuchin, Braulio Montalvo, Bernard G. Guerney, Jr., Bernice L. Rosman, and Florence Schumer, *Families of the Slums: An Exploration of Their Structure and Treatment* (New York: Basic Books, 1967). See also Ivan Boszormenyi-Nagy and Geraldine M. Spark, *Invisible Loyalties: Reciprocity in Intergenerational Family Therapy* (Hagerstown, MD: Harper & Row, 1973).

10 Val Gillies, "Parenting, Class and Culture: Exploring the Context of Childrearing," *Community Practitioner* 79, no. 4 (2006): 114–117.

11 For a sociological overview of school bullying that includes gender differences, see C. J. Pascoe, "Notes on a Sociology of Bullying: Young Men's Homophobia as Gender Socialization," *QED: A Journal in GLBTQ Worldmaking* no. 1(2013): 87–104. For a discussion of school bullying that explicitly centers race/

ethnicity, see Melissa Fleschler Peskin, Susan R. Tortolero, and Christine M. Markham, "Bullying and Victimization among Black and Hispanic Adolescents," *Adolescence* 41, no. 63 (2006): 467–484.

12 We know school bullying is intricately related to masculinity, as noted in Pascoe, "Notes on a Sociology of Bullying." See also CJ Pascoe, *Dude, You're a Fag: Masculinity and Sexuality in High School* (Berkeley: University of California Press, 2007).

13 This is not surprising, given research by those who have studied teachers and are not afraid to expose the violence they can enact on their students. See Irwin A. Hyman and Pamela A. Snook, *Dangerous Schools: What We Can Do About the Physical and Emotional Abuse of Our Children* (San Francisco, CA: Jossey-Bass Inc., Publishers, 1999). More recently, sociological work has documented similar patterns of teachers actively bullying Black and immigrant girls of color, as noted in Ranita Ray, "School as a Hostile Institution: How Black and Immigrant Girls of Color Experience the Classroom," *Gender & Society* 36, no. 1 (2022): 88–111.

14 For a discussion of the negative effects of psychotherapy, see Bernhard Strauss, Romina Gawlytta, Andrea Schleu, and Dominique Frenzl, "Negative Effects of Psychotherapy: Estimating the Prevalence in a Random National Sample," BJPsych Open 7, no. 6 (2021): e186.

15 Minuchin et al., *Families of the Slums*. See also Boszormenyi-Nagy and Spark, *Invisible Loyalties*.

16 Joanne E. Coster, Janette K. Turner, Daniel Bradbury, and Anna Cantrell, "Why Do People Choose Emergency and Urgent Care Services? A Rapid Review Utilizing a Systematic Literature Search and Narrative Synthesis," *Academic Emergency Medicine* 24, no. 9 (2017): 1137–1149.

17 See Office of the Assistant Secretary for Planning and Evaluation, "Trends in the Utilization of Emergency Department Services, 2009–2018," U.S. Department of Health & Human Services, March 2, 2021, https://aspe.hhs.gov/pdf-report/utilization-emergency-department-services.

18 Research shows a correlation between being bullied and academic performance. See, for example, Jaana Juvonen, Yueyan Wang, and Guadalupe Espinoza, "Bullying Experiences and Compromised Academic Performance Across Middle School Grades," *Journal of Early Adolescence* 31, no. 1 (2011): 152–173. See also Dewey Cornell, Anne Gregory, Francis Huang, and Xitao Fan, "Perceived Prevalence of Teasing and Bullying Predicts High School Dropout Rates," *Journal of Educational Psychology* 105, no. 1 (2013): 138–149.

19 For an account of just how racist the criminal legal system is, see Nicole Gonzales Van Cleve, *Crook County: Racism and Injustice in America's Largest Criminal Court* (Redwood City, CA: Stanford University Press, 2016). See also Reuben Jonathan Miller, *Halfway Home: Race, Punishment, and the Afterlife of Mass Incarceration* (New York: Little, Brown and Company, 2021); Michael L. Walker, *Indefinite: Doing Time in Jail* (New York: Oxford University Press,

2022); Michelle Alexander, *The New Jim Crow: Mass Incarceration in the Age of Colorblindness* (New York: The New Press, 2012); and Matthew Clair, *Privilege and Punishment: How Race and Class Matter in Criminal Court* (Princeton, NJ: Princeton University Press, 2020).

20 For a conservative discussion of eminent domain, see Ellen Frankel Paul, *Property Rights and Eminent Domain* (New Brunswick, NJ: Transaction Books, 1987).

2. FAT FREAK

1 A continuance is a postponement or delay of a court hearing to a later date that can be requested by the defense or prosecution and is approved by a judge. For an overview of the criminal justice system, see "The Justice System," Bureau of Justice Statistics, https://bjs.ojp.gov/justice-system.

2 Kate Shuster, "Teaching Hard History: American Slavery," Southern Poverty Law Center, 2018, www.splcenter.org/sites/default/files/tt_hard_history_american_slavery.pdf.

3 As with other teenage girls from the working class, sex for me—at least with Chuck—wasn't about romance but was instead about performing working-class white femininity. See Julie Bettie, *Women Without Class: Girls, Race, and Identity* (Berkeley: University of California Press, 2002).

4 Jaana Juvonen, Leah M. Lessard, Hannah L. Schacter, and Luisana Suchilt, "Emotional Implications of Weight Stigma Across Middle School: The Role of Weight-Based Peer Discrimination," *Journal of Clinical Child & Adolescent Psychology* 46, no. 1 (2017): 150–58.

5 For a contemporary discussion of fatphobia, see Kate Manne, *Unshrinking: How to Face Fatphobia* (New York: Crown, 2024). For a sociomedical take on how the numbers on the scale have been pathologized by the medical community, see Annemarie Jutel, "The Emergence of Overweight as a Disease Entity: Measuring Up Normality," *Social Science & Medicine* 63, no. 9 (2006): 2268–2276. See also Annemarie Jutel, *Putting a Name to It: Diagnosis in Contemporary Society* (Baltimore, MD: Johns Hopkins University Press, 2011).

6 Michael T. Vallis and Michael A. Ross, "The Role of Psychological Factors in Bariatric Surgery for Morbid Obesity: Identification of Psychological Predictors of Success," *Obesity Surgery* 3, no. 4 (1993): 346–59. See also Nancy Puzziferri, Thomas B. Roshek, Helen G. Mayo, Ryan Gallagher, Steven H. Belle, and Edward H. Livingston, "Long-Term Follow-up After Bariatric Surgery: A Systematic Review," *JAMA* 312, no. 9 (2014): 934–42.

7 See Charles W. Breaux, "Obesity Surgery in Children," *Obesity Surgery* 5, no. 3 (1995): 279–284.

8 For a study on the high failure rate of the bariatric surgery I underwent, see Ruben Schouten, Dorothee C. Wiryasaputra, Francois M. H. van Dielen, Wim G. van Gemert, and Jan Willem M. Greve, "Long-Term Results of Bariatric

Restrictive Procedures: A Prospective Study," *Obesity Surgery* 20, no. 12 (2010): 1617–26.

9 For a discussion of race and fatness, see Sabrina Strings, *Fearing the Black Body: The Racial Origins of Fat Phobia* (New York: New York University Press, 2019). See also Da'Shaun L. Harrison, *Belly of the Beast: The Politics of Anti-Fatness as Anti-Blackness* (Berkeley, CA: North Atlantic Books, 2021), and Manne, *Unshrinking*. Medicine's role in perpetuating anti-fatness is discussed by Jutel, "The Emergence of Overweight as a Disease Entity"; and Jutel, *Putting a Name to It*. For a discussion of the ideal body, see Susan Bordo, *Unbearable Weight: Feminism, Western Culture, and the Body* (Berkeley: University of California Press, 1993). See also Joan Jacobs Brumberg, *The Body Project: An Intimate History of American Girls* (New York: Random House, 1997).

10 See Robert E. Brolin, Lisa B. Robertson, Hallis A. Kenler, and Ronald P. Cody, "Weight Loss and Dietary Intake After Vertical Banded Gastroplasty and Roux-en-Y Gastric Bypass," *Annals of Surgery* 220, no. 6 (1994): 782–90.

3. NEIGHBORS

1 Sociological research shows that mothering isn't hard-wired. See Barbara J. Risman, "Can Men 'Mother'? Life as a Single Father," *Family Relations* 35, no. 1 (1986): 95–102.

2 See Gillies, "Parenting, Class and Culture: Exploring the Context of Childrearing."

4. MONKEY SHIT GREEN

1 For a discussion that identifies the problems in academic searches, see Damani K. White-Lewis, "The Facade of Fit in Faculty Search Processes," *The Journal of Higher Education* 91, no. 6 (2020): 833–857.

2 See Miri Song, *Helping Out: Children's Labor in Ethnic Businesses* (Philadelphia, PA: Temple University Press, 1999).

3 For a discussion of gender within gangs, see Jody Miller, *One of the Guys: Girls, Gangs, and Gender* (New York: Oxford University Press, 2000).

4 For a discussion of empowerment among women drug dealers, see Heidi Grundetjern and Jody Miller, "'It's Not Just the Drugs that are Difficult to Quit': Women's Drug Dealing as a Source of Empowerment and its Implications for Crime Persistence," *The British Journal of Criminology* 59, no. 2 (2019): 416–434. For a white woman's experience from elite college student to convicted drug dealer, see Keri Blakinger, *Corrections in Ink: A Memoir* (New York: St. Martin's Press, 2022).

5 The #CrimingWhileWhite viral hashtag has been criticized. See Sarah Galo, "#CrimingWhileWhite vs. #AliveWhileBlack: Twitter Weighs in On Garner Decision," *The Guardian*, December 4, 2014, www.theguardian.com/us-news/2014/dec/04/eric-garner-twitter.

6   Kara Brown, "The Problem With #CrimingWhileWhite," *Jezebel*, December 4, 2014, https://jezebel.com/the-problem-with-crimingwhilewhite-1666785471.

5. EVICTION

1   JD Vance, (@JDVance), *X*, June 12, 2024, https://x.com/JDVance/status/1800889737718505697.

2   For a contemporary empirical study of networks, see David S. Pedulla and Devah Pager, "Race and Networks in the Job Search Process," *American Sociological Review* 84, no. 6 (2019): 983–1012. See also Francis Kramarz and Oskar Nordström Skans, "When Strong Ties are Strong: Networks and Youth Labor Market Entry," *The Review of Economic Studies* 81, no. 3 (2014): 1164–1200.

3   For a popular press piece on why some people become obsessed with cleaning, see Julie Stewart, "Why Cleaning Makes Some People Feel Less Anxious," *Vice*, October 3, 2018, www.vice.com/en/article/598wn8/why-cleaning-makes-some-people-feel-less-anxious.

4   For another sociologist's personal encounter with housing eviction, see Krystale E. Littlejohn, "I Know The Horror of Childhood Eviction," *Medium*, August 29, 2021, https://krystalelittlejohn.medium.com/i-know-the-horror-of-childhood-eviction-we-have-to-make-it-stop-a1eca23c0b80.

5   After housing eviction, many folks end up in motels because they do not have the security deposit, application fees, etc. to secure rental housing. See Christopher P. Dum, *Exiled in America: Life on the Margins in a Residential Motel* (New York: Columbia University Press, 2016). See also Matthew Desmond, *Evicted: Poverty and Profit in the American City* (New York: Crown, 2016).

6   For an introductory discussion of the flawed ideologies of sex, gender, and sexuality, see Anne Fausto-Sterling, *Sex/Gender: Biology in a Social World* (New York: Routledge, 2012).

6. SURGERY

1   For a sociological discussion of workplace racial discrimination in medical settings, see Adia Harvey Wingfield and Koji Chavez, "Getting In, Getting Hired, Getting Sideways Looks: Organizational Hierarchy and Perceptions of Racial Discrimination," *American Sociological Review* 85, no. 1 (2020): 31–57.

2   "Communication" and "personality and demeanor of provider" are defined as key characteristics that shape a patient's satisfaction with medical care providers, in Roger Anderson, Angela Barbara, and Steven Feldman, "What Patients Want: A Content Analysis of Key Qualities that Influence Patient Satisfaction," *The Journal of Medical Practice Management* 22, no. 5 (2007): 255–61.

3   See Pedulla and Pager, "Race and Networks in the Job Search Process."

4   For a discussion of the relationship between Greek immigration and their overrepresentation in the food industry, see Stamatina Mylonas, "Tribute to Greeks who Feed America," *Greek City Times*, January 30, 2020, https://greek-citytimes.com/2020/01/30/the-greeks-who-feed-america/.

7. AN EDUCATION

1   For a critical discussion of the GED, see James J. Heckman, John Eric Humphries, Paul A. LaFontaine, and Pedro L. Rodríguez, "Taking the Easy Way Out: How the GED Testing Program Induces Students to Drop Out," *Journal of Labor Economics* 30, no. 3 (2012): 495–520.

2   See Timothy R. Levine, Kim B. Serota, Frankie Carey, and Doug Messer, "Teenagers Lie a Lot: A Further Investigation into the Prevalence of Lying," *Communication Research Reports* 30, no. 3 (2013): 211–220.

3   For an overview of these gangs, see George W. Knox, "The Satan's Disciples: A Gang Profile," National Gang Crime Research Center, 2008, www.ngcrc.com/ngcrc/sataprof.htm; and National Drug Intelligence Center, "Drugs and Crime Gang Profile—Gangster Disciples," U.S. Department of Justice (February, 2003), https://cryptome.org/gangs/gangster.pdf.

4   For a sociological overview of fashion, see Patrik Aspers and Frédéric Godart, "Sociology of Fashion: Order and Change," *Annual Review of Sociology* 39 (2013): 171–192. For a discussion of "taste," see Pierre Bourdieu, *Distinction: A Social Critique of the Judgement of Taste* (Cambridge, MA: Harvard University Press, 1987).

5   Medical scrubs are associated with pride, professional identity, and self-image, among other things. See Kate Shaw and Stephen Timmons, "Exploring How Nursing Uniforms Influence Self Image and Professional Identity," *Nursing Times* 106, no. 10 (2010): 21–23.

6   For a cultural critic's take on the ongoing popularity of *Friends* despite its polarizing cringeworthiness, see Kelsey Miller, *I'll Be There For You: The One About Friends* (New York: Hanover Square Press, 2018).

7   See Judith Scott-Clayton, "Do High-Stakes Placement Exams Predict College Success?," Community College Research Center, February 2012, https://files.eric.ed.gov/fulltext/ED529866.pdf.

8   See Tatiana Velasco, John Flink, Mariel Bedoya, and Davis Jenkins, "Tracing Transfer: Community College Effectiveness in Broadening Bachelor's Degree Attainment," *Community College Research Center*, February 2024, https://ccrc.tc.columbia.edu/publications/Tracking-Transfer-Community-College-and-Four-Year-Institutional-Effectiveness-in-Broadening-Bachelors-Degree-Attainment.html.

9   Juliana Menasce Horowitz, Anna Brown, and Kiana Cox, "The Role of Race and Ethnicity in Americans' Personal Lives," in *Race in America 2019* (report), Pew Research Center, April 9, 2019, pewresearch.org.

10 See "GED® Test Performance," American Council on Education, accessed September 12, 2024, www.equityinhighered.org/indicators/secondary-school-

completion/ged-test-performance/#:~:text=White%20and%20Asian%20stu-
dents%20had,American%20students%20had%20the%20lowest.

11 See Katherine L. Milkman, Modupe Akinola, and Dolly Chugh, "What Happens Before? A Field Experiment Exploring How Pay and Representation Dif-
ferentially Shape Bias on the Pathway into Organizations," *Journal of Applied
Psychology* 100, no. 6 (2015): 1678–1712. For a discussion of how whiteness
is an asset for first-gen college students, see Jenny Marie Stuber, "Integrated,
Marginal, and Resilient: Race, Class and the Diverse Experiences of White
First-Generation College Students," *International Journal of Qualitative Studies
in Education* 24, no. 1 (2011): 117–36.

12 See, for example, Pedulla and Pager, "Race and Networks in the Job Search Process." See also Kramarz and Nordström Skans, "When Strong Ties are Strong:
Networks and Youth Labor Market Entry."

13 See the chapter "Mobility through Marriage: The Cinderella Effect," in Stephen J.
McNamee, *The Meritocracy Myth*, 4th edition (Lanham, MD: Rowman & Littlefield, 2018), 153–70. See also Jessi Streib, *The Power of the Past: Understanding Cross-Class Marriages* (New York: Oxford University Press, 2015); Laura
T. Hamilton and Elizabeth A. Armstrong, "Parents, Partners, and Professions:
Reproduction and Mobility in a Cohort of College Women," *American Journal
of Sociology* 127, no. 1 (2021): 102–151; and Daniel Lichter, Joseph P. Price, and
Jeffrey M. Swigert, "Mismatches in the Marriage Market," *Journal of Marriage
and Family* 82, no. 2 (2020): 796–809.

14 For a broader discussion of how white people, in particular women, benefit
from white supremacy, see Jessie Daniels, *Nice White Ladies: The Truth About
White Supremacy, Our Role in It, and How We Can Help Dismantle It* (New
York: Seal Press, 2021).

8. REDACTED

1 Personal medical records, December 23, 1997.

2 Personal medical records, November 26, 1997.

3 See Anderson et al., "What Patients Want: A Content Analysis: of Key Qualities
that Influence Patient Satisfaction."

4 I would learn more than a decade later that my experience discovering my intersex diagnosis, and the lies and deception that surround it, are not unique. See,
for example, Sharon E. Preves, *Intersex and Identity: The Contested Self* (New
Brunswick, NJ: Rutgers University Press, 2003). For a historical discussion of
intersex experiences, see Elizabeth Reis, *Bodies in Doubt: An American History
of Intersex* (Baltimore, MD: Johns Hopkins University Press, 2009).

5 Georgiann Davis, "The Power in a Name: Diagnostic Terminology and Diverse
Experiences," *Psychology & Sexuality* 5, no. 1 (2014): 15–27.

9. DAVIS

1 For a sociological analysis of weddings, see Chrys Ingrahams, *White Weddings: Romancing Heterosexuality in Popular Culture*, 2nd ed. (New York: Routledge, 2008).

2 See Pamela J. Smock, "Cohabitation in the United States: An Appraisal of Research Themes, Findings, and Implications," *Annual Review of Sociology* 26 (2000): 1–20.

3 I've been to enough Dave Matthews Band (DMB) concerts to confidently agree with the claim that the DMB fanbase is predominately college educated white, cis, and straight folks born in the 1970s or 1980s.

10. FIVE STAR DREAMS

1 See "Reconsidering the Use of the Graduate Record Examination (GRE) in Graduate School Admissions Decisions" (report), American Sociological Association, March 2021, www.asanet.org/sites/default/files/gre_statement_march_2021-final_format.pdf.

2 For a discussion of the uniqueness, and necessity, of intense intimate relationships for queer folks, see Jeffrey Weeks, Brian Heaphy, and Catherine Donovan, *Same Sex Intimacies: Families of Choice and Other Life Experiments* (New York: Routledge, 2001).

11. SERVED

1 See John C. Navarro and George E. Higgins, "Familial Identity Theft," *American Journal of Criminal Justice* 42, no. 1 (2017): 218–30.

12. STOLEN

1 For a now classical sociological analysis on views of residential integration, see Lawrence Bobo and Camille Zubrinsky, "Attitudes on Residential Integration: Perceived Status Differences, Mere In-Group Preference, or Racial Prejudice?," *Social Forces* 74, no. 3 (1996): 883–909.

2 Research consistently shows that the majority of those who survive a suicide attempt will not die by suicide at a later date. For more information, see Bingjie Tong, Andrew Devendorf, Vanessa Panaite, Rose Miller, Todd B. Kashdan, Thomas Joiner, Jean Twenge, Marc Karver, Roshni Janakiraman, and Jonathan Rottenberg, "Future Well-Being Among U.S. Youth Who Attempted Suicide and Survived," *Behavior Therapy* 53, no. 3 (2022): 481–291. For a discussion of the relationship between firearms, suicide, and gender, see Michael Siegel and Emily F. Rothman, "Firearm Ownership and Suicide Rates Among US Men and Women, 1981–2013," *American Journal of Public Health* 106, no. 7 (2016): 1316–1322.

3 My ability to independently work with the credit reporting agencies, involved banks, and law enforcement personnel to repair my credit is an example of

how I enacted my acquired cultural capital to navigate identity theft. For a discussion of cultural capital, see Pierre Bourdieu, "The Forms of Capital," in *Handbook of Theory and Research for the Sociology of Education*, ed. John G. Richardson (Westport, CT: Greenwood, 1986), 241–58.

4 See, for example, Judith Lewis Herman, "The Mental Health of Crime Victims: Impact of Legal Intervention," *Journal of Traumatic Stress* 16, no. 2 (2003): 159–66.

5 There are substantial societal pressures to maintain parent-child relationships, which contributes to the guilt one experiences when they attempt to distance themselves from their family of origin. See Kristina M. Scharp, Lindsey J. Thomas, and Christina G. Paxman, "'It Was the Straw that Broke the Camel's Back': Exploring the Distancing Processes Communicatively Constructed in Parent-Child Estrangement Backstories," *Journal of Family Communication* 15, no. 4 (2015): 330–348. See also Kristina M. Scharp and Elizabeth Dorrance Hall, "Reconsidering Family Closeness: A Review and Call for Research on Family Distancing," *Journal of Family Communication* 19, no. 1 (2019):1–14.

6 The FBI has labeled this practice "illegal property flipping." See "Illegal Property Flipping," Federal Bureau of Investigation, accessed September 10, 2024, www.fbi.gov/video-repository/newss-property-flipping/view#:~:text=This%20is%20how%20they%20work,the%20property%20from%20him%20quickly.

7 For a discussion of predatory lending, see Gregory D. Squires, *Why the Poor Pay More: How to Stop Predatory Lending* (Westport, CT: Praeger, 2004).

8 See "Coping with the Shock of Intrafamilial Sexual Abuse," *The National Child Traumatic Stress Network*, accessed September 14, 2024, www.nctsn.org/sites/default/files/resources/coping_with_intrafamilial_sexual_abuse_parents.pdf. See also Camille Warrington, Helen Beckett, Elizabeth Ackerley, Megan Walker, and Debbie Allnock, "Making Noise: Children's Voices for Positive Change After Sexual Abuse," *University of Bedfordshire, The Making Noise Project*, 2017, accessed September 12, 2024, www.beds.ac.uk/media/86813/makingnoise-20042017.pdf.

9 I define medically induced bulimia as vomiting induced by a medical procedure—in this case bariatric surgery—that affects one's health and causes dangerous weight loss.

10 Colleen Flaherty, "Barely Getting By," *Inside Higher Ed*, April 19, 2020, www.insidehighered.com/news/2020/04/20/new-report-says-many-adjuncts-make-less-3500-course-and-25000-year.

13. SUPERSTITIOUS FORGIVENESS

1 Juan Carlos Jorge, Leidy Valerio-Pérez, Caleb Esteban, and Ana Irma Rivera-Lassen, "Intersex Care in the United States and International Standards of Human Rights," *Global Public Health* 16, no. 5 (2021): 679–91.

2 It has been found that slot machines often offer some of the worst odds. Depending on the game, the chances of hitting the top jackpot can range

from one in 5,000 to one in 34 million when playing maximum coins. While significant wins do happen, the longer you play, the more the odds favor the house, increasing the likelihood of leaving with less money than you started with. Chris Neiger, "Casino Stats: Why Gamblers Rarely Win," Investopedia, September 23, 2024, www.investopedia.com/financial-edge/0910/casino-stats-why-gamblers-rarely-win.aspx.

3 For an in-depth journalistic account of the U.S. opiate epidemic, see Sam Quinones, *Dreamland: The True Tale of America's Opiate Epidemic* (New York: Bloomsbury Press, 2015). For a sociological analysis of how pharmacists navigate the epidemic, see Elizabeth Chiarello, "The War on Drugs Comes to the Pharmacy Counter: Frontline Work in the Shadow of Discrepant Institutional Logics," *Law & Social Inquiry* 40, no. 1 (2015): 86–122. See also Elizabeth Chiarello, *Policing Patients: Treatment and Surveillance on the Frontlines of the Opioid Crisis* (Princeton, NJ: Princeton University Press, 2024).

14. REMORSE

1 For a sociological critique of meritocracy, see Stephen J. McNamee and Robert K. Miller, Jr., *The Meritocracy Myth: Who Gets Ahead and Why* (Lanham, MD: Rowman & Littlefield, 2004).

2 For a timeline of the Blagojevich ordeal, see Jonathon Berlin and Kori Rumore, "Rod Blagojevich Saga Timeline: From Arrest to Donald Trump's Commutation to the End of His Supervised Release," *Chicago Tribune*, June 1, 2021, www.chicagotribune.com/2021/06/01/rod-blagojevich-saga-timeline-from-arrest-to-donald-trumps-commutation-to-the-end-of-his-supervised-release/.

3 I'm using the definition of "third-party custodian" provided by Marie Van-Nostrand and Gena Keebler, "Pretrial Risk Assessment in the Federal Court," *Federal Probation* 73, no. 2 (2009): 3–29.

15. ARREST

1 For a sociological analysis of the racist "spectacle of abuse" in U.S. criminal courts, see Nicole Gonzalez Van Cleve, "Due Process & the Theater of Racial Degradation: The Evolving Notion of Pretrial Punishment in the Criminal Courts," *Dædalus, the Journal of the American Academy of Arts & Sciences* 151, no. 1 (2022): 135–52.

2 For an overview of disparities in the criminal legal system, see "Racial and Ethnic Disparities in the Criminal Justice System" (report), National Conference of State Legislatures, 2022, www.ncsl.org/civil-and-criminal-justice/racial-and-ethnic-disparities-in-the-criminal-justice-system.

16. PRISON TOUR

1 My search for information about FCI Greenville began with the Federal Bureau of Prisons. I quickly went down an internet search rabbit hole, reading all about the facility from various sources, ranging from official sites to random

social media posts by those with personal experience, working or otherwise, at FCI Greenville.

17. GROWTH

1 Georgiann Davis, *Contesting Intersex: The Dubious Diagnosis* (New York: New York University Press, 2015).

2 For an updated report on faculty salaries in sociology and adjacent disciplines, see John W. Curtis and Michael Kisielewski, "Faculty Salaries in Sociology and Other Disciplines, 2016 Update," *American Sociological Association*, August 2016, www.asanet.org/research-and-publications/research-sociology/research-briefs/faculty-salaries-sociology-and-other-disciplines-2016-update.

3 For a discussion of survivor's guilt, see Geraldine K. Piorkowski, "Survivor Guilt in the University Setting," *The Personnel & Guidance Journal* 61, no. 10 (1983): 620–22. See also Rebecca Covarrubias, Andrea Romero, and Michael Trivelli, "Family Achievement Guilt and Mental Well-Being of College Students," *Journal of Child and Family Studies* 24 (2015): 2031–2037.

4 See Katie Robertson, "Nikole Hannah-Jones and University Settle Hiring Dispute," *The New York Times*, July 15, 2022, www.nytimes.com/2022/07/15/business/media/nikole-hannah-jones-unc-settlement.html.

5 See Robert Mackey, "Professor's Angry Tweets on Gaza Cost Him a Job," *The New York Times*, September 12, 2014, www.nytimes.com/2014/09/13/world/middleeast/professors-angry-tweets-on-gaza-cost-him-a-job.html.

6 See Sara Ahmed, *Complaint!* (Durham, NC: Duke University Press, 2021).

7 For a cultural critique of the mobilizing of diversity in colleges and university, see "Black Is Over (Or, Special Black)," in Tressie McMillan Cottom, *Thick: And Other Essays* (New York: The New Press, 2019).

8 See Kiese Laymon, *Heavy: An American Memoir* (New York: Scribner, 2018).

9 For a sociological overview of some of the issues faced by marginalized academics in sociology, see *Social Problems* 64, no. 2 (2017). This special issue of *Social Problems* is titled *Voices from the Margins: Inequalities in the Sociological House*, and is edited by Aldon D. Morris. See also Kyle K. Moore, Ismael Cid-Martinez, Jermaine Toney, Jason A. Smith, Amber C. Kalb, Jean H. Shin, and Roberta M. Spalter-Roth, "Who Climbs the Academic Ladder? Race and Gender Stratification in a World of Whiteness," *The Review of Black Political Economy* 45, no. 3 (2018): 216–244. Also see Victoria Reyes, *Academic Outsider: Stories of Exclusion and Hope* (Redwood City, CA: Stanford University Press, 2022).

10 For a discussion of how racism and sexism infiltrate sociological theory courses, see Victoria Reyes and Karin A. C. Johnson, "Teaching the Veil: Race, Ethnicity, and Gender in Classical Theory Courses," *Sociology of Race and Ethnicity* 6, no. 4 (2020): 562–567. With respect to the teaching of sexualities, see Salvador Vidal-Ortiz, "A Sea of Whiteness: Teaching Sexuality through a New Sociology at a U.S. American University," *Teaching Sociology* 49, no. 3 (2021): 223–232.

11 See, for example, Angela Y. Davis, Gina Dent, Erica R. Meiners, and Beth E. Richie, *Abolition. Feminism. Now.* (Chicago: Haymarket Books, 2022). See also Derecka Purnell, *Becoming Abolitionists: Police, Protests, and the Pursuit of Freedom* (New York: Astra House, 2021).

12 For a discussion of the complicated family dynamics of those incarcerated, see Megan Comfort, *Doing Time Together: Love and Family in the Shadow of the Prison* (Chicago: University of Chicago Press, 2008). See also Patrick Lopez-Aguado, *Stick Together and Come Back Home: Racial Sorting and the Spillover of Carceral Identity* (Berkeley: University of California Press, 2018).

13 See "Frequently Asked Questions," *Bureau of Justice Statistics*, accessed September 16, 2024, https://bjs.ojp.gov/frequently-asked-questions#faq-how-much-do-federal-state-and-local-governments.

14 See Angela Y. Davis, *Are Prisons Obsolete?* (New York: Seven Stories Press, 2003).

15 Georgiann Davis, "When Feminists Mentor," *SIUE Women's Studies Program*, October 21, 2013, https://siuewmst.wordpress.com/2013/10/21/when-feminists-mentor/.

16 "Mama's Little Boy or Daddy's Little Girl: Identity Confusion or Brainwashing?," *Dr. Phil*, Season 14, Episode 55, CBS, November 30, 2015.

17 "Gender Revolution: A Journey with Katie Couric," *National Geographic Documentary Films*, 2017.

18. STILL FAT

1 Marilyn Wann, *Fat!So? Because You Don't Have to Apologize for Your Size!* (Berkeley, CA: Ten Speed Press, 1998).

2 For a sociological discussion of stigma, see Erving Goffman, *Stigma: Notes on the Management of a Spoiled Identity* (New York: Prentice-Hall, 1963).

3 For a contemporary discussion of the internalization of fatphobia and its consequences at the interactional and institutional levels of society, see Manne, *Unshrinking*. For a now classic empirical piece on fat discrimination, see Rebecca Puhl and Kelly D. Brownell, "Bias, Discrimination, and Obesity," *Obesity Research* 9, no. 12 (2001): 788–805.

4 Keith Devlin, "Top 10 Reasons Why the BMI is Bogus," *NPR*, July 4, 2009, www.npr.org/templates/story/story.php?storyId=106268439.

5 For a scholarly critique of the tools used to measure body size, see Sonya Satinsky & Natalie Ingraham, "At the Intersection of Public Health and Fat Studies: Critical Perspectives on the Measurement of Body Size," *Fat Studies: An Interdisciplinary Journal of Body Weight and Society* 3, no. 2 (2014): 143–54.

6 See "Fat Shaming in the Doctor's Office Can Be Mentally and Physically Harmful," *American Psychological Association*, accessed September 18, 2024, www.apa.org/news/press/releases/2017/08/fat-shaming.aspx.

7 David Griffiths, Peter Hegarty, and Kamila Hawthorne, "After the Recognition of Intersex Human Rights: Symposium Report," University of Surrey, accessed

July 12, 2022, www.ias.surrey.ac.uk/wp-content/uploads/2019/11/Intersex-Symposium-IAS-Report.pdf.

8   The Intersex Day Project was founded in 2015 by Morgan Carpenter and Laura Inter. See "About the Intersex Day Project," Intersex Day, accessed September 16, 2024, https://intersexday.org/en/about/.

9   Adapted from materials provided by my bariatric surgeon's office (2016).

10 Roxane Gay, *Hunger: A Memoir of (My) Body* (New York: HarperCollins, 2017). For another discussion of the complicated decision to have bariatric surgery, see Gabourey Sidibe, *This Is Just My Face: Try Not to Stare* (New York: Houghton Mifflin Harcourt, 2017).

11 Roxane Gay, "What Fullness Is: On Getting Weight Reduction Surgery," *Medium*, April 24, 2018, https://medium.com/s/unrulybodies/the-body-that-understands-what-fullness-is-f2e40c40cd75.

19. ASHES

1   For one example, see Contessa Brewer and Scott Zamost, "Gift Card Crime Fueling Opioid Addiction Across the US," *CNBC*, December 7, 2017, www.cnbc.com/2017/12/07/gift-card-crime-fueling-opioid-addiction-across-the-us.html.

2   See Piorkowski, "Survivor Guilt in the University Setting." See also Covarrubias et al., "Family Achievement Guilt and Mental Well-Being of College Students."

3   See John M. Eason, *Big House on the Prairie: Rise of the Rural Ghetto and Prison Proliferation* (Chicago: University of Chicago Press, 2017).

4   Julie Netherland and Helena B. Hansen, "The War on Drugs That Wasn't: Wasted Whiteness, 'Dirty Doctors,' and Race in Media Coverage of Prescription Opioid Misuse," *Culture, Medicine, and Psychiatry* 40, no. 4 (2016): 664–686. See also Alexander, *The New Jim Crow*.

5   William H. Pryor, Jr., Rachel E. Barkow, Charles R. Breyer, Danny C. Reeves, Zachary C. Bolitho, J. Patricia Wilson Smooth, Kenneth P. Cohen, and Glenn R. Schmitt, *Demographic Differences in Sentencing: An Update to the 2012 Booker Report* (Washington, DC: United States Sentencing Commission, November 2017), www.ussc.gov/sites/default/files/pdf/research-and-publications/research-publications/2017/20171114_Demographics.pdf.

6   Sociologist Steven Seidman has shown the experience to be far less uniform, and instead shaped by race, class, and gender. See Steven Seidman, *Beyond the Closet: The Transformation of Gay and Lesbian Life* (New York: Routledge, 2002).

7   For a discussion of U.S. divorce rates over time by educational attainment as well as by race and ethnicity, see Valerie J. Schweizer, "Divorce: More than a century of change, 1900–2018," *National Center for Family & Marriage Research, Family Profile*, FP-20-22, 2020, https://doi.org/10.25035/ncfmr/fp-20-22.

8   Richard N. Velotta, "Four Years Ago, Las Vegas' Casinos Shut Down for 78 Days. The Fallout Was Brutal," *Las Vegas Review-Journal*, March 14, 2024, www.reviewjournal.com/business/casinos-gaming/four-years-ago-las-vegas-casinos-shut-down-for-78-days-the-fallout-was-brutal-3017034/.

ABOUT THE AUTHOR

GEORGIANN DAVIS is an intersex scholar-activist whose research, teaching, and activism are at the intersection of medical violence and feminist theories. She is the author of *Contesting Intersex: The Dubious Diagnosis*, which was recognized with the American Sociological Association's Section on Sex and Gender Distinguished Book Award and the Medical Sociology Section's Donald W. Light Award for Applied or Public Practice of Medical Sociology. She is also a past recipient of the Feminist Activism Award from Sociologists for Women in Society as well as a Feminist Scholar-Activist Award from the American Sociological Association's Section on Sex and Gender.